A HISTORY OF
WESTERN EDUCATIONAL IDEAS

Woburn Education Series
General Series Editor: Professor Peter Gordon
ISSN 1462-2076

For over twenty years this series on the history, development and policy of education, under the distinguished editorship of Peter Gordon, has been evolving into a comprehensive and balanced survey of important trends in teaching and educational policy. The series is intended to reflect the changing nature of education in present-day society. The books are divided into four sections – educational policy studies, educational practice, the history of education and social history – and reflect the continuing interest in this area.

For a full series listing, please visit our website: www.woburnpress.com

History of Education

The Victorian School Manager: A Study in the Management of Education 1800–1902 *Peter Gordon*

Selection for Secondary Education *Peter Gordon*

The Study of Education: Inaugural Lectures
Volume I: Early and Modern   Volume III: The Changing Scene
Volume II: The Last Decade   Volume IV: End of an Era?
edited by Peter Gordon

History of Education: The Making of a Discipline
edited by Peter Gordon and Richard Szreter

Educating the Respectable: A Study of Fleet Road Board School, Hampstead, 1879–1903 *W.E. Marsden*

In History and in Education: Essays Presented to Peter Gordon
edited by Richard Aldrich

An Anglo-Welsh Teaching Dynasty: The Adams Family from the 1840s to the 1930s
W.E. Marsden

Dictionary of British Educationists *Richard Aldrich and Peter Gordon*

Biographical Dictionary of North American and European Educationists
Peter Gordon and Richard Aldrich

The Making of the Backward Pupil in Education in England, 1870–1914
Ian Copeland

Social History

The First Teenagers: The Lifestyle of Young Wage-earners in Interwar Britain
David Fowler

James Kay Shuttleworth: Journey of an Outsider *R.J.W. Selleck*

Targeting Schools: Drill, Militarism and Imperialism *Alan Penn*

The English Higher Grade Schools: A Lost Opportunity *Meriel Vlaeminke*

A HISTORY OF

WESTERN EDUCATIONAL IDEAS

DENIS LAWTON
and
PETER GORDON

WOBURN PRESS
LONDON • PORTLAND, OR

First published in 2002 in Great Britain by
WOBURN PRESS
Chase House, 47 Chase Side, Southgate
London N14 5BP

and in the United States of America by
WOBURN PRESS
c/o ISBS
5824 N.E. Hassalo Street
Portland, Oregon 97213-3644

Website: www.woburnpress.com

British Library Cataloguing in Publication Data

Lawton, Denis, 1931–
   A history of Western educational ideas – (The Woburn
   education series)
   1. Education – Western influences – History 2. Education
   – Europe – History 3. Education – Aims and objectives –
   Europe – History
   I. Title II. Gordon, Peter, 1927–
   370.9′1812

ISBN 0-7130-0219-0 (cloth)
ISBN 0-7130-4041-6 (paper)
ISSN 1462-2076

Library of Congress Cataloging-in-Publication Data

Lawton, Denis.
A history of western educational ideas / Denis Lawton and Peter Gordon.
   p. cm. – (Woburn education series, ISSN 1462-2076)
Includes bibliographical references (p.) and index.
ISBN 0-7130-0219-0 (cloth) – ISBN 0-7130-4041-6
   1. Education – Philosophy – History. I. Gordon, Peter, 1927–
II. Title. III. Series.

LB14.7 .L39 2002
370′.1 – dc21   2001057514

Typeset by Frank Cass Publishers
Printed in Great Britain by
MPG Books Ltd, Bodmin, Cornwall

Contents

1
Introduction: A History of Western Educational Ideas

INTRODUCTION

Our focus upon the history of ideas in this book is partly an attempt to move history of education away from an approach based on 'great men' to technological, economic, social and political influences on ideas and beliefs. In our view many books on the history of education have moved all too easily from one famous writer to another without sufficient regard for the general historical context of the ideas.

The history of education has, in the past, not only concentrated too much on the story of great thinkers but also on the history of institutions, for example, on topics such as 'The Rise of the University' rather than examining the changes in society which gave rise to those institutions or to changes in them. In reality the twelfth-century universities of Paris and Oxford had very little in common with twentieth-century higher education. One of our purposes will be to explore the reasons for change without ignoring the contributions made by individuals.

We have specified 'Western' in the title because it is not the intention of this book to try to cover aspects of oriental philosophy and education. The Buddhist, Hindu and Chinese traditions are very rich, but beyond the scope of a single volume and beyond our expertise. We will make some reference to Islamic education though mainly to the influence of those ideas on Western education, which were considerable, but do not take us outside the general narrative of this book. Islamic culture shared many aspects of the Judaeo-Christian tradition and benefited from the writings of authors such as Aristotle.

Many historians have suggested that if an individual is ignorant of the history of his or her own country, he or she is rather like someone without a memory: we need the past in order to make sense of the present, or at least to know how we arrived at this point. The same is true for anyone involved in education: there are many aspects of an education system that only make sense if we know how that system has developed over time.

Part of that development is the story of how institutions (schools, colleges and universities) have changed, but it is also important to understand how ideas in education have developed.

THE DEVELOPMENT OF EDUCATION

All societies have the problem of bringing up their young in such a way that they will become the kind of people who will be wanted and accepted in that society. In simple, pre-literate societies this process is usually in the hands of the family, probably the extended family. Parents and other close adults can pass on all the skills, knowledge and values that are needed. This is sometimes referred to as 'informal education'. In pre-literate societies there is usually little discussion about education or the purpose of education: it is taken for granted that the young need to be brought up in certain ways and that the elders know best.

As societies become more complex, and especially when writing is adopted or invented, it may become necessary for some specialist teachers to be employed, often in institutions called schools or universities. It is at this point that ideas about education begin to be developed and discussed. Prior to this, the upbringing of children would have been regarded as commonsense and taken for granted; but when schools exist, those involved in teaching the young, and those who want to criticise the failures of the system, begin to theorise about teaching methods, about the curriculum, about the purpose of education and possibly even about the education of teachers. Different societies, at different times, throw up all kinds of ideas about education and training. It is interesting to relate these ideas to the social conditions and events that have generated them, and also to see how ideas develop and change over time.

The approach taken in this book is not to attempt the history of education over a period of about 2,500 years, but to concentrate on educational ideas, how these ideas have emerged from certain social conditions and how they have developed and influenced each other. We shall not be looking at the history of schools and other institutions in any great detail: we will be more concerned with educational thinking.

CULTURAL CHANGE AND EDUCATIONAL IDEAS

It should be clear from later chapters of this book that the purpose as well as the practice of education differs from time to time and place to place.

This variation is partly due to the kind of society it is – agrarian societies have different priorities from industrial ones, for example. However, some differences in priorities are also due to different ideas about knowledge and truth: you will find that Plato thought that mathematics was the key to truth, but his pupil Aristotle believed that science was more important. Later on, the Jews, Christians and Muslims believed that they possessed sacred books which provided the Truth. By the end of the sixteenth century most people thought that there was one answer, and many believed that they knew what it was. In more recent centuries, social scientists and educationists have tended to believe that each culture provides its own solution to these eternal problems of knowledge and truth. We have the benefit of hindsight in as much as we can look at Greece and Rome, for example, from a distance. When we do this we should be careful, though, not to be judgmental – that is, to apply twentieth-century knowledge and values to cultures that were very different from our own. We shall see, however, that it is difficult for educationists not to believe in some principles which are timeless and universal.

What is history?

In writing this book we became increasingly conscious of the fact that over the centuries there have been vigorous, sometimes acrimonious, debates about the nature of history, but rather less discussion about the nature of the history of education. We have in mind two aspects of that debate. First, the specific question of the extent to which historians and history books are themselves a product of their time, reflecting current attitudes and values. Or can historians really establish a degree of objective truth? The second aspect of the debate is an extension of the first. It deals with the more general attack on history by various post-modernist writers, particularly over the last 20 years.

Many writers, including Richard Evans,[1] begin by contrasting the two approaches represented by E.H. Carr[2] and Geoffrey Elton.[3] Carr adopted a moderate sociological, even relativist, approach, advising students of history to 'study the historian'. In other words, historians could not be expected to be totally unbiased but inevitably represented some kind of viewpoint. Elton, on the other hand, saw the historian as a trained seeker for objective truth; history would always have a backbone of political events and historians should focus on documentary records as their evidence. Both Carr and Elton believed in historical truth and objectivity but interpreted those terms differently.

Evans in his book felt it necessary to take the argument some way beyond the Carr–Elton contrast because, especially since the 1980s, some postmodernist writers have questioned whether history was any use at all. One of the problems with using a word like postmodernism is that it is not only extremely vague, but those who describe themselves, or are referred to as postmodernist adopt more or less extreme points on the spectrum of postmodernism.

MODERNISM, HIGH MODERNISM, POSTMODERNISM

Modernism began as a description of architectural style, often also applied to art and music. It was a description of attempts to reject the traditional and invent something new. Modernism was sometimes a self-conscious expression of the functional and a demonstration of control over the environment (Le Corbusier is often quoted as an example). In the world of intellectual ideas, modernity and modernism began to be identified with the questioning of traditional beliefs and values which, as we shall see in later chapters, can be associated with the eighteenth-century Enlightenment and the elevation of scientific rationality as the highest possible authority. Modernity was not an event but a gradual process; modernism was a belief in modern styles and a rejection of the old.

In the twentieth century there was a realisation that science did not provide all the answers, that human beings were characterised by limited rationality, and that emotions and the unconscious mind had to be taken into account. This was accompanied by work in the social sciences, particularly social anthropology, which described cultures with beliefs and values very different from those in Western industrial capitalist societies. At first, Christian missionaries had tried to convert such peoples to their 'superior' way of life, but social anthropologists preached the doctrine of respect for other cultures. This simple expression of social science being 'value-free' led to the equally simple belief in moral and cultural relativism: we should not talk of inferiority/superiority but of cultural differences. For some social scientists this developed into the belief that there were no absolute values or principles: everything was relative, including truth itself.

The debate sometimes focused on the interpretation of the concept of cultural relativism which could be held in moderate or very extreme forms. Moderate relativists, including perhaps a majority of scientists and social scientists, accepted relativism as applied to other societies but would draw the line at tolerating cannibalism or female circumcision. All

4

cultures should be respected, but a high modernist[4] might well assert the technological superiority of science over witchcraft in such practical matters as landing on the moon. Other late modernists might accept the general idea of tolerating and respecting cultural differences but retain some absolute or near absolute values, such as respect for persons, which would not tolerate genocide or individual offences against others' 'rights'.

Clearly, one of the characteristics of high modernity is that views stretch right across the relativist spectrum, and at the extreme end are those who deny all absolutes, and even refuse to accept rationality itself as anything more than part of liberal bourgeois ideology. It would be convenient if those at the extreme end of relativism could be called postmodernist whilst those in more moderate position could be safely referred to as high modernists. Unfortunately, the terminology is confused by some of quite moderate views preferring to call themselves postmodernist.[5] Postmodernist views usually include all or some of the following: a disbelief in absolute values, a questioning attitude to scientific rationality, progress and truth. They tend to dislike general theories or 'grand narratives' preferring local explanations of reality. Many postmodernists have thus questioned the validity of history as an intellectual discipline. We shall return to the debate about postmodernism and history later in this chapter.

Meanwhile, what cannot be ignored in a book like ours is that over the period covered, the nature or theory of history has changed, and yet we still rely, to some extent, on what historians like Thucydides and Livy tell us. 'To some extent' is a reasonable qualifier only if we go a little further in specifying the criteria by which we decide what to accept and what to reject. One useful rule is certainly to accept Carr's advice and to be aware of the purpose or intention of the historian in question. We will discuss other 'rules' in the course of this chapter. One of the additional complexities is that not only is the historian influenced by the society in which he lives, but also by what history is thought to be.

A NOTE ON CHANGES IN HISTORIOGRAPHY

In Greece and Rome, history was generally not distinguished from literature: it was telling a story about the past. Those who told a good story, dramatically and with style, were admired. Many Greeks (more than 1,000) wrote about past events but we would not regard them as historians. Only a few writers showed a concern to distinguish between factual events and legends. One exception was Herodotus (484–424 BC) who was regarded by Cicero as the 'father of history'. Herodotus was influenced by the Ionian philosophers who wanted to understand the universe by means of reason, and made a distinction between myths and truly historical accounts. Herodotus wrote about his studies as 'enquiry' or *historia*. The Ionian approach contrasted with earlier attitudes to the past (including the Babylonian and Egyptian accounts) where the writing was intended to preserve and glorify heroic deeds, an expression of nationalism which we might now classify as propaganda.

Some of the well-known Roman historians, for example, Livy (59 BC – AD 17) regressed to some extent by using historical accounts for 'moral' and nationalistic purposes. Livy also frequently failed to distinguish between history and legend. However, Julius Caesar, despite a tendency always to present himself in a good light, generally provides an accurate record. One way in which the Greek and Roman historians were later criticised was for their failure systematically to quote their documentary sources. They did, however, see the need to doubt the accuracy of their sources and to check them against other evidence wherever possible. Perhaps for this reason many Greek and Roman writers usually preferred to keep close to their own times.

The Jews were interested in writing history because it was seen as the story of the gradual unfolding of God's plan for humanity. This view was carried over from the Old Testament to the New Testament by Christians, but the historical accuracy of the Gospels is, to say the least, open to question. We can assume that whoever wrote the Gospels were more concerned with the moral messages of Christianity than with accuracy about historical detail; and since part of the story was depicting the life of Christ as a fulfilment of Old Testament prophecies it would be surprising if some distortions did not creep in.

Eusebius (AD 264–340), a bishop who wrote a history of the church, despite his difficult task of handling the role of divine providence in establishing Christianity within the Roman Empire, provided valuable accounts of the early church and also developed techniques for checking one source against others wherever possible. However, he did not always exclude what we would now regard as fiction. Medieval Christian 'history' was based on very definite assumptions about the relation between God and the world created by Him: divine intervention was a legitimate 'explanation' of events. The early centuries of Christianity were not a high point of historical accuracy.

Later, the Venerable Bede (AD 673–735) was, however, notable for carefully checking sources, particularly in his *Ecclesiastical History of the English People*. He is regarded as one of the greatest historians of the

Middle Ages. The influence of Bede and other Anglo-Saxons who carefully quoted sources in historical writings also affected the revival of learning on the continent where scholars in Charlemagne's court became conscious of the need for historical accuracy, and this tradition survived despite frequent lapses when history was sacrificed to propaganda.

Renaissance historians consciously moved away from using divine intervention as an explanation and tended to move back to the pagan world. They also had an interest in social change and were aware of the fact that medieval writers operated in a different social context and world view from the Greeks and pre-Christian Romans: they valued accuracy of detail and looked critically at source material; they even began to write about the Bible as a text that might need to be interpreted and corrected in the light of studies of earlier (Greek) versions. It would not be an exaggeration to say that humanist historians rewrote much of the history of Europe on the basis of new translations of Greek and Latin texts and a more 'historical' attitude to past events.

With the Reformation came a period of disputed interpretation of historical texts based sometimes on revisions of the Bible. Eventually the history of Christianity was rewritten by Protestant scholars. The existence of two versions of historical reality, Protestant and Catholic, stimulated more critical views of texts and textual analysis, but impartiality was difficult to sustain and two rival versions of history tended to develop.

From the sixteenth century onwards history grew in popularity as a university subject and began to be seen as an essential aspect of high culture for the educated man. Stone[6] suggested three reasons for this: apart from history being a source of entertainment (better than most novels) it provided a means of moral instruction for the young, and civic training about politics and power. Between 1870 and 1930 history developed into an independent professional discipline. Political history was central, was concerned with the truth, and was value-free. These were bold statements, dangerous trends inviting the backlash that came later. History was also attempting to be more scientific in other respects, and from about 1930 was increasingly influenced by economics, sociology and later by anthropology. History had also moved away from narrative to more analytical approaches; historicism (in the form of the Whig interpretation of history, that is the inevitable progress towards parliamentary monarchy and liberty) was eventually rejected and there were even attempts to merge history into the social sciences. Nevertheless, history maintained its independence and even developed new specialisms.

In the last quarter of the twentieth century, however, postmodernist writers have questioned not only the status of history as a subject, but whether it should exist at all as a useful form of knowledge. On one famous occasion historians were invited by Ankersmith[7] to abandon their discipline and adopt the postmodernist view of reality. Historians would then be judged by aesthetic criteria, by literary form rather than by its approximation to truth. Ankersmith received a scholarly response from Zagorin[8] who rejected the postmodernist attack for a number of reasons. First, historians should be wary of postmodernism because, having passed out of its own historicist phase, they should not now be taken in by the essentially historicist position of postmodernism asserting that this was an inevitable stage in the evolution of culture. Second, Zagorin objected to postmodernism because, in many cases, postmodernist writers had not only criticised the values of modernism but repudiated such important aspects of modern culture as 'logocentrism', that is, the centrality of language and knowledge in a meaningful world. Third, postmodernists also tended to be hostile to humanism on the grounds that it was an outmoded relic of bourgeoise ideology: humanism was elitist in its rejection of some aspects of human cultures. Zagorin continued his attack with the charge that postmodernism was associated with the decline and exhaustion of civilisation, foretelling the end of mankind. He concluded his critique with a list of the characteristics of postmodernist writing: it was essentially superficial (depthless); it was fixated on the image; it paid too little attention to the emotions; it regarded truth as metaphysical baggage; it encouraged the disappearance of the autonomous individual; and it risked the loss of the past and the disintegration of time sense into 'unrelated presents'. He also criticised the prevalence of pastiche, imitation and cannibalisation of style. More seriously, in abandoning the concepts of explanation and cause, postmodernism trivialised history.

We have spent some time on postmodernism and history in this chapter, and we shall return to the topic in our final chapter, simply because it cannot be ignored in a book about the history of educational ideas. However irrational extreme versions of postmodernist ideology may seem to be, it has influenced educational theory and practice as well as being a continuing theme within historiography. For the rest of this book we have tried to tread a middle path between traditional historical approaches and some aspects of new history. We retain conventional historical 'periods', for example, but stress the inevitable artificiality involved. We avoid concentrating on the 'great thinkers' of education by looking more generally for social, economic and political causes in the history of education, without accepting historicist or deterministic explanations. Ideas clearly owe much to political and economic factors but it would be difficult to ignore the contributions of individuals in their

8

social context. One difficulty of this approach is that almost anything existing in a culture is relevant to educational ideas, but it is only possible to analyse a few of the factors. There will be, however, a companion volume in which we look at specific, more limited, educational topics in greater detail.[9]

REFERENCES

1. R.J.Evans, *In Defence of History* (Granta Books, 1997), pp. 1–4.
2. E.H. Carr, *What is History?* (George Macaulay Trevelyan Lectures delivered at the University of Cambridge January–March, 1961).
3. G. Elton, *The Practice of History* (Sydney University Press, Sydney, 1967).
4. The terms 'high' or 'late' modernist are often used interchangeably, but some prefer 'high' on the grounds that 'late' assumes more knowledge about timing than we actually possess.
5. Another complication is that some writers comment favourably on some postmodernist beliefs but reject the title for themselves – for example, A. Hargreaves, *Changing Teachers, Changing Times: Teachers' Work and Culture in the Postmodern Age* (Cassell, 1994).
6. L. Stone, *The Past and the Present Revisited* (Routledge & Kegan Paul, 1987), pp. 3–44.
7. F.R. Ankersmith, 'Historiography and postmodernism', *History and Theory*, 28, 1989, pp. 137–53.
8. P. Zagorin, 'Historiography and postmodernism: reconsiderations', *History and Theory*, 29, 1990, pp. 263–74.
9. P. Gordon and D. Lawton, *Lessons From the Past*, forthcoming.

Further Reading

Bronowski, J. and Mazlish, B., *The Western Intellectual Tradition: From Leonardo to Hegel* (Harper and Row, 1960).
Tarnas, R., *The Passion of the Western Mind: Understanding the Ideas That Have Shaped our World View* (Pimlico, 1991).

2
The Greeks

It is important to remember that during the period we shall be discussing in this chapter (from the ninth to the third centuries BC) there was no such country as Greece as we know it today. The area now shown on the map as Greece, as well as many hundreds of islands and large parts of Asia Minor (modern Turkey), was occupied by groups who possessed some cultural features in common but who thought of themselves as Spartans or Athenians or Cretans rather than Greeks. Only occasionally did these various city-states (and there were more than 1,000 of them) unite in the face of a common enemy, such as Persia. For most of the time, as we shall see, the Spartans and Athenians were hostile to each other and tended to emphasise their cultural differences. Nevertheless, it is possible to generalise to some extent about the Greeks: in particular, they shared a common language (with some local variations and dialects): those who did not speak Greek were termed 'barbarians' because the words they uttered sounded like 'ba..ba..ba' to the Greeks. They also had a common religion – or at least they shared the same pantheon of gods and a mythology; and they shared a great literary heritage, most importantly the Homeric tales of the *Iliad* and the *Odyssey*, which had been converted from an oral to a written form in the eighth century BC and were used for hundreds of years as educational texts for the improvement of the young.

We shall have space to compare only two of the many Hellenic nations: Sparta and Athens. The differences in their ideas on education are often very surprising. In addition, we shall make a brief reference to Alexander the Great and his Macedonian Empire, not least because Aristotle was Alexander's tutor.

We have started with the Greeks because their views have, fortunately, survived in written form, and because some of those views have continued to be influential for over 2,000 years. Education may be said to start to exist when some teachers cease to accept traditional beliefs automatically and begin to ask 'why?' Before that time teaching (or at least training) can exist together with learning, but *what* is transmitted is taken for granted:

children learn occupational skills from their elders together with beliefs about the environment, but such learning is assumed to be true as part of a traditional belief system. Very often such beliefs form part of a religious or magical worldview that is sacred and unquestioned. The earliest Western philosophers, in seventh-century BC Greece, started asking questions that called for logical thought rather than mere repetition of traditional folk knowledge. Some of the questions were focused upon the natural environment. For example, Thales (624–546 BC) of Miletus (in Asia Minor) is sometimes referred to as the first philosopher. He asked questions about the nature of the universe, studied astronomy and successfully predicted an eclipse of the sun in 585 BC. The fundamental question that puzzled Thales was 'What is the world made of?' He incorrectly came to the conclusion that water was the basis of all matter. However, his importance lies not in the answer but in the fact that he found it necessary to ask a question for which the answer was derived from observation and logical reasoning rather than from myth. The educational significance of this was that the young should be taught to think and ask questions rather than be given information (true or false) to memorise.

Thales was not the only philosopher to ask such questions. He had a group of followers, known as the Milesian School, which included Anaximander (610–545 BC) who, like Thales, was an astronomer, asking scientific questions about the universe. He was also a geographer, or at least a map-maker, who produced useful charts despite being handicapped by believing the world to be flat. Another of the pre-Socratic philosophers was Heraclitus (544–483 BC) who lived some time after Thales at Ephesus. He asked similar questions to those of the Milesian School, including the nature of matter. He came to the conclusion that fire was the basic element causing all change and motion: nothing stays the same over time, everything is in a state of flux, hence his famous axiom 'it is not possible for anyone to step in the same river twice'. He was also concerned with moral questions, saying that a person's character is his destiny. Better known than any of the above is Pythagoras (580–500 BC) of Samos who combined work in philosophy and mathematics. He applied logical (mathematical) thinking to the solution of practical problems, and Pythagoras' theorem about triangles is still part of the geometry curriculum. There were many other philosophers in the Greek world. One whose name we should mention is Protagoras (485–410 BC) of Abdera who is remembered above all for his bold statement 'man is the measure of all things'. In many respects such thinkers paved the way for Socrates whose Athens, unlike Sparta, was ready to be taken into the real world of philosophy.

SPARTA

The Spartans lived in that part of the Peloponnesian peninsula known as Laconia. For many centuries they were successful as warriors and brought up their male children to become good soldiers. Some hostile writers have described the whole of Sparta as a kind of military training camp. Life for all the Greeks was hard, but for young Spartans it was designed to be tough, even brutal.

Soon after birth a child was presented by his father to an official inspection committee who would permit only healthy specimens to live. Those who failed the test were disposed of, usually by being exposed on the mountainside. (Infanticide was not uncommon among the Greeks, but outside Sparta the decision was the family's, not the State's.)

When the boy was seven years old the State took over from the family, and at the age of 14 state education became total in military-style boarding schools or training camps. The boys learned the basics of literacy but most of the curriculum was dedicated to physical fitness and training for war: the ability to tolerate pain and hardship and to be self-sufficient was prized. Food was deliberately kept in short supply so that the boys would have to steal, and if they were caught stealing they would be severely whipped – not for the crime of stealing but for their lack of skill and for being caught. They remained in the camp until the age of 18 or 20 when they became soldiers, and as they approached manhood the training programme became even more harsh and militaristic. They would be required to survive in the wild on their own and might be encouraged to kill a few slaves to prove their manliness.

What was the explanation for this harsh Spartan regime? Some have blamed a ninth-century leader and law-giver named Lycurgus, but it is doubtful whether such an individual ever existed: it is more likely that the regime developed over quite a long period, from the ninth century to the seventh century BC. Most writers have agreed on two factors: first, war between the Greeks and against common enemies was frequent; and second, the Spartans had defeated the neighbouring Messenians, who out-numbered them by about ten to one, and kept these neighbours, nominally free, in a state of subordination. The Spartan style of rule was to treat their subject peoples and slaves (*helots*) very harshly, making them do all the hard work in fields, for example. This provided the Spartan elite with leisure time but no security, as they were always anxious that their subject peoples and slaves might rise up against them, or worse still, combine with other enemies. The Spartan solution was to use their leisure time for prolonged military training; education for young Spartan males was

12

dominated by social structure and was little more than preparation for becoming a warrior.

Spartan educational ideas were simple and very limited. The purpose of education was training – for physical fitness and military proficiency. It was a conservative educational policy in the sense that it did not change, and it looked back to a semi-mythical golden age; it fitted a culture where foreigners were disliked and foreign trade not tolerated; Spartans were forbidden to travel outside Sparta as foreign ideas were seen to be dangerous, encouraging weakness and a desire for luxury; obedience was stressed rather than imagination, creativity or improvement. The Spartans were good athletes, winning far more than their fair share of Olympic prizes, and they had an efficient army. But was it a life worth living? Despite the harshness of Spartan society and its education system, Plato admired some aspects of the regime, especially the subordination of individual desires to the greater good of the State, a view reflected in the *Republic*.

ATHENS

The people of Athens shared some of the Spartan ideas and practices, but the differences were more important than the commonalities. One major contrast was that whereas the Spartans were suspicious of new ideas and disliked foreigners, the Athenians were seafarers and traders who admired innovation and who welcomed many aliens into their society. Admittedly the aliens were not citizens but they were respected as members of Athenian society: at the beginning of the fourth century BC, when the citizens of Athens numbered about 21,000 (counting only men), there were also some 10,000 resident foreigners as well as 20,000 slaves.

In the early days of Athenian history (ninth century BC) ideas on education were in some respects similar to those in Sparta albeit less extreme. Education was still largely physical but with a greater emphasis placed on music, poetry and general literacy. From the fifth century BC, Athenian culture developed significantly and this influenced their educational thinking and practice. A major difference was that Athenian boys were educated for democratic citizenship, as all adult Athenians were liable to be drawn, by lot, for public office, or they might need to plead a legal case in front of their fellow citizens, there being no professional lawyers to plead for them. Thus education for citizenship took the form of public speaking or rhetoric, with wealthy parents paying large sums for good training under expert teachers. From the sixth and fifth centuries BC, to precede that kind of post-school education, schools for the 7–14 age group developed and began to flourish. The male children of most citizens went to school at the age of seven and about one in ten proceeded to more advanced education at the age 14. Schools in Athens were private, although some fees might be paid by the State, and the children of more affluent parents tended to go to the better schools and remain there longer. Girls were educated at home where the training concentrated on their future role as wives and mothers while including some aspects of the boys' practical activities. The curriculum reflected the Athenian concern for physical development and music. (Music, derived from the Greek *muse,* included poetry and dance; poetry was intended to be accompanied by a lyre, and all were encouraged to learn to play.)

It is important to bear in mind that the key subject of rhetoric or oratory was much more than speaking clearly and grammatically, although both of these were considered very important. It amounted to presenting an argument logically and elegantly, without notes. Unscrupulous teachers might have concentrated on instructing their pupils on how to win an argument by trickery, by scoring points, or to win a case even if the evidence pointed the other way. On the other hand, the best teachers advocated honesty, and taught an ethical approach to rhetoric as well as how to exploit the beauty of language as a kind of prose poetry.

In the fifth century BC, Athens not only produced their own teachers of rhetoric but attracted many from overseas who set up schools or taught small groups in the open air. Some of these teachers have been collectively referred to as the Sophists. They developed a philosophy of a kind, although some Athenians, including Socrates, criticised many of them for their methods, their superficiality and for their lack of true principles. Others claim that the Sophists made a contribution to both philosophy and education. What they certainly succeeded in doing was creating an ethos in Athens in which discussion of crucial issues flourished. An important difference between them and philosophers like Socrates and Plato was that Sophists tended to deny absolutes such as Truth and preached a kind of moral relativism.

Athens was not perfect but it was a society in which the majority of the citizenry (which did not include women or slaves) participated in political and social life. This participation involved such educative events as attending the plays of Sophocles and Euripides, which provided a kind of adult moral education as well as being written in magnificent poetry. What concerned Plato as well as many others, including the dramatists, was that the mythological stories about the gods provided very poor role models for human behaviour. By the end of the fifth century, many, like Socrates, were looking for `reasonable' explanations for the world and the human position within it.

SOCRATES (470–399 BC)

One of the paradoxes of the Greek world was that Socrates has been accepted as one of its greatest thinkers despite the fact that if he ever wrote anything it has not survived. We know about Socrates largely through the Dialogues written by Plato. We do not know how accurately Plato reported on Socrates' life and philosophical position. He may have simply used Socrates as a convenient way of expressing his own ideas, but it is likely that the earlier Dialogues reflect more of the genuine Socrates than the later writings where Plato was probably developing his own ideas. That Socrates was a real historical figure, with remarkable ideas, is beyond dispute: other writers including Xenophon (435–354 BC) have also written accounts of Socrates' life and work, though not in such detail as Plato.

One of the features of Socrates' life on which there is agreement is his style of teaching, now sometimes referred to as 'Socratic method', a system of intellectual enquiry based on questioning fundamental assumptions or beliefs. This technique involved an expression of ignorance. When the Oracle at Delphi proclaimed Socrates to be the wisest of all men, Socrates interpreted this to mean that he was wiser than those who thought they knew the answers because he knew that he did not. So when Socrates asked 'What is justice?' it was not to lead his audience to a correct definition, but to illustrate the fact that such questions did not lend themselves to simple or even complex definitions. The interesting aspect of this kind of 'teaching' was that it abandoned the notion of knowledge being acquired by the process of the transmission of ideas or information from one who knows (the teacher) to one who has space in his mind to receive it (the student), a view of education that has been difficult to transcend even in the twenty-first century. To put forward this view in the fourth century BC was truly remarkable.

THE INFLUENCE OF PLATO (428–347 BC)

Plato's ideas on education are probably more widely discussed than any other pre-twentieth-century writer, the reason being that Plato had very clear ideas about the purposes of education which were closely connected with a social philosophy that has since been copied and adapted by many groups in a variety of countries. For example, in England after the Second World War some local education authorities adopted the practice of separating secondary school pupils into three different schools according to their performance on a test at the age of 11. Some of those who advocated this tripartite system of secondary schooling justified their practice partly by reference to Plato's *Republic*.

Plato's theory of education was presented in the context of a much broader question 'What is the good life?' In the *Republic* the answer, significantly, begins with a long discussion about the nature of justice which Plato eventually replaced by 'How are men to live their lives so as to live well?' To answer that question Plato found it necessary to embark upon an analysis of the relation between the individual and society: all individuals have needs, some of which are only satisfied in co-operation with other individuals. The answer about the good life was therefore a social question as well as a matter of personal morality; education is a basic component of a good society.

Education was seen by Plato as essentially a process of nurturing what we might now call an individual's 'human nature'. Plato's ideas on education were much influenced by the fact that Athens had experienced a good deal of social unrest and political instability by the time that Plato was writing. Plato came from an aristocratic family, one which in pre-democratic times would have been part of the ruling oligarchy. That oligarchic regime had been overturned and replaced by 'democracy'. Plato himself was never convinced that democracy could work: under an enlightened leader like Pericles (490–429 BC) democracy worked reasonably well, but after his death, Plato became very critical of the democratic leaders, who, he thought, pandered to the wishes of the masses.

Plato's *Republic* was a kind of Utopian recipe for a stable, just society in which the citizens could enjoy a 'good life'. Plato's central idea was that his ideal society would have three levels of citizens: the workers or men of bronze; the warriors or men of silver; and the guardians or philosopher-leaders, the men of gold. Each of these three groups would be carefully educated and trained specifically for their future roles in society. A good society was one in which all individuals played a useful part. Clearly, the education required for the guardians or rulers would be a philosophical training to help them decide on policy, and to rule wisely, whereas warriors and workers needed much more practical vocational training. In such a society everyone would know their place and everyone would be trained to do their duty according to their rank. From a very early age they would have been prepared for their adult role according to their rank. There would be different curricula for each of the three groups. (We should note that in Plato's *Republic* there would be no slaves, women could be guardians and the system was what we now call 'meritocratic', that is, based on ability rather than rank.)

Those who praise Plato's ideas should realise that Plato was making his recommendations for a very specific (but non-existent) community: a city-state with a simple agrarian and trading economy where there was little technology and therefore little technological change. There was no need for social mobility to promote further changes. In fact, Plato wanted to have as little change as possible: social and political stability were, for him, very high priorities along with justice, although his ideas for the Republic would have involved major changes in Athenian culture. Such a system would not be possible in a twentieth-century industrial country with a rapid rate of social and technological change. The other point that needs to be stressed is that Plato was not in favour of democracy. He believed that democracy had failed in Athens, and his *Republic* was an alternative, utopian, proposal for social stability and justice – of a kind.

Plato also continued a debate that has dominated the philosophy of knowledge for centuries: Plato was an idealist who argued that the evidence of the senses was unreliable: the use of such evidence had to be reviewed critically by the mind. He agreed with Parmenides (515–450 BC) that appearance and reality are essentially different; Plato argued that knowledge or truth and what can be perceived with our senses may be contradictory. He believed that nothing in the world is 'knowable' except in so far as it corresponds to an intelligible 'reality' and reality for Plato was a set of abstract ideas: round objects could be grouped together and generalised because there is an abstract – ideal – concept of roundness as a Form. Good exists as an ideal or abstract idea in the same way. This idealist view contrasted, as we shall see, with Aristotle's realism, but they both agreed that Socrates had made two major contributions: inductive arguing and generalising. They also agreed that the prime purpose of education was to produce a better person, in terms of virtuous behaviour and service to the State.

ALEXANDER THE GREAT (356–323 BC) AND ARISTOTLE (384–322 BC)

Alexander was the son of Philip of Macedon, an area of the Balkans that was Greek-speaking but regarded as somewhat less civilised by the

Athenians and the Greeks in other more southern city-states. Philip had been a successful general who inherited the throne of Macedonia in 336 BC when he was only 20. He came to the rescue of the Greek city-states when they were threatened by the Persian Empire. Later, his son Alexander decided to invade Persia and in the process took command of a united Greek Army. He conquered Persia and also occupied Phoenicia, Palestine and Egypt. As a result of Alexander's conquests, Greek ideas were established in many parts of the world, such as Alexandria where education flourished. Aristotle was Alexander's tutor for a while and Alexander's curriculum was said to include philosophy, rhetoric, biology and medicine. Aristotle's influence on Alexander should not be exaggerated, but many writers have claimed that Alexander retained his interest in some of the subjects he had been taught by Aristotle, and it may be true that he took scholars with him on his Asian expeditions who reported back to Aristotle. After the death of Alexander in 323 BC his empire began to disintegrate with important political and cultural consequences.

Aristotle's influence on philosophy and education was, however, enormous. His scientific writings, including ideas about the human mind and how children learned were hardly challenged for hundreds of years. Aristotle was educated at Plato's Academy in Athens, remaining there for some 20 years. Later, in 336 BC, he founded his own school in Athens, the Lyceum. Although greatly indebted to Plato, Aristotle rejected one major thesis, that of idealism. Unlike Plato, he was a realist who believed that what we think depends entirely on the sensations we have experienced. This gave rise to the later interpretation, possibly misinterpretation, of his view of the mind as a blank space which needed to be filled up with educative experiences – an excuse for much bad practice throughout the centuries, including the twenty-first. Aristotle's writings (in Latin translation) were studied in medieval Spain and in schools in France set up by Charlemagne.

Like Plato, Aristotle believed that education should be controlled by the State and that the control should include school inspectors. This debate about state control has continued ever since. It would be impossible to attempt to summarise all of Aristotle's contributions to Western ideas here. We will concentrate on those that have had a direct influence on education. Like Plato, Aristotle saw education in terms of preparation for 'the good life'; education was essentially a moral process, and his writings on ethics are still worthy of study today. The study of ethics is not only close to education but also to politics: Aristotle gave us the famous definition of 'man, the political animal'. All human beings have to learn to achieve their own happiness in the context of a society in which it is essential to co-operate with others, which Aristotle saw as the major task of education. Part of the secret of human happiness, therefore, is what is now often referred to as the 'golden mean', a balanced position between two extremes: temperance is the happy mid-point between extravagance and meanness; courage is between cowardice and recklessness. Balance is always the key to happiness and adjustment to social norms. According to Aristotle, moderation in all things is in keeping with the natural laws of the universe, and with the norms of a good society.

Aristotle's *Ethics*[1] does not present us with a working system of universal principles. Such a system would have been impossible for Aristotle because he realised that difficult ethical issues are those where principles come into conflict with each other. What he left was a set of 'roughly accurate generalisations',[2] which may be superseded in time by superior principles. This has become the basis of moral education in schools in several countries.

When Alexander died in 323 BC, Aristotle, perhaps mindful of the death of Socrates, fled from Athens to Chalcis where he died a year later. His Lyceum School, however, survived for about 500 years. In the Middle Ages, Aristotle's ideas were adopted by Islamic scholars such as Avicenna (979–1037 AD) and Ibn Rushd Averroes (1126–98 AD) and were, remarkably, incorporated into Christian philosophy in the form of scholasticism. His ideas on philosophy and education also influenced many of the Renaissance reformers. We shall return to his influence in later chapters.

CYNICS, SCEPTICS, EPICUREANS AND STOICS

At least four kinds of philosophers emerged at about the time of Alexander: their ideas were of educational importance for many years in a variety of countries that came under Greek influence. In different ways they were all trying to make sense of a bewildering world which, particularly after the death of Alexander, seemed to be characterised by uncertainty.

Cynics

The philosophy associated with the Cynics can be dated from about 400 BC in Athens. Antisthenes (c. 455–360 BC), a pupil of Socrates, is regarded as the first of the Cynics, and he advocated a simple moral code not based on personal pleasure or happiness. The most famous of the

Cynics was Diogenes (412–323 BC), who believed that individual self-sufficiency in moral behaviour should take priority over social conventions. The extreme simplicity of his life earned him the title of 'cynic': he lived like a dog rather than a human being. (Cynic originally meant 'like a dog' but is now applied to those who tend to believe the worst of others and do not trust what they say.)

Sceptics

Sceptics believed that absolute knowledge was not attainable; the most appropriate behaviour was to doubt all dogma and doctrines; peace of mind was a reasonable goal and it could best be obtained by not claiming to know anything, but to base judgments on the balance of probability. The search for certainties was a waste of time. The origin of this scepticism went back hundreds of years in Greek thought, but it was Pyrrho (365–270 BC) who developed scepticism into a philosophical school of thought.

Epicureanism

Epicurus (341–270 BC) taught in Athens from about 306 BC. His message was that the rational pursuit of happiness provided a worthy purpose in life. Epicurus taught that at a time when the fame of public life might be dangerous, it was more sensible to achieve happiness in the fulfilment of a worthwhile private life. He recommended 'living unknown' as a key to the contented life. He did not deny the existence of a god or gods, but advised that we should not rely on their intervening in our world – we must look after ourselves physically and spiritually. This independence was, of course, later to be condemned by the Christians and others. Epicureanism survived its originator and was further developed in Rome by Lucretius (99-55 BC) who wrote *De Rerum Natura* (On the Nature of Things) which was an early version of atomic theory.

Stoicism

Stoicism was founded about 300 BC by Zeno (335–262 BC), a Greek born in Cyprus. Stoics believed that happiness is achieved by accepting the world as it is rather than wasting energy trying to change it. Nevertheless, they preached the brotherhood of all human beings and opposed slavery. Stoicism was a major influence on the development of Roman thought, especially that of Marcus Aurelius (121–180 AD) and Seneca (4 BC– 65 AD) and on Roman education (see Chapter 3). Stoics believed that we should rely completely on reason – there could be no higher authority. Stoics were also later criticised by Christians for committing the sin of thinking that human reason was superior to the authority of tradition, especially the Bible. A much later Stoic, Epictetus (55–138 AD) encouraged his followers to put the common good before individual self-interest.

Throughout this book there will be many occasions when we refer back to the ideas that were being discussed in Ancient Greece and particularly in Athens during the fifth and fourth centuries BC. Both Plato and Aristotle shaped European ideas about politics and ethics which encouraged later generations to think of education as much more than a matter of the acquisition of skills and useful information. In addition, both Plato and Aristotle established 'schools' in Athens which not only contributed in a practical way but also served as an example of teaching method. Plato's Academy survived for hundreds of years until it was closed by Justinian, for ideological reasons, in 529 AD.

CONCLUSION

We have already seen that Greek educational ideas of various kinds have survived into the modern world. Plato's 'utopian' solution of different kinds of education for different levels of a meritocracy is still being argued about in Western Europe. Perhaps more significantly, the views of both Aristotle and Plato that the State should control education was disputed in the nineteenth century and opposed vigorously in the 1980s and 1990s, to such an extent that even left-wing regimes in the West have accepted partial privatisation of some educational services. Aristotle's ideas on education for citizenship were also revived in England during the implementation of a new national curriculum from the year 2000 onwards.

REFERENCES

1. Aristotle, *Ethics* (Introduction by J. Barnes) (Penguin Classics, 1976).
2. Ibid., p.21.

Further Reading

Aristotle, *Ethics* (Introduction by J. Barnes) (Penguin Classics, 1976).
Marrou, H.I., *A History of Education in Antiquity* (Mentor, 1964).
Nettleship, R.L., *The Theory of Education in Plato's Republic* (Oxford University Press, Oxford, 1935).
Plato, *Republic* (trans. by D. Lee) (Penguin Classics, 1987).
Plato, *Plato's Dialogues* (trans. by F.M. Cornford) (Routledge & Kegan Paul, 1935).

3
The Romans

The traditional date for the foundation of the city by Romulus was 753 BC; the Romans used that date, which was probably mythical, as the basis of their calendar. Rome was originally a farming community and this background was always an important aspect of Roman culture, but the prosperity of the city was the result of trade, especially with the Etruscans in the north and the Greek colonies in the South.

At first the Romans were ruled by kings, and at some stage, probably in the sixth century BC, the Etruscans occupied Rome. In 510 BC the Roman patricians or aristocrats organised a revolt against the Etruscan tyrants and succeeded in replacing the foreign kings with a republic. From that time the Roman preference for a republic to any kind of monarchy was a powerful aspect of their culture. By the third century BC, Rome had expanded gradually, eventually controlling the whole of Italy. This inevitably brought Rome into conflict with another expansionist society: Carthage, based in North Africa (modern Tunisia). After long periods of warfare (the Punic Wars of 264–241 and 218–202 BC), Rome was victorious and dominated the whole Mediterranean region. The Greek colonies and city states were no match for the well-organised Roman Army, but in time the Romans learned to admire many aspects of Greek culture.

By the first century BC, Rome had become extremely wealthy, but the Republic of what had been a city-state was not an efficient means of running a vast empire. Only powerful generals such as Sulla, Marius and finally Julius Caesar were able to control the empire, and even then there were frequent civil wars. Caesar was assassinated in 44 BC, not least because some republicans feared that he intended to become king in fact if not in name. However, Caesar's nephew, Octavius, took over and eventually became the Emperor Augustus (63 BC–14 AD). The Empire based on Rome lasted until the fourth century AD, spreading Graeco-Roman culture to most of Western Europe as well as North Africa and Asia Minor. In the east the Roman Empire based on Constantinople survived until 1453, but its culture was different from the Roman in many respects, and we will consider education separately in Chapter 4 under the heading of Byzantium.

ROMAN EDUCATION

The Romans were not great cultural innovators, hence the frequency of the term 'Graeco-Roman' to describe their cultural artefacts and ideas. However, cultural domination by Greece was never complete: from the sixth to the third century BC, Rome had established its own cultural traditions, based on a rural economy in which the Roman landed aristocracy were firmly in control. Although the Romans took over many Greek ideas on education, they never relinquished their Roman cultural heritage based on a rural economy. One famous Roman exemplifying these ideals was Cato (234–148 BC) who wrote a manual on farming, probably the earliest surviving work in Latin prose. Cato also had firm views on many social issues, including education, and his respect for the rural life made him disagree with those Greeks who thought that manual labour was unworthy. Cato claimed that he had personally taught his son to read, write, fence and swim. He would have also introduced him to some of the techniques of farming. E.B. Castle[1] wrote:

> The average Roman had none of the mental agility of the Athenian and no strong political sense. His political struggles had always been utilitarian, centred on some definite freedom, legal or economic. He was almost devoid of philosophical curiosity. On the other hand the Romans had very definite views and standards concerning legal obligations, and, more than any other people before or since, a respect for constituted authority and a capacity for accepting intelligent and courageous leadership, qualities which were to make them masters of the civilised western world. But the most significant characteristic of early Roman society… is the position of the family in Roman domestic and civil life. It is here that the student of Roman education must begin.

Education began at home – in the family – and the father was responsible. In the early days of the Republic he had been legally entitled to flog his wife and children, even to execute them. By the time of Augustus that right had been lost, but not forgotten. Education at home would include learning to read and write, but probably not much arithmetic. (Until Arabic numerals were acquired, ciphering using Greek or Roman letters was very cumbersome and limited.) History hardly existed, but some tales of Roman grandeur would have been transmitted orally. If the boy grew up in the country he would, early on, be introduced to farming and its market economy. Music was not regarded as necessary nor the gymnastics once so important to the Greeks. Cicero (106–43 BC), who thought that education should concentrate on rhetoric, was contemptuous of certain Greek traditions: music and gymnastics were no preparation for war or government. Above all, traditional Roman morality stressed the family and the importance of education within the family.

EDUCATING FOR *GRAVITAS* AND *PIETAS*

The qualities that Romans admired most were *gravitas* and *pietas,* both closely connected with respect for family. *Gravitas* means possessing qualities of seriousness, earnestness, responsibility and probably a certain rigidity and distrust of innovation. *Pietas* was a devoted loyalty to family, nation and the gods. Bearing in mind those values and the possibility of their disappearance, Tacitus (55–120 AD), described traditional education in the following way:

> In the good old days, every man's son, born in wedlock, was brought up not in the chamber of some hireling nurse, but in his mother's lap, and at her knee. And that mother could have no higher praise than that she managed the house and gave herself to her children. Again, some elderly relative would be selected in order that to her, as a person who had been tried and never found wanting, might be entrusted the care of all the youthful scions of the same house; in the presence of such a one no base word could be uttered without grave offence, and no wrong deed done. Religiously and with the utmost delicacy she regulated not only the serious tasks of her youthful charges, but their recreations and their games.[2]

The French scholar, Carcopino, however, tells us that the practice of hiring a nurse (often Greek) to care for and educate young children became more and more common, a practice deplored by Cato and others.[3] At the age of seven the child's education passed from mother to father who would be particularly concerned with values: as well as *gravitas* and *pietas*, he would seek to inculcate *justitia* (love of justice and moderation), *fortitudo* (manliness), *constantia* (steadfastness or constancy) and *prudentia* (practical judgement). As with the Greeks, academic studies would be a much lower priority than what we might now call social and moral education. At about the age of 16, the boy's name would be placed on the list of citizens, he would be allowed to wear the adult toga, and would become available for military service. He would probably be placed under the tutelage of a respected man outside the family, a custom that survived into the middle ages as the squire–knight relationship.

SCHOOLS IN ROME

The earliest schools in Rome began around 200 BC when there was some reference to Spurius Cavilius, an ex-slave who was the first teacher on record in Rome to charge fees. Schools, as in Greece, were for seven-year-old boys and girls, and the curriculum was very basic, concentrating on reading, writing and simple calculations, as well as the elementary values of *pietas* and *gravitas*. This kind of regime lasted until the child was aged about 12. For the more affluent it was followed by a grammar school where the curriculum included Greek and Latin grammar, and later on literature: Homer, the fables of Aesop, in Greek, plus some Latin authors such as Horace, Virgil and Livy. Memorisation was the standard teaching method. Some practical geometry and simple ciphering would also be included.

At around the age of 16 the major subject became rhetoric, either with a private tutor or in a school of some kind. At this point Roman education was much indebted to Greek tradition and also to teachers who were often Greek and taught in Greek, despite the protests of conservative Romans such as Cato who objected to that kind of foreign influence. In 161 AD the Senate even attempted to ban foreign philosophers and rhetoricians but not for very long. The later emperors, Hadrian, for example, set up scholarships to encourage the teaching of rhetoric. It was not uncommon for the sons of the rich to go overseas to attend a famous school: Caesar went to Rhodes, Brutus to Athens; Cicero, perhaps the greatest of the Roman orators, went to both. Such education, at home or abroad, was very much an experience reserved for a wealthy elite.

CICERO (106–43 BC) ON EDUCATION

Cicero wrote extensively on education. His major work was *De Oratore* (On Oratory or Rhetoric) written in 55 BC. The title may give a misleading impression of the book which concerned the ideal upbringing of a young man, destined to play a part in government. Cicero emphasised the importance of the family and early child-rearing as well as the kind of education required to produce an orator who was imbued with the traditional values of a Roman statesman. Despite his emphasis on Roman traditions, it is clear that Cicero was greatly influenced by some of the Greek philosophers, particularly Isocrates (436–338 BC), a leading Athenian teacher of rhetoric. Cicero advocated the imitation of traditional Roman virtues as well as the acquisition of the best of Greek literature and philosophy. The key word in the text was *humanitas* which conveyed more to the Romans than the English word 'humanity': *humanitas* signified all the best qualities of civilised and well-educated men – courtesy, unselfishness and generosity as well as *pietas* and *gravitas*. *De Oratore* was a philosophical text, setting out a prescription for a good, worthy life in an almost ideal society. It was left to Quintilian about 150 years later to translate that philosophy into a teaching programme.

QUINTILIAN (35–96 AD)

The most famous teacher and educational theorist of Roman times was Marcus Fabius Quintilianus (Quintilian). He was the son of a teacher of rhetoric and not only followed his father's profession but established a very successful school. Little is known of his own education, except that he made some reference in his writing to his good teachers. Although he was in many respects very Roman, he was steeped in Greek literature, and was particularly influenced by Aristotle.

Quintilian was not simply a teacher but a practising rhetorician – he pleaded professionally in the courts in Rome. After some time in Spain where he had been born, he was summoned to Rome in 68 AD by the Emperor Galba. He then established his own school, receiving an imperial salary. He continued pleading in the courts, and was apparently successful in both careers. He attempted to retire from teaching in 88 AD, and on the strength of 20 years experience he wrote *The Institutes of the Orator*. While writing this major work he was recalled to teaching and given the task of tutoring two of the Emperor Domitian's great-nephews. He nevertheless managed to complete his book, which was published in 96 AD shortly before his death. It was based partly on the pedagogical ideas of Domitius Afer of Nimes, and partly on the philosophical writings of Cicero. The result was much more than a treatise on the training of orators; it has been regarded by successive generations as a classic text on early education theory. Quintilian's successful rhetorician was not simply a skilful orator but a wise man. The book is about education for wisdom rather than training for verbal skills. According to Quintilian, the perfect orator would be a man of integrity – a good man as well as a clever pleader. To achieve this end, Quintilian postulated three stages of training: up to the age of seven at home; general education at grammar school up to the age of around 16; finally, specific instruction in the art of rhetoric for several years.

For the first stage, Quintilian recommended that both parents should be 'cultured' and the nurse should speak well. Boyhood companions should be chosen carefully with a view to the development of good language habits. If any of these factors were in doubt, Quintilian recommended hiring a good 'master of language' to correct any faults. Quintilian believed strongly in developing good habits, especially in language, at an early age, however, little formal instruction was envisaged before the age of seven, just the correction of errors and bad habits of speech. Quintilian was anxious that if formal instruction started too soon it would be counter-productive. The repetition of rhymes and even the beginnings of reading and writing might start before the age of seven, but in the form of a kind of game. He was clearly operating with an early version of a 'stages of development' theory which cautioned against making difficult demands before the child was ready.

For the second stage, Quintilian favoured education at home with a tutor rather than what was beginning to be provided by the State in schools. The reason for this preference appears to be moral as well as pedagogical: at the time Roman schools were generally of doubtful quality and lacked adequate supervision, both in terms of behaviour and learning. Quintilian was unhappy about large classes and other aspects of public schools, although he also pointed out the limitations of a boy learning alone with a tutor. At school a boy could learn from what others were taught. Quintilian had a good deal to say about the grammar school: he subdivided his advice under two headings, moral and intellectual. At a time when corporal punishment was common, Quintilian strongly expressed his dislike of 'the whipping of children'. It was also counter-productive educationally: children should be encouraged to learn because learning was useful and enjoyable, not for fear of punishment. If children lacked interest that was at least partly the fault of the teacher. He did not use a word for 'motivation' but he had a good intuitive feel for the concept. He also understood the need to be aware of individual differences and aptitudes.

Quintilian's curriculum emphasised language: both Latin and Greek were essential; poetry was a high priority, as well as clear speaking and arguing. Children should be exposed only to material that was beautiful as well as eloquent: Homer and Virgil came first, then others who were considered to encourage the habit of reading. Music was also strongly recommended, partly because it was associated with poetry and therefore reinforced the teaching of language. Geometry too was essential. Physical education would have received separate attention in a specialist school for physical culture, where deportment and possibly dancing would be taught. As for converting this curriculum into a timetable, Quintilian favoured switching from subject to subject during the course of a day, partly to provide variety and partly to enable the co-ordination of learning.

Finally, the boy proceeded from the grammar school to the school of rhetoric. Once again, the character of the master was all-important. This was much more important to Quintilian than the quality of the facilities in the school. Quintilian listed the qualities of a good teacher: severe but not harsh; affable but not lax (familiarity breeds contempt); moderate in both criticism and praise, but prompt in responding to questions. He thought that the plainest methods were always the best. The final sections of the *Institutes* dealt in detail with the technicalities of rhetoric.

How influential was Quintilian? Pliny, Juvenal and Suetonius all referred to his work with respect, but his writings may not have been widely read in the Roman Empire itself. In 1416 a complete manuscript was discovered by the Italian humanist Gian Poggio at St Gall, Switzerland and became a classic text on education during the Renaissance. In 1512 Erasmus even apologised for mentioning teaching methods because he thought Quintilian had settled such questions long before.

MARCUS AURELIUS (121–180 AD) AND THE STOIC PHILOSOPHERS

Marcus Aurelius was influenced by the Stoic philosophy of Zeno (335–262 BC) of Citium in Cyprus, and closer to his own time, by Seneca and Epictetus (55–138 AD) who wrote nothing, but whose discourses were recorded by his admiring pupil, Flavius Arrian. The ideals of Epictetus have been compared with those of Christ although at this time Christianity was still forbidden in Rome and Christians were from time to time persecuted. A central theme was the brotherhood of man which included slaves. Pleasure was not a worthy aim in life: the Stoic ideal was to achieve happiness even when immediate pleasures were lacking.

As emperor, Marcus Aurelius led a life that avoided luxury and pleasure-seeking, performing his duties conscientiously. He reflected on his life in the *Meditations,* written in Greek. Stoic philosophy was fashionable among a minority of Romans before and after Aurelius but, unlike Christianity, had little appeal as a mass movement among the poor.

CONCLUSION

It would seem that popular education was not a great success in Rome. Recently, Carcopino has criticised the schools for failing to educate the young in a way that might have enabled them to save society, but was it fair to expect teachers to salvage a society in decline? Was the problem that Roman society had generally lost any sense of purpose? It may also have been the case that rhetoric became debased: instead of being a philosophy of life based on high principles and ideals, it became a game to be played and won, judged in terms of criteria concerned with verbal trickery, rhetorical devices and superficial debating skills rather than sound philosophical ideas. Seneca may have struck the right note when he criticised teachers for concentrating on the classroom rather than on life, but there were certainly very deep-rooted problems in society itself which schools and teachers could not be expected to solve. The poor quality of schools may have been a symptom rather than a cause of the decline of Roman standards.

Rome must take some of the credit – or the blame – for the spreading of the notion of the school. The Emperor Agricola (AD 37–93) exported the idea of the school to Britain, and it is very probable that by then it was general policy to introduce schooling into conquered regions in order to Romanise the population. In later years, the Emperor Diocletian wanted the State to take complete control of schools, and by the time of Theodosius, in 425 AD, all education was supervised by the State and teachers were only permitted to teach if licensed. This was another idea which was to spread throughout Western Europe. The Roman 'grammar' schools did not survive the Barbarian invasions but the model was remembered and revived in the eighth and ninth centuries AD, particularly at the time when Charlemaigne wanted to revive learning and improve the quality of the clergy.

REFERENCES

1. E.B. Castle, *Ancient Education and Today* (Penguin, 1961), p. 108.
2. Quoted by Castle, p. 112.
3. J. Carcopino, *Daily Life in Ancient Rome* (Penguin, 1962), p. 119.

A History of Western Educational Ideas

Further Reading

Boardman, J., Griffin, J. and Murray, O. (eds), *The Roman World* (Oxford University Press, Oxford, 1986).
Carcopino, J., *Daily Life in Ancient Rome* (Penguin, 1962).
Castle, E.B., *Ancient Education and Today* (Penguin, 1961).

4

The Judaeo-Christian Tradition

INTRODUCTION

It is important to keep in mind that early Christianity arose directly out of Judaism; at first it was regarded as just another Jewish sect. But Judaism, from about the third century BC, had been strongly influenced by Greek culture, especially language and philosophy. Later Christianity, including educational thought and practice, may be seen as a mixture of that Judaeo-Christian tradition and subsequent Graeco-Roman influences.

Background

For the Jews religion was part of their defence against foreign domination and oppression: theirs was a culture of a persecuted but chosen people. Their traditions told them that they had been led out of pagan Ur by Abraham who took them to Canaan. Later, the Old Testament contains a vivid description of the Israelites' captivity in Egypt, and their being rescued by Moses and given the law in the form of the ten commandments. If this happened, it probably took place in the thirteenth century BC. Later still, the Assyrians took over as the heathen oppressors: Nebuchadnezzar destroyed Jerusalem and began the `Babylonian captivity' (the Jews were in exile from 586–536 BC). In the fourth century BC Alexander conquered Palestine; not only did the Jews remain subjugated, but in the second century BC Antiochus of Syria attempted to abolish Judaism and replace it with Greek ideas. This produced the famous revolt of the Maccabees in 168 BC. In 63 BC the Romans, led by Pompey, took Judea and made it part of the Roman Empire; from AD 66–70 there was a revolt against Rome, and, as a punishment, Emperor Titus ordered the destruction of the Temple in Jerusalem and the expulsion of the Jews from their country.

Thus pre-Christian Jewish culture possessed a number of distinctive features. It was a nation frequently without a homeland; the Jews regarded themselves as superior, a chosen people, worshipping the one true God,

Jehovah, and they were often persecuted for this. They derived many of their religious laws and customs from a sacred text, the Torah, which included the five books of Moses (the Pentateuch). A powerful aspect of their culture was the need to transmit sacred knowledge and practices to succeeding generations. It was a culture in which learning was greatly respected.

JEWISH CULTURE AND CHRISTIANITY

The pre-Christian Jews had survived persecution by emphasising their `differentness': they were chosen, they were monotheistic, they had distinctive values, partly derived from their prophets. The early Christians adopted some, but not all, of these values. The Jews had a sacred text; the Christians would later add their own, the New Testament. Education was inevitably connected with these authoritative texts. Religion permeated the whole of life, and religion was identified with morality in a way that was unknown to the Greeks and Romans.

Castle[1] makes much of the distinction between priests and prophets. The priest represented organised religion, controlling ritual and worship; his influence was conservative – looking back to better days – and his function was to preserve existing forms. The prophet was a reformer, a directly inspired spiritual leader often with political powers: Jehu was proclaimed king by the prophet, Elijah. The prophets could also be social reformers and moralists: Amos (c. 750 BC) denounced racketeers who lived in luxury in the midst of poverty; Isaiah, son of Amos, preached about the obligation of the rich to care for the poor. However, this morality was presented as the will of God, not as part of a philosophical system of ethics. The prophets were messengers carrying God's word.

Later, the emotional preaching of the prophets was counterbalanced, to some extent, by the calm, detached wisdom of the sages, some of whom were influenced by Greek philosophy. For example, Ben Sirach (c. 200 BC) was sympathetic to a good deal of Greek culture but felt obliged to point out the superiority of traditional Hebrew wisdom. The sages were on the side of the oppressed and spoke of 'righteousness' as well as obedience. Another significant difference between Hebrew and Greek values was that the Jews did not disdain manual work. Yet another aspect of Jewish culture that has become part of Western civilisation is historical consciousness: God not only intervened in history but also had an historical plan for His people. Time is thus forward-looking as well as involving a record of the past – the idea of the promised land was a dominant feature of Jewish culture. It is not unconnected with the idea of progress which became so important in Western European notions of history and education.

Sadducees, Pharisees and Christian Values

From the second century BC, the Jews in Palestine were beginning to divide into two groups. First, the Sadducees who were 'fundamentalists', accepting only the Torah, the 'written law', but who occasionally flirted with some Greek ideas, including philosophy, as long as such notions were kept separate from religion. The second group, the Pharisees, accepted the Torah but believed that the laws needed to be interpreted to deal with social change; they advocated living by a combination of the Torah and the Talmud (the oral tradition of the Mishna in its written form), as well as being willing to discuss further interpretations of the Torah and the Talmud. Although the Pharisees were, in this way, more `progressive', they tended to be hostile to non-Jewish innovations, including Greek ideas. The greatest of the Pharisees was Hillel (60 BC–20 AD) who was credited with a version of the golden rule 'Do unto others as you would have them do unto you'.

Beliefs shared by Jews and Christians include the following:

- One God, the creator of the universe;
- the unity of mankind;
- the individual's sacred right to be protected from exploitation;
- the future as God's time, in which His rule will be established.

Education

There were elementary schools in Old Testament Palestine, but it is difficult to know how important they were. Many Jews could read but the skill was officially confined to a limited number of families since reading Hebrew was a difficult and specialised skill. For most young people, education was probably oral and took place mainly within the family. Synagogues were used for education as well as worship, but not as schools at this period; they were more like centres of education for adults, not children. Judaism was still a religion of 'The Book' but not all adults had direct access to the word: most needed to be told the stories from the Bible and have them interpreted by rabbis who were teacher-scholars rather than priests, owing their authority to their learning rather than their status.

From the second century on, the Jews in Alexandria read Greek rather than Hebrew, and had the Old Testament translated into Greek for their own educational purposes. For a time the revolt of the Maccabees separated Jewish education from Graeco-Roman ideas but it may have helped to persuade the Jews that they needed schools for their young. Simon Ben Shetah, the Pharisee leader, set up schools for boys aged about 16, mainly to encourage scriptural study. They flourished until 70 AD when the Temple was destroyed. After that they continued to exist for the Jews in their dispersal, or diaspora, as part of the means of inculcating Jewish values and beliefs. Nearly all boys attended: schooling was religious education of a nationalist kind designed to secure the survival of a religious culture. The family was probably an even more important institution for that purpose, the father being a priest for the whole family, and included an advanced ethical code. The Mishna (oral tradition) was very important as a source and was eventually written down as part of the Talmud. But the Torah was even more important, specifying details of everyday behaviour including diet. Children learned these rules from about the age of three. By the age of 13 boys were expected to understand and practise the law: texts were memorised and interpreted. There were also many feasts to be celebrated each with distinctive rituals which had to be mastered.

Jewish teachers tended to copy the schooling methods of the Greeks, but not their aims. The purpose of Jewish schools was essentially religious and nationalist: reading Hebrew was important for both purposes; however, interpretation of the texts was also stressed. At this stage writing did not feature on the curriculum: boys were simply not allowed to copy sacred scripture which was a highly specialised sacred adult role. For the young, reading the Torah was quite enough – it was extremely difficult. Arithmetic was not taught as it had no religious value; it was acquired as vocational training only by those who needed it. There was no music or physical education but health education in the form of bodily cleanliness was stressed, both at home and at school.

Schools from the third century AD

From the third century AD the elementary curriculum was broadened to include texts other than the Torah: for example, the Psalms and the Book of Proverbs. Post-elementary schools for boys 13–17 were less formally organised, in some cases resembling the Greek style of learning dating back to Socrates. Their subject matter was discussion of the Mishna. This kind of education was probably received by about 10 per cent of boys. The emphasis on memorisation and repetition continued. Teachers did not charge fees but accepted contributions from parents: they were greatly respected but were sometimes poor.

The Jewish tradition of education had a very clear purpose: it was religious-moral education, based on sacred texts and interpretations of the texts which were largely concerned with the survival of a persecuted but elite people. The curriculum was concerned with the pupil now, not as a preparation for his adult role and profession. Rich and poor children were educated together. It was a narrow curriculum but it focused on the child in a community and gave pupils exactly what parents valued.

EARLY CHRISTIAN EDUCATION

We have already discussed the Greek influence on Jewish educational ideas from about the second century BC. The simplicity of Hebrew monotheism and the morality of the prophets were enriched by such Greek ideas as those of the Stoics which stressed willing acceptance of hardship and difficulties, submission to Nature rather than domination of it. In the first century AD, Philo, a Jewish philosopher in Alexandria, attempted a synthesis of Greek and Jewish thought which began a tradition that was also of some importance in the development of Christian ideas. Early Christian education was therefore a mixture of several different traditions: Greek, Roman, Hebrew and the teachings of Christ and his followers. This is exemplified by St Paul: originally a devout Jew (a Pharisee) living in the Roman Empire, speaking and writing in Greek, but preaching a message that was distinctively different – some would say revolutionary – a set of Christian doctrines.

Schools

It is unlikely that before the capital of the Roman Empire transferred to Constantinople in the fourth century that there were many schools that could be described as Christian. The first converts to Christianity had tended to be poor, but during the second century there was a gradual change and more educated Romans began to be attracted. Generally, they would have continued to send their sons to traditional secular schools and endeavoured to have their children taught about Christianity at home and in church. This sometimes created a problem: the early Fathers disputed among themselves about the acceptability of the traditional curriculum based on Greek and Roman texts. St Justin Martyr (100–185 AD) had claimed that Christianity and Platonic philosophy shared the same God and the same process of reasoning: Socrates was a 'Christian before Christ'. Others like Tertullian (160–220 AD) regarded pagan texts as very dangerous, but better than no education.

In most cases, Christian parents used the traditional schools that were available, probably according to their social class. There were, however, a few notable exceptions where Christian school systems developed, for example in Alexandria and Syria where there were catechetical schools, interpreting the scriptures to the young (and to older converts). Such examples were rare, and even they were modelled to some extent on Greek schools. Teachers such as Origen (AD 185–254) of Alexandria expounded key texts and established a tradition of exegesis which lasted until the late Middle Ages.

THE DECLINE OF ROME

Meanwhile, the Roman Empire was facing a number of crises. First, we have already mentioned the problems of internal cohesion. The government machinery had been set up to run a republican city-state, not a vast empire. There were also social problems: in Rome and elsewhere the gap between rich and poor had grown to a dangerous extent, and there was little to bind citizens together, no religious faith, no philosophy of life, no great philosophical ideal. Moreover, corruption was the order of the day, and self-appointed moralists bemoaned the decline of traditional values and family life. Second, there were increasing external pressures on the Empire, including the city of Rome itself, from `Barbarians' of various ethnic origins coming from the north and the east. Finally, the defence of the Empire was increasingly in the hands not of Romans but of previously conquered peoples, some of whom were now supposedly subject to Roman rule.

The Move to Byzantium

The whole social and philosophical situation was so unstable that in the fourth century the Emperor Constantine decided to leave Rome and make a new capital in Greek-speaking Byzantium which he renamed Constantinople. This was the first of two momentous steps taken by Constantine; the second was to relax the prohibition of Christianity and later to become a Christian himself. From the fourth century AD the centre of Graeco-Roman civilisation, including education, shifted from Rome to Constantinople. Eventually there were two versions of Graeco-Roman civilisation and two versions of Christian teaching: Latin and Rome in the West, Greek in the east. The Roman Catholic and the Greek orthodox churches gradually grew further apart.

It is not part of our task to detail that aspect of the history of Christianity, and we shall only refer to it as it relates to the history of education. It is, however, important to emphasise that although Christ's religious message was unique, Christian education owed much to two earlier traditions – the Hebrew and the Greek. The Hebrew tradition contributed not only the literary approach of the Old Testament, but also a set of spiritual attitudes to life, death and dependence on one God. The Greek tradition contributed a powerful feeling for the wholeness of Man and the contrast between ideal and what passes for reality. Part of the story of the development of Christian education is the tension of those two traditions. We shall return to that development later.

EDUCATION: THE DEVELOPMENT OF A CHRISTIAN TRADITION

At first there was a lack of complete unity of belief among the Christians. This problem was countered by establishing a central authority for what was later (about 115 AD) called Catholic Christianity. As the original Apostles died out, it was important to have some sources of authoritative belief, in the absence of eye-witnesses. Catholic Christianity in each community was organised under a bishop (*episcopos* or supervisor). The theory was that each of the original Apostles had been directly `appointed' by Christ and the Holy Spirit; their successors were appointed by apostolic succession, that is, indirectly appointed by God himself. In 115, Bishop Ignatius of Antioch, who was shortly to be martyred by the Romans, wrote to his flock telling them to unify by supporting their bishop. He stressed the importance of obedience to priests and bishops if Christian unity was to be preserved. Thus an early traditional belief was the importance of obeying the authority of the church. One practical aspect of this belief was the Creed which converts had to memorise and repeat regularly. The Creed was a minimum statement of belief laid down by authority and about which there could be no dissent. If there was any dispute between bishops it was, somewhat later, resolved by the Bishop of Rome, the Pope, who had a direct line of succession back to St Peter. A feature of Catholic Christianity was thus established, namely, hierarchical authority: it had clear implications for Christian education.

From about 248 AD, persecution of Christians increased when there were attempts to enforce emperor-worship. Diocletian (245–313 AD) was particularly zealous: churches were demolished, scriptures burned and Christians executed or maimed. However, by the early fourth century, numbers had increased to such an extent that Constantine demanded that persecution cease completely. By 380, the Emperor Theodosius (346–95 AD) made Christianity the official state religion: paganism and heresy were forbidden by law. In this church of the late Roman Empire (fourth to sixth centuries) Christianity flourished – the age of the Western Church Fathers, Ambrose, Jerome and Gregory. Some historians have suggested that Constantine's motive in encouraging Christianity was that it would help unify the Roman Empire: he was astute enough to realise that the Empire lacked ideological consensus and that some kind of unifying force was needed. Despite its hierarchical organisation, however, Christianity was prone to differences in belief, especially doctrines about the Trinity and the Nature of Jesus Christ (was he God or man or both?). Emperors and church leaders called councils to resolve differences, but public debate sometimes had the opposite effect. Christianity began to adopt the Roman answer to heresy – persecution. The idea of tolerating dissent was rarely expressed: it was regarded as essential to know what was 'right' and to eliminate error on the basis of the authority of the Church. This was another social belief that influenced educational theory and practice.

The hierarchy necessary for enforcing orthodoxy also became more complex and more rigid. One result of such meetings as Councils was Canon Law, separate from traditional Roman law but legally enforceable. Priests and bishops needed to be educated about Canon Law as well as about Christian doctrines.

Another important development for education was the growth of monasticism. Monks living in isolation and poverty seemed to many to express Christian ideals better than bishops with their increasing wealth. The values of monasticism were, however, accommodated by the Church. (More will be said about monasticism in Chapter 5).

Schools

In most cases Christians probably took over existing Roman schools and modified their practices to some extent. This may have been a disadvantage because many of the schools were unsatisfactory in terms of organisation, curriculum and pedagogy. Nevertheless, the strength of existing arrangements and practices, such as corporal punishment, persisted and proved to be more powerful than Christ's own commandments about love and forgiveness. Moreover, in the west from the fourth century, schools and other institutions were declining or disappearing with the advance of the Barbarians and the collapse of the Roman regime.

ROME AND BYZANTIUM

In the fifth century, Rome began to withdraw armies from parts of the west, including England. The Empire effectively split in two: the Byzantine East based on Constantinople, and the West based on Rome which was gradually taken over by Germanic tribes and such kings as Odovacar and Theodoric. The Empire in Constantinople still claimed the whole of the Roman heritage and recovered some of the lost territories in Italy: for example, Justinian's famous General Belisarius won back most of Italy in the mid sixth century, but when he left, the territory slipped back to the local control of Goths or Vandals. Under these circumstances schools and education were not very high priorities. This remained the political situation of the Empire until the rise of Islam. Before embarking upon that narrative we should say more about Byzantium.

Education in Orthodox Byzantium

Although Latin remained the official language of the Byzantine Empire, by the fifth century Greek had become dominant linguistically and culturally. The majority of the population was Greek. This was important because Byzantium became a new culture, part Roman, part Greek, and from a religious point of view strongly Christian, sometimes fanatically so. Constantinople was a very large city at the centre of the Empire and needed vast numbers of literate officials and priests. Byzantine schools had two major purposes: first, to maintain Christian orthodoxy; second, to provide for the bureaucratic manpower needs of the Court and Empire.

Despite the destruction of records about secular life in Byzantium, including schools, we can be sure that schools were dominated by Christian beliefs, tempered by Greek and Roman pedagogical traditions. At first the secular and the sacred were kept separate, but later this proved impossible.[2] In the fourth century, St Basil had been in favour of all children being allowed to attend those schools intended for future priests. Despite some opposition from the Church this custom became common, but those parents who were wealthy enough usually preferred to hire personal tutors (often priests or monks) for their own children. By the sixth century, schools were catering for a large proportion of children, although there was considerable regional variation. By the eleventh century, free schools were available to all children, including orphans for whom the state assumed responsibility.

Before attending school, children would have been educated at home in the Roman tradition: mothers provided elementary instruction in speaking, reading and writing. Passages from the Bible would be learned by rote. Most boys would attend school from about the age of 14 and study grammar, which included correct reading and writing and the beginnings of rhetoric. They would learn 50 lines of Homer each day and read the commentaries on the passages. In the final year at school pupils would be studying philosophy, science and the four liberal Arts – arithmetic, geometry, music and astronomy (the *quadrivium*). Each bishop would control a religious school for future monks and priests where theology was included in the curriculum. Some would also learn to copy texts in the scriptoria.

Christianity remained a minority religion in most places in the Empire, and even within Christian areas heresies of various kinds continued to flourish. The old pagan superstitions and customs were extremely difficult to eradicate. Schools were much better at encouraging drills and rote learning than understanding the ideals of Christianity. In some places the only really effective educational institutions were the monasteries (see Chapter 5).

ST AUGUSTINE OF HIPPO (354–430)

Augustine is better known as a theologian and philosopher, but his ideas on education are important. He was born in Tagaste, in North Africa, modern Algeria, into a reasonably prosperous family: his father wanted him to have a good education. Augustine followed a course similar to what was described in Quintilian's *Instituteo*. He received elementary instruction in reading, writing and ciphering at the school of a *ludi magister*. His memories of his schooling were not entirely favourable: he did not like study and admitted he had to be forced to work. Whether this was due to incompetent teaching or Augustine's self-confessed idleness is not clear. He passed on to a grammar school and after a while did get interested in some of his studies, but his masters were not all followers of Quintilian, and Augustine frequently suffered the rod. He was forced to study Homer in Greek, and wondered why he could not have read it in Latin, which he loved.

As he got older he read widely: he especially appreciated Virgil but arithmetic did not attract him. Augustine began to think that it was better not to be forced to learn subjects which lacked interest for the student. Finally, he was sent to a school of rhetoric at Carthage. While he was pursuing these higher studies, Augustine flirted with the Manichean heresy, the belief that God and the devil were equally powerful. He remained interested in this belief for about nine years. For a while he became a teacher of rhetoric at Tagaste until he moved to Carthage where he was worried by the unruly behaviour of the students. He left to teach in Rome where he found the students less difficult, but when he opened his own school he was troubled by the dishonesty of the students who avoided paying their fees.

By now Augustine had found and understood Aristotle's work on logic. When he moved school yet again – to Milan – he met St Ambrose (340–97), became interested in Christianity and was introduced to the Neo-Platonists. He was converted to Christianity in 386, ordained in 391 and became Bishop of Hippo in 396. He now encountered a practical educational problem involving teaching methods. It was then the policy to recruit local priests from areas targeted for conversion, but the native Numidian trainee priests knew no Latin and found difficulty in mastering liturgical music. Augustine reflected on the problem and came up with solutions based partly on his experience and partly from 'the pagan world'. In Augustine's time some Christians were opposed to making use of any pagan ideas and literature, and disapproved of sending Christian children to pagan schools. However, the Fathers had learned to make good use of pagan culture, some even pointing out similarities between Plato and St Paul. Augustine was attracted by that kind of solution and concentrated on bringing classical learning into the service of Christianity. Part of pagan culture treated in this way was the curriculum based on the seven liberal Arts: arithmetic, geometry, astronomy and music (the *quadrivium*); and grammar, rhetoric and logic (the *trivium*). Augustine worked hard to harmonise the two traditions and largely succeeded. Uneducated trainee priests had to learn Latin by traditional methods as part of their Christian education.

Apart from one book, *De Magistro* (On the Teacher), which is devoted to an exposition of some basic educational problems in the form of an imaginary dialogue with his son, Augustine's educational ideas are scattered throughout his other writings. *De Magistro* is partly an enquiry into the origin of our ideas: are these ideas in the mind itself or as a result of an external agency such as sense experiences? Popular thinking in Augustine's day favoured the idea of the child with an empty mind that needed filling by means of verbal communication from teacher to pupil. Augustine saw the question in a more complex way: he did not accept the straightforward correspondence between language and thought, and recognised the need for the pupil to be actively involved in the learning process. The true function of language in learning was not to bring ideas into our minds but to stimulate and awaken those that were already there.

Teaching had to start with the familiar and proceed to the unfamiliar. Augustine saw teaching as the activity of causing pupils to learn, but the learning process was in itself necessarily an active process. He thought that when learning did take place it was the result of 'divine illumination'.

A second problem that Augustine attempted to solve was the nature of universality in our thinking: for example, the shift from saying that three sticks added to five sticks make eight sticks to the more abstract $3 + 5 = 8$. Augustine brought Platonic thinking to bear on this: namely the relation between ideal and reality, adding that God was the source of all our knowledge. He also had much to offer on the question of curriculum: the seven liberal arts of the *trivium* and *quadrivium*, which he used in a much more flexible way than his teaching contemporaries. He apparently wrote extensively on six of the liberal arts, but the only one to survive is *De Musica*.

One aspect of Augustine's theology which had unfortunate implications for education was his view of predestination and original sin. He thought that Adam, before the Fall, had free will and the capacity for good but that once he and Eve had sinned, the human race lost this capacity and deserved eternal damnation. All who died unbaptised would go to hell because they were essentially wicked as a result of Adam's sin. By God's grace, according to Augustine, some people were chosen to go to heaven. There was no hope for the others. This pessimistic view of humanity, which was eventually rejected by the Catholic Church but adopted by the seventeenth-century theologian, John Calvin, might also suggest that some could learn but others were destined to eternal ignorance. This did not fit in well with Augustine's more enlightened views of education, and in particular how children learn.

CONCLUSION

Whereas in Greece and Rome moral education was a powerful element in the curriculum, in Judaism, education was religious education: history, literature, indeed the whole of knowledge was filtered through a religious ideology. Rabbis were essentially scholar-teachers operating within a strict religious context centred on the synagogue. This tradition, which identified education almost totally with religious education was, eventually, taken over by the Roman Catholic Church in the West and by the Byzantine (Orthodox) Church in the East, which passed on the same tradition to Russia by way of the Orthodox Church. This total identification of religious belief and education encouraged a static view of knowledge and proved to be an impediment to necessary changes on several occasions, as we shall see in later chapters. If we define education as being essentially open-ended, then systems of schooling which emphasise conformity and obedience run the risk of becoming anti-educational, even anti-humanistic. The memorisation and exegesis of sacred texts is not, in the long run, a satisfactory alternative to the development of powers of thinking and critical understanding.

REFERENCES

1. E.B. Castle, *Ancient Education and Today* (Penguin, 1961) p. 155.
2. T.T. Rice, *Everyday Life in Byzantium* (Barnes and Noble Books, New York, 1967), p. 192.

Further Reading

Foss, C. and Magdalino, P., *Rome and Byzantium* (Elsevier-Phaidon, Oxford, 1977).
Norwich, J.J., *Byzantium: The Apogee* (Penguin,1991).

5

Medieval Europe and the Influence of Islam

INTRODUCTION

The period of European history covered in this chapter (roughly the fifth to the thirteenth centuries) was once neglected compared with the Renaissance, for example, but it is important for the history of educational ideas for two reasons. First, we need to know which ideas survived and developed; and, second, the new influences that emerged, such as monastic education, the rise of Islam, scholasticism and the development of universities.

Background

Rome fell to Barbarian invaders from the north in AD 410. Even earlier, as we saw in the last chapter, Constantine had taken the precaution of moving his capital city to the east – to Byzantium, which he renamed Constantinople (now Istanbul). Christianity survived in the West, however, and some of the invaders were converted to Christianity. Meanwhile Constantinople and the Eastern Empire (Byzantium) continued to flourish. Monasticism also developed, preserving traditional religious values and developing new ones.

From the fifth century, Roman culture and education were disrupted by barbarian invasions but did not disappear, and in some cases Roman institutions were taken over by the invaders. For example, in Italy the Ostrogoths did not abolish the schools of grammar and rhetoric in Rome, Milan or Ravenna. In Spain and Gaul, schools virtually disappeared but the classical tradition and culture continued into the seventh century. Latin texts were now more likely to be used than Greek. The classical tradition was sufficiently alive in Italy to produce great scholars such as Boethius (AD 470–524), a Roman senator from an aristocratic family who was well versed in the Greek as well as the Latin writers and stimulated the continued study of the classics, not least by his own translations of Aristotle and others into Latin.

MONASTIC EDUCATION

The major educational development was, however, the monasteries. St Benedict (AD 480–547) founded the monastery at Monte Cassino in Italy and established the Benedictine monastic rule; he also converted Totilla, King of the Ostrogoths. The Benedictine rule became a model for other orders of monks. St Augustine of Canterbury (d. 605) brought the rule to England where it continued as an important religious and educational influence until the Reformation.

During the sixth century, monasteries developed as a major religious and educational influence, and by the seventh century individual Christian scholars such as the Venerable Bede (673–735) at a monastery in Jarrow devoted their lives to scholarship and teaching. Bede, for example, produced the *Ecclesiastical History of the English People* (731) which is probably the single most valuable source for early English history. In addition, Bede wrote homilies, lives of the saints, epigrams and his own commentaries on the Old and New Testaments. Not long before he died he translated St John's Gospel into Anglo-Saxon or Old English. He had a good knowledge of Latin, Greek and Hebrew. It would be foolish to pretend that Bede was a typical monk: he was certainly exceptionally able and devout; but it is true that the best of monasteries were excellent centres of scholarship and education. From the sixth to the eighth centuries, the Church was the main means of preserving continuity in education, although it was often education of an exclusively religious kind. The main purpose of education was to train future monks and priests. The extent to which the classics featured in the curriculum is not clear. Mention has already been made of Boethius; other scholars such as Isidore of Seville (c. 560–36) also helped to keep the classical tradition alive.

CATHEDRAL SCHOOLS

The monasteries were, however, by no means the only providers of schools. Bishops often continued the tradition of Roman grammar schools in the form of cathedral schools, probably boarding schools for future clergy. In the case of these schools, as with the monastic schools, the purpose of education was clearly vocational: the first priority was to ensure that future priests and monks would be educated to a suitably high standard. The curriculum tended to be dominated by Bible studies and the Fathers of the Church but might also include carefully selected Latin authors.

The teacher in a cathedral school, as in a monastic school, was as much concerned with discipline and moral development as with academic achievement; they would very probably not have made any distinction between them. Some teaching manuals have survived which stress the importance of inculcating the four virtues: prudence, justice, fortitude (courage) and temperance. The instructional texts, religious and pagan, would not have been taught in isolation from the four virtues. Sometimes physical education was also mentioned, a healthy mind in a healthy body. Frequently the sacred text, the Bible was preferred to any other literary source.

For those not destined to be priests or monks education was usually very basic; just enough religious knowledge to understand the sacraments and the main aspects of the church services. The educational objectives were on two levels: elementary understanding of faith for the majority, with higher levels of understanding and knowledge for priests and monks, including some Latin. There were, nevertheless, constant complaints about the inadequate education of the clergy throughout the Middle Ages.

IRELAND

A major centre of educational development was Ireland where Rome had never been very influential. Irish monks not only spent their lives copying and illuminating texts, such as the famous Book of Kells, but also preserved some non-religious books for study. Irish monks, acting as missionaries, brought their learning to England and to other parts of Europe such as St Gall where a very important monastic centre was established.

The celebrated saints of Ireland included Patrick (389–461) and Columcille (or Columba) (521–597) who founded schools at Armagh and Iona. There was also a prestigious school and what we would now call a university at Clonmacnoise which attracted students from all over Europe, and from the seventh to the tenth centuries Ireland sent monks to many parts of the continent to establish monasteries and schools. Although the major purpose was to convert the heathen and to strengthen the Church, the curricula of schools often included such subjects as mathematics, poetry and astronomy.

ENGLAND AND FRANCE

In time, England also became a centre of scholarship and missionary training. Northumbria, in particular, possessed notable monasteries such as Jarrow, which was mentioned above in connection with Bede. Slightly later, York produced Alcuin (735–804) who in 780 went to France to the school in the palace of Charlemagne at Aix, now Aachen. The motive was always the same: to spread the Gospel and save souls by means of education. Alcuin himself went on from the palace school at Aachen to become Abbot of Tours in 796. He was a powerful influence throughout Charlemagne's Empire and helped to encourage the Carolingian revival of education and Christian culture.

CHARLEMAGNE AND THE CAROLINGIAN CULTURAL REVIVAL

Charlemagne, Charles the Great (742–814) was King of the Franks from 768, and was crowned Emperor of the Romans by the Pope in 800. It has sometimes been said that the Holy Roman Empire (a term not used at the time but by historians and critics later) was neither holy, Roman, nor an Empire; but the title was greatly valued by some of the Emperors. It was 'holy' because it was Christian: one of Charlemagne's achievements was to conquer and Christianise most of Western Europe; it was 'Roman' because many regarded the Carolingian Empire as the successor to Roman central control in Europe.

In addition, Charlemagne has often been given the credit for reinvigorating education at the end of the eighth century. In reality his contribution built on the developments of the church which had taken place earlier in monasteries and cathedrals. Charlemagne was, however, a genuine enthusiast for education and was concerned when he became King of the Franks in 768 to find that Latin standards in the court and elsewhere, even among the bishops, were extremely low. Charlemagne ordered that the clergy be instructed more vigorously and standards be strictly enforced. He felt it necessary for all priests to have a good command of Latin so that they could be confident in their transmission of the Bible – the sacred text – to their congregations and pupils. Accuracy was essential. To accommodate the teachers of teachers, the school at Aachen was expanded to cater for advanced studies for true scholars.

The school at Aachen became what would now be called a university, as it was devoted to higher levels of learning. As well as having English scholars like Alcuin, there were refugees from Moorish Spain, monks from Ireland and many other learned men. A central feature of the university was its library, and a *scriptorium* where books could be copied. (The catalogue at Aachen still exists.) Charlemagne thought that every school should have a *scriptorium*; as Abbot of Tours, Alcuin instituted a school of calligraphy to ensure that scripts were copied clearly and beautifully. This revival of culture and education continued under Charlemagne's sons, especially Louis the Pious, and his grandsons.

KING ALFRED THE GREAT AND THE REVIVAL OF LEARNING IN ENGLAND

In Wessex, Alfred became king in 871 and was, like Charlemagne a century earlier, disappointed with contemporary educational standards. Few priests really understood Latin well enough to translate the messages from the Bible into English in a way that their flock could understand them. Alfred's solution was to attract to his court scholars from England and the rest of Europe to promote higher standards of learning and also to translate some key texts into English. He was said to have translated the famous book by Boethius, *De Consolatione Philosophiae*. Young monks were encouraged to be scholarly as well as pious; this was not seen as a distraction from their religious duties, but as an enrichment of their studies. At this time there was also a good deal of cross-fertilisation between English and French schools and monasteries.

During the ninth and tenth centuries, although the first priority was still to educate the clergy, there was a growing tendency for some noble laymen (and women) to develop literary skills, extending the purpose of education from the purely religious towards the courtly accomplishments of the Christian knight which were later to become even more important (and which we shall discuss further in Chapter 6). The majority of the population, of course, remained totally illiterate. In some parts of Europe where a knightly tradition was beginning to develop, Latin texts of such classical moral writers as Cicero also became part of the curriculum, supplementing the scriptures.

During the twelfth century, there was a tendency in some European countries for the Church to become stronger and to want to reinforce this strength by restricting access to monastic schools to future monks. Monasteries became more exclusive and other groups, especially in cities, took on the responsibility for educating laymen and sometimes priests. The Church often wanted to retain control of education and reacted by saying that only those teachers licensed by bishops could be permitted to teach. The Lateran Council (1179) made this an official requirement for all Christendom. This ostensibly gave some credibility to the developing non-monastic schools and perhaps improved the quality of some of them. The schools adopted a 'liberal' curriculum of the classical *trivium* (grammar, rhetoric and logic) and the *quadrivium* (geometry, arithmetic, astronomy and music) which became the accepted advanced curriculum for the later Middle Ages. Philosophy and discussions about knowledge and how it should be structured into curricula were also beginning to be more common at this time, not least in the new universities.

THE UNIVERSITIES

We have already used the word 'university' to refer loosely to post-school education, but 'university' has developed into a more precise meaning and form of organisation. It may be helpful now to clarify the concept of the university. By the end of the twelfth century in several places in Europe, it had been found expedient for a bishop, or cathedral chancellor, to license groups of teachers to organise higher level, post-school, studies for clerics. Such licensed teachers and their students would commonly have certain privileges as a group which would enable them to run their own affairs without interference from civil authorities or others. This concept of a university was very far reaching and highly significant. We shall return to the topic towards the end of this chapter, here we simply note that there was a need, perceived by the Church authorities, for improved methods of educating the future clergy at a higher level after they had passed through school; several of the universities emerged out of this need.

The division of educational stages into primary, secondary and higher is now taken for granted, but in the Middle Ages it was far from clear what was needed, it was felt that the future leaders of a Christian society should understand Christian beliefs and the scriptures and be able to pass them on to their less educated flock. The university was not suddenly invented: it emerged gradually to meet social needs. It was greatly stimulated by the rediscovery of Aristotle, initially by Islamic scholars. Aristotle became *the* philosopher for universities and virtually the curriculum for the Arts faculty, but not the Theology faculty. We shall return to this topic later in this chapter.

ISLAM

Mohammed (570–632), the founder of Islam, was born in Mecca and in about 610 he proclaimed himself a prophet and said that the divine word of God had been directly revealed to him. This set of religious ideas was later written down as the Koran. Islam, like Judaism and Christianity, became a religion based on a sacred text and this was to have important educational implications. In 622 Mohammed fled from his persecutors to Medina; this flight, or *hegira*, became a significant date in the Islamic calendar. In 623 Mohammed and his followers defeated the traditionalist heathens at the battle of Badr; this was followed by a series of victories and Mohammed re-entered Mecca in 630, acknowledged as the great prophet of Arabia.

Islam shares many of the beliefs of Judaism and Christianity: for example, the Old Testament version of the Creation and the fall of Adam, but Mohammedans believe that both the Old and New Testaments were superseded by the Koran which did not accept the divinity of Christ. Despite a disputed succession when Mohammed died in 632, the Islamic empire expanded across North Africa into Spain and southern Europe: the successors to Mohammed's authority were the Caliphs.

Muslim scholars have correctly been given credit for preserving and developing the classical heritage of Greece and Rome. This process of Islamic educational development began during the Umayyad Caliphate (661–750): Greek science was encouraged in Syria; schools were patronised in Alexandria, Beirut and Antioch, and several other cities where the classical tradition had survived in schools. The encouragement of classical cultural traditions was intensified during the Abbasid Caliphate (750–1100): Greek texts, such as Plato and Aristotle as well as Galen's medical works were translated into Arabic, sometimes by Hebrew and Persian scholars. In addition, the famous ninth-century mathematician, al-Khwarizmi (c. 780–850), developed Arabic numerals from the Hindu notation and recorded the earliest version of trigonometric tables. He was also responsible for a geographical encyclopaedia. Thus it was not only a question of passing on Greek texts to those in the West who had lost them; it also involved developing them in the context of Persian and Hindu scholarship and Islamic culture. In such an intellectual climate Islam produced its own group of original thinkers.

From the ninth to the eleventh centuries, there was an interesting tension within Islam between the orthodox religious idea that the Koran was the ultimate source of all wisdom and a secular pressure to take advantage of other kinds of knowledge, including foreign knowledge, past and present. There were good social and economic reasons for the development of non-religious knowledge: the expansion of Islam encouraged such technical innovations as irrigation, for which the Arabs became famous in Sicily and elsewhere, architecture, ironwork, gunpowder, textiles and leather, as well as shipping. Although many of those technical and commercial developments took place independently of education, there were clear education and training needs if the Arabs were to be able to exploit these developments. The traditional forms of Arabic schools needed to be modified.

Prior to this era there had been many types of schools in the Arabian peninsula: circle schools, writing schools, palace and mosque schools as well as schools of public instruction. Their names indicate their functions. Some universities also emerged between the ninth and the eleventh centuries: not only in Baghdad but also in Spain there were many that were to become significant in the history of European education, including Cordoba, Seville, Granada, Cadiz and Valencia. The curriculum was wide and geared to some extent to practical requirements such as medicine, mathematics, science and technology.

From the tenth to the twelfth centuries there was a golden age of Islamic scholarship which included the poetry of Omah Khayyam, as well as the writings of Avicenna (979–1037), a philosopher, scientist and writer of the standard text on medicine. Slightly later, Averroes (1126–98) flourished in Cordoba. He was a philosopher who wrote appreciations of, and commentaries on, Plato and especially on Aristotle and did much to reconcile Greek and Islamic thinking. He was also a physician who was determined to keep science separate from religious dogma. This was seen as dangerous and he was exiled for heresy in 1195, but later rehabilitated, perhaps because his medical skills were so important. The teachings of Averroes were difficult to reconcile with the Koran and the Bible and led to later heresies.

THE DEVELOPMENT OF THE IDEA OF THE MEDIEVAL UNIVERSITY

The first university in Europe was possibly Salerno in the ninth century but there are problems of retrospective definition. Bologna, founded in the twelfth century, may be less controversial since it is closer to what came to be regarded as a university structure in the Middle Ages. The University at Bologna was soon followed, and possibly copied, by such places as Paris, Oxford and Cambridge. At first the term in use was not university, but *studium generale*. The first use of the term *universitas magistrum et scholarum* (university of teachers and scholars) was at the beginning of the thirteenth century, in Paris. Early *studia* were developed as a response to the need for institutions to educate priests and monks when it was considered by the Church authorities or other leaders that the monastic or cathedral schools were not providing education at a sufficiently high standard for future clerics and administrators.

It was thought that the schools were adequate up to a certain level but that some students should be encouraged to continue their studies. Since such *studia* were few and far between, it became common for students to travel long distances, even to other countries. *Studia* were then regarded as universal rather than local institutions. It was necessary for the groups of teachers and students to organise themselves partly for protection and partly for social and academic purposes. As the students were all clerics they were entitled to immunity from civil courts but were subject to ecclesiastical legal authority. It became convenient for universities to have their own courts: the first example may have been when the Holy Roman Emperor, Frederick I, in 1158 granted the students of Bologna protection against civil arrest and the right to trial by their peers.

Other privileges gradually followed, and eventually developed into the important concept of 'academic freedom' which is still interpreted as the right to work in a university without being subject to State censorship or control. That idea took a long time to develop fully, and is still subject to dispute, but by the fourteenth century a university certainly meant that there was a community of scholars, but not necessarily a building, that was recognised by the local civil and ecclesiastical authorities as possessing autonomy of some kind. Originally the Chancellor of the local cathedral granted licences to teach, and, somewhat later, his authority was partly delegated to a Vice-Chancellor who tended to be the elected head of the teachers (in much the same way as an abbot was elected to be first among equals of the monks in a monastery). By the thirteenth century, a bishop's authority was often not enough: it became necessary to have authority granted by the Pope or the Emperor.

One version of the history of Cambridge University is that in about 1209 a group of scholars in dispute with the Oxford University authorities simply left and set up a new establishment in the cathedral city of Cambridge. The issue at stake may well have been autonomy of teachers and students, an early example of a dispute about academic freedom. Tension was inevitable because universities often wanted freedom from interference from the Church itself, which was its licensing authority. Part of the story of the Reformation was a desire by universities to gain freedom from ecclesiastical control. For similar reasons, Protestant states, such as Marburg (1527) created new universities. Later one aspect of the Counter-Reformation was the action by Jesuits to gain control over existing universities or to establish new ones.

SCHOLASTICISM AND THE UNIVERSITIES

'Scholasticism' is the term used by later historians to describe the dominant approach to education between the eleventh and the fifteenth centuries. Scholasticism arose in reaction to a considerable problem: how to resolve the apparent contradictions between different authorities, for example, in theology the authorities were the Holy Scriptures as interpreted by the Church fathers; these might seem to contradict the legal authority of an emperor or the philosophy of Aristotle. The task of scholasticism was to harmonise these authorities; the method which developed was derived from Aristotle's system of logic.

Some writers place the origins of scholasticism earlier than the eleventh century. Pieper,[1] one of the great authorities on scholasticism, has suggested that we should attach great importance to the year 529, when the Byzantine Emperor, Justinian, closed the Platonic Academy in Athens, thus signalling disapproval of pagan writers and providing an impetus for the development of a philosophy which would be distinctively Christian. In that same year, 529, the first Benedictine Abbey was founded at Monte Cassino which provided a suitable location for the development of Christian scholastic thinking and writing, the search for the 'whole of attainable truth'. An even earlier date suggested by Pieper is 524 when Boethius, awaiting execution, produced his masterpiece *The Consolation of Philosophy* which referred to the pursuit of wisdom and the love of God as the two sources of happiness. Some have noted that this book is not specifically Christian, although Boethius himself was a Christian, and his work became widely read by Christians for several centuries. Boethius had also translated Aristotle's *Organon* and other texts into Latin. Cassiodorus, the first biographer of Boethius, founded a monastery and established in it his Roman library which included the works of Boethius. Aristotle, as translated by Boethius, became part of the monastic heritage and kept alive a limited view of Aristotelian philosophy until further works were, much later, made available by Islamic scholars.

The pedagogy of scholasticism was based on the study of authoritative texts as well as mastery of the techniques of formal logic. In this way any inconsistencies could be argued away. At university a master would read a chosen text out loud and slowly. Books were, of course, in very short supply prior to the invention of printing. This reading or *lectio,* the origin of the modern lecture, was followed by explanation of the meanings of any difficult words and discussion of obscure passages. The master would then pose questions about the text and resolve any difficulties that arose: this was the method known as *quaestio* which was followed by the *disputio,* a carefully conducted argument during which the rules of logic had to be scrupulously obeyed. University students thus carefully internalised the texts corporately chosen by the masters and became confident in the art of argument. This process had something in common with Greek and Roman rhetoric training, except that in scholasticism supreme attention was paid to the idea of truth as represented by authorities and tested by logic. No other kind of test was permitted or perhaps even contemplated: for example, Aristotle's work on biology might be tested 'logically' against the Bible, but not empirically. The world of words and ideas was much more important than things.

The High Point of Scholasticism: St Thomas Aquinas (1224–74)

Thomas Aquinas was not only a philosopher and theologian but a poet. Born in Italy he spent some time as a boy at the monastery of Monte Cassino, but was later sent to the University of Naples and then to the University of Paris. At Naples, he found the philosophical and scientific texts of Aristotle that were being translated from Greek and Arabic. He became a Dominican and went to the University of Paris in 1245 where he studied under the famous scholar Albertus Magnus. He began teaching in Paris in 1256, and after a period as advisor to the Papal *Curia,* he returned to Paris to develop his thesis concerning faith and reason, namely, that reason is able to operate within faith yet according to its own principles. He was at first opposed not only by traditional theologians but also by those influenced by Averroes who saw faith and reason as completely independent of each other. Siger of Brabant was a notable opponent of Aquinas, who claimed that Siger's over-rational views were not only wrong but compromised the Christian interpretation of Aristotle.

In his *Summa Theologiae* and *Summa Contra Gentiles,* Aquinas produced the definitive systematisation of theology in the form of a synthesis of reason and faith, philosophy and theology, university and monastery. In 1272 Aquinas returned to the University of Naples to establish a Dominican House. At this point, once again, he had to face the opposition of the traditionalist followers of Augustine who stressed the idea of Man as fallen. Aquinas saw Man situated at the juncture of two different universes: the corporeal and the spiritual (the body and the soul; matter and form).

Aquinas died in 1274, and three years later the theology masters of Paris University, in a zealous outburst of 'reform', condemned 219 propositions, including 12 of Aquinas'. Ultimately, however, Aquinas was reinstated and canonised in 1323. Meanwhile, orthodox scholasticism was dominated by discussions of the spiritual without the benefit of Aquinas' resolution of the problem of the two universes.

Aquinas is important in the history of educational ideas not least because he saw the learner as being at the centre of the educational process – the learner capable of self-education but within the context of faith and authority. Aquinas' interpretation of Aristotle was to have a far-reaching influence on Roman Catholic thought: he accepted Aristotle's dictum that Man was by nature a political animal and rejected the pessimistic view of political authority as a necessary means of restraining Man's sinful tendencies derived from original sin. Instead, Aquinas emphasised Man's social nature and saw government as a means of promoting Man's social well-being. This view had enormous educational implications.

The world of scholasticism was eventually threatened by a number of factors including the beginning of empirical enquiry by early scientists such as Roger Bacon (c. 1214–92) and, later, the scepticism of fourteenth- and fifteenth-century Renaissance ideas. It is easy to criticise scholastic education in retrospect, but for about 400 years the logical training involved was useful and productive in what was the most efficient higher education available. Minds were trained by this linguistic and logical set of exercises; in addition the young were taught to respect authorities and to regard logical argument as a high priority. Above all, it was open-ended education: sacred texts were central but not exclusively important.

CONCLUSION

It has sometimes been argued that the period covered in this chapter included the Dark Ages, a kind of cultural vacuum in between the splendours of ancient Greece and Rome and the revival of civilised ideas in the Renaissance. This is an over-simplification which underestimates the continuing intellectual activity in Europe and the progress made from the fifth to the thirteenth centuries, despite the havoc caused by the Barbarian invasions. One scholar has expressed the problem in this way:

> Adventurousness and dogmatism certainly exists in every age, even if the balance between them shifts, and in the long run one no doubt

spurs the other. In any case, a more general psychological comparison between the medieval and the classical ages would be more just and perhaps show less disparity.[2]

It may also be the case that outside influences have been underestimated. So strong was the Islamic influence on Western ideas that some modern historians have wanted to date the origins of the Renaissance much earlier than the fourteenth or fifteenth century. It is certainly true that the eleventh and twelfth centuries should not be regarded as uncivilised: Romanesque architecture, Gregorian chant, chivalry, poetry, monasteries, universities and such enlightened figures as St Francis of Assisi all indicate the development of civilisation.

There were, of course, other factors: around the year 1000 there were many technological developments. In agriculture, the heavy-wheeled plough as well as windmills and water wheels appeared; and even the efficiency of the horse was greatly improved by the invention of the stirrup and the horse collar. All this helped to support an expanding population, which in turn encouraged the revival of urban life, eventually providing, as we shall see in Chapter 6, an alternative world view to that of the Church in Rome. It also encouraged the eventual breakdown of a rigid feudal social structure by the growth of a prosperous merchant class eager for the education of their children.

REFERENCES

1. J. Pieper, *Scholasticism* (trans. R. and C. Winston) (Faber & Faber, 1961), p. 29.
2. R. Tarnas, *The Passion of the Western Mind: Understanding the Ideas that have Shaped our World View* (Random House, 1991), p. 168.

Further Reading

Huyghe, R. (ed.), *Byzantine and Medieval Art* (Paul Hamlyn, 1958).
Keen, M., *Medieval Europe* (Penguin, 1968).

6
Humanism and the Renaissance

In Italy, the rediscovery of many Greek and Latin texts had, throughout the fourteenth and fifteenth centuries, been of some influence in changing attitudes and tastes in a variety of fields, not simply the literary. In England and in other parts of Western Europe, there had also been indications of dissatisfaction with the religious establishment, including the Papacy, from at least as far back as John Wycliffe (1320–84) and the Lollards in the last quarter of the fourteenth century. The effects of the Renaissance were enormous, and had a profound influence on the theory and practice of education at all levels. In this chapter we will examine Renaissance and Humanist ideas and show how they had an effect on education throughout Europe.

Ideas are, however, often generated or changed as a result of technological advances. In his discussion of the history of ideas, Tarnas[1] stressed the importance of four inventions: the magnetic compass, the mechanical clock, gunpowder and printing. Narrowing the focus to educational ideas, in this chapter and the next we shall have many opportunities to mention the crucial role of the printing press.

THE RENAISSANCE AND HUMANIST THINKING

It is important to think of the Renaissance not as an event but as a very gradual process. Some historians now locate the origins of the Renaissance as far back as the fourteenth century or even earlier. The Renaissance as the transition from the age of Faith to the age of Reason was only part of the education story. Similarly, Humanism involved more than the emergence of individualism, or the spirit of criticism challenging simple acceptance of doctrines and beliefs.

The term Renaissance is ambiguous and we should remember that it was not used until the eighteenth century. The origins of the Renaissance were associated with the rediscovery and revival of interest in classical

Greek and Latin texts:

> Generally ... the Humanists are thought of as an army of scholars, untiring researchers, collectors of texts, whose historic merit consists essentially in having enriched and restored our knowledge of the Classical cultural heritage. If that had been all (and it was not) modern civilisation's debt to the Humanists would still be inestimable. Without their discoveries, and their recovery of the past, their work of restoration, the later developments of European culture would be unimaginable. It is enough to think how much the Humanists' introduction of the study of Greek philosophy has meant to modern culture. By way of the Greek scholars who were asked to come and teach in the Italian schools and academies from the time of the fall of Constantinople, the whole great heritage of Byzantine learning and philosophy ... became a part of Western culture.[2]

The transition to a new era effectively began when writers and artists started to transform the classical models into new forms and styles; for example, Petrarch (1304–74) unearthed the lost letters of Cicero which influenced the style of Petrarch's friend Boccaccio (1313–75). Moreover, the discovery of Cicero's letters stimulated Poggio Bracciolini and others to go on searching for more lost texts, and fortunately Poggio found Quintilian whose work on education influenced Erasmus and others discussed later in this chapter.

Many writers have stressed Renaissance achievements in art, architecture and sculpture, but the Renaissance was also significant for changing ideas – especially of the kind that cast doubt on traditional accepted truths or 'commonsense', for example, Machiavelli (1469–1527) in statecraft (political philosophy), or, later, Francis Bacon (1561–1626) and Galileo (1564–1642) in science. In his book on the Renaissance, J.H. Plumb put art into a wider cultural context, stressing also the availability of knowledge to a much wider readership:

> Yet art was only one aspect of the brilliance of Renaissance Italy, which created an image of man, a vision of human excellence, that still lies at the heart of the Western tradition. Rarely achieved, it has nevertheless haunted men like a mirage. The Italians, particularly the Florentines, revered antiquity – its wisdom, its grace, its philosophy and its literature. Sensitive and deep-thinking men had done so, of course, ever since the Roman world had crumbled into decay; in monastic schools and universities Plato, as well as

Aristotle, had been studied intensively. Yet such knowledge had been largely part of the private world of scholars. At the time of the Renaissance these humanistic studies spread through the upper and middle ranks of society and became a formidable part of the education of those who were to wield power and authority. The timely invention of the printing press not only multiplied the works of antiquity so that they were readily available to hundreds of thousands of men and women, but also helped to create a public for their study.[3]

HUMANISM AND EDUCATION IN ITALY

Fifteenth-century Italy experienced a rise in prosperity and a generally increased demand for the educated and qualified. Universities failed to keep up with this demand, and most were extremely old-fashioned in what they offered. New schools were founded, often in the homes of scholars, where there was direct communication between teacher and student, and new material was taught. The word 'humanist' was in use as early as the fifteenth century (in Italian *umanista* from the Latin *humanista*) originally denoting a teacher of the humanities, but later in a broader way to include beliefs such as the uniqueness of human beings in possessing free will and power over nature. Some Humanists taught in universities, or as private tutors, others founded schools. One famous example was the Academy of Vittorino Rambaldone da Feltre at Mantua which set a pattern for the education of Italian aristocrats of both sexes that influenced many later writers such as Castiglione, Sir Thomas Elyot, Roger Ascham and Richard Mulcaster, all of whom contributed to new thinking about the content and methods of education.

The Transition from the Medieval Curriculum to Educating the Renaissance Man

Vittorino da Feltre (1378–1446) had established boarding schools in Padua and Venice before starting in 1423 his most celebrated academy in Mantua, La Casa Giocosa, the name of which ('the playful, or merry, house') was indicative of his pedagogic style – for example, practising mathematics by playing games. The *trivium* and *quadrivium* were not abandoned but were balanced by literature and philosophy, as well as by recreation and physical education; moral education pervaded the whole curriculum and everything studied was considered to have a positive moral influence on the learner. Plumb was in no doubt about Vittorino's importance:

> Vittorino's ideas were to influence European education profoundly for centuries. He believed that education should concern itself with the body as well as the mind, with the senses as well as the spirit. Wrestling, fencing, swimming and riding alternated with hours devoted to Virgil, Homer, Cicero and Demosthenes. Luxury was eschewed, and Vittorino educated the poor with the rich. Nor was he prejudiced about the sexes; the Gonzaga princesses enjoyed the same extensive education as the princes. Above all, he encouraged the belief that individual greatness was part of the nature of man, and a desirable part, one that was in no way in opposition to the obligations which men had to their fellow men. To Vittorino the virtues were innate; they were human. Although a devout Christian and insistent on regular religious practices, he nevertheless cherished an optimistic view of man's capacities. Certainly in Lodovico, as in the great Federigo da Montefeltro, Vittorino found an apt pupil, and the traditions which he helped to create kept the Gonzaga from gross excesses and saved Mantua from the terrible sufferings which were so frequently the lot of other Italian cities.[4]

One of the most celebrated Italian writers on education was Baldassare Castiglione (1478–1529) who wrote *Il Cortegiano* (The Courtier) between 1513 and 1518, although it was not published until 1528. It set out the requirements for an accomplished (educated) nobleman. The courtier had to know how to fight, play, dance and make love, as well as being well-versed in the Classics, poetry and oratory. *Il Cortegiano* was quoted and copied throughout Europe, including Tudor England where it was translated by Sir Thomas Hoby and published as *The Courtyer* in 1561. Sir Philip Sidney was said to have taken a copy with him whenever he travelled.

For both da Feltre and Castiglione education was more than learning: it was 'breeding' (which was not the same as birth or blood, but was more like the English word 'upbringing'). Gentility was not a matter of correct conversation or clothes, what we might now call etiquette, it was, as J.H. Plumb has remarked, 'the whole being of man'. These qualities could be taught: suitable sports could give the body suppleness and grace. The gentleman must excel without seeming to do so: Castiglione talked of *sperzatura* or nonchalance (which survived into twentieth century England as the public school and Oxford man's 'effortless superiority').

HUMANISM AND EDUCATION IN FRANCE

The existence of the University of Paris, which was flourishing in the fifteenth century and developing a dynamic form of scholasticism, probably delayed the spread of Renaissance ideas in France. However, there were exceptions, and two of the early supporters of humanistic ideas were Rabelais and Montaigne.

François Rabelais (1495–1553) was probably the son of a lawyer who deposited Francois, aged nine, in a Franciscan community. Some years later Rabelais moved to the relative freedom of a Benedictine monastery; later still he changed again to become a secular priest and qualified as a physician. Rabelais' ideas on education owed something to Erasmus. Despite the enlightened kind of scholasticism being developed in Paris, Rabelais rebelled against it as well as criticising conventional education in schools. In his famous satire, *La Vie très horrificque du grand Gargantua* (Life of the Great Gargantua), Rabelais attacked teachers for packing Gargantua's mind with useless information and turning him into a well-informed fool rather than developing his reason; it required a massive purge to bring Gargantua back to humanity. Gargantua's father then criticised the kind of schooling which did nothing but practice memorising, and instead sought a tutor who would follow the Renaissance ideal of developing the whole person.

In describing Gargantua's curriculum, however, Rabelais depicts an almost impossible programme of work, so wide as to tax all but the most able. Rabelais goes one stage further, satirising the excesses of the new humanist education. When Gargantua prescribed a curriculum for his own son, Pantagruel, he lists Greek, Latin, Hebrew and also Chaldee and Arabic; these linguistic studies were supplemented by literature, music, athletics, nature study, art, manual work and the Bible, all intended to encourage Pantagruel to think for himself. Rabelais was presumably criticising a curriculum which was so packed with knowledge that the pupil would have no time to think. For Rabelais education meant liberation; in his utopian Abbey of Theleme the freedom of pupils was a priority. They could follow their own interests, but they had been so imbued with a love of learning that no time was wasted.

Michel de Montaigne (1533–92) was writing a generation later than Rabelais. He shared many of his attitudes towards education, but not his satirical style of writing. Above all, he stood for tolerance in an age of increasing denominational strife, particularly the French Wars of Religion in the sixteenth century.

Montaigne was critical of the medieval pattern of education, but, like Rabelais, he was also wary of the excesses of some forms of Humanist education. He disliked the kind of education which concentrated on amassing knowledge: he said that as lamps are extinguished from too much oil, so is the mind from too much information. In his essay *Du Pedantisme* ('On Pedantry'), he said that too often teachers aimed at the wrong targets: Greek and Latin or prose and verse, when the aim should have been to encourage wisdom and virtue. His aims were spiritual freedom and independence of judgment. Montaigne agreed with the humanist idea of educating the whole person, body and mind. Understanding was more important than memorisation. Montaigne's *Essais* (1580–88) were widely read, especially in France and England. They included his reflections on education and his criticisms of pedantic excesses. Some of his ideas on education were taken up by Locke and Rousseau.

HUMANISM AND EDUCATION IN NORTHERN EUROPE

Erasmus (1466–1536), a Dutch Humanist, brilliantly exemplified Renaissance thought spreading to the north-west of Europe. He studied in Paris in the 1490s and after 1499 paid a number of significant visits to England, for example, lecturing in Cambridge in 1511 and 1513. His edition of the New Testament in Greek (1516) provided an interesting link between Humanism and the Reformation. Study of the Greek version showed up errors of translation in the Latin Vulgate text which provided some support for those potential reformers who wished to claim that it was the Bible, not the Church or the Pope, which should be regarded as the authority in religion.

Erasmus also applied a similar critical attitude in a number of educational texts: *De Ratione Studii* (1511, On the Correct Method of Study); *De Civilitate Morum Puerilium* (1526, On the Politeness of Children's Manners); *De Pueris Statim ac Liberalitur Instituendis* (1529, On the Liberal Education of Boys). The study of Latin and Greek texts, with a concentration on the discussion of meaning, was the basis of Erasmus' educational programme, but he also advocated the critical study of good modern literature. Like other Humanist teachers he believed that pupils should enjoy learning and that it was part of the task of the teacher to know how to make the work interesting to individuals with different backgrounds. He apologised for mentioning this because he believed that Quintilian had already settled the issue.

John Colet (1467–1515) had travelled widely in France and Italy before becoming Dean of St Paul's Cathedral and founding St Paul's

School in 1510 as a grammar school for about 150 boys, which rapidly became an influential centre for English Humanism. Colet encouraged more enlightened methods of learning Latin and Greek, which he considered to be essential; but he also introduced new methods of studying the Scriptures. He departed from the medieval search for mystical and allegorical meanings in the Bible and sought instead to use the Scriptures as a model for real life behaviour. Colet believed that the New Testament was the best guide for living a good life. In his school, which he financed out of his own fortune, Colet showed a very practical concern for such matters as cleanliness (many sixteenth-century schools were described as squalid, and disorderly) and he forbade such popular leisure pursuits as cock-fighting.

Sir Thomas More (1478–1535) was perhaps the most famous of the English Humanists, probably best known for being executed for refusing to accept Henry VIII as Head of the Church. He had not been to Italy and did not stay long enough at Oxford to get a degree (his father wanted him to study law instead); he was nevertheless a key figure in the development of Greek studies in England. He was careful to have his own son and three daughters educated according to the modern Renaissance methods, at home with selected tutors. In his *Utopia* (1516) he discussed pedagogy in the context of social and political change. There were some 'utopian' rules in More's own household: gambling and idleness were not permitted; education was seen as a life-long process for male and female members; and everyone was expected to do some work in the garden. More was a close friend of Erasmus, and between 1515 and 1520 he strongly supported his programme of Greek studies as a basis for theological reform.

Sir Thomas Elyot (1490–1546) is best known for *The Boke Named the Governour* (1531) which was dedicated to Henry VIII. It was a programme designed for the upbringing and education of the sons of gentlemen. It was not very original from an educational point of view, but being written by someone who was an enthusiast for the English language, it made Renaissance ideas on education available to a wide readership.

Roger Ascham (1515–68) also emphasised the importance of the English language, although as a teacher of Greek at Cambridge he did not neglect the Classics. *The Scholemaster,* published posthumously in 1570, introduced double translation as a method of teaching Latin and Greek. (Double translation meant starting with a text in the original language, translating it into English, and finally, after a suitable lapse of time, translating it back into Latin or Greek.) Like several other Humanist tracts, *The Scholemaster* touches upon the psychology of learning:

Ascham was opposed to corporal punishment and advocated educating the whole person, accepting the Renaissance view that good literature had moral effects. He also shared the Renaissance enthusiasm for certain kinds of physical activities and he wrote a very famous book on archery, *Toxophilus* (1545). He was tutor to Elizabeth from 1548 to 1550 and Latin Secretary to the Queen until his death.

Richard Mulcaster (1530–1611) is an excellent example of a schoolmaster who reflected on the educational practices of his day and theorised about education based on his own experience as well as on the writings of others. He was Master of the Merchant Taylors' School from 1561 to 1586, followed by 12 years as High Master of St Paul's. He changed the curriculum in both schools by adopting Humanist ideas and by including English language and literature. His two major educational publications were *Positions, Wherein Those Primitive Circumstances be examined which are necessie* [sic] *for the Training up of Children either for Skill in their Boke or Health in their Bodie* (1581); and *The Elementarie which entreateth Cheeflie of the right writing of our English tung* (1601). He stressed the need to recognise individual differences in children and to adjust teaching to meet their needs. Mulcaster wanted an efficient system of teacher education, comparable in status to that of doctors and lawyers. He saw school teaching not as a mechanical process of encouraging the memorisation of knowledge but of finding suitable experiences for all young people, including physical education, not only for boys but also for girls who should also be admitted to universities.

Another important Humanist influence was Joan Luis Vives (1492–1540), a Spaniard who spent most of his life elsewhere in Europe. He was greatly influenced by Erasmus but was also interested in popular education, and by no means despised practical education. Like Erasmus, he related teaching method to the psychology of the child and advocated individual programmes; he agreed with da Feltre and others in the psychological advantages of learning through playing games. He favoured a curriculum which balanced the classical and the modern, including the vernacular language. In 1523 Vives was invited to England to be the preceptor for the Princess Mary, and in the following years he lectured in philosophy at Oxford University. However, he offended Henry VIII by expressing sympathy with Catherine over the divorce issue, and had to leave the country.

THE RENAISSANCE CURRICULUM

In many of the examples mentioned above, views about education shifted away from a total concern for the medieval *trivium* (grammar, rhetoric and logic) and the *quadrivium* (arithmetic, geometry, astronomy and music) to a balanced programme of physical, intellectual, spiritual and aesthetic development. Although it may be anachronistic to think of such clearly defined areas of experience at this stage, literature and music were thought to have moral purposes, as were physical activities of the right kind. The physical included fencing, riding, hunting, hawking and dancing; the intellectual focused on Greek and Latin texts but also on contemporary poetry and prose. The arts were also important, and it was regarded as desirable not only to appreciate music and painting but also, if possible, to be a performer.

However, the most important difference between Renaissance education and the medieval *trivium* and *quadrivium* was that in all aspects of the curriculum pupils were encouraged to understand and to exercise their critical faculties rather than emphasising memorisation. In addition, the Renaissance curriculum opened up a much wider range of literary styles and subject matter.

SCHOOLS IN SIXTEENTH-CENTURY ENGLAND

We have seen that the Renaissance created demands for education throughout Europe. To what extent did schools in England match up to the new standards? As is so often the case, schools lagged behind: monastic, chantry and cathedral schools were inadequate both in terms of the numbers they catered for and in terms of the curriculum.

It has sometimes been suggested that the Reformation helped by diverting funds away from the monasteries to new grammar schools that were endowed by patrons who had benefited financially from the Reformation, particularly the dissolution of the monasteries. This may have been an example of Tudor propaganda. In his discussion of schools and the Reformation, R.H. Tawney has this to say:

> As for the schools, what it did for them Mr Leach has told us. It swept them away wholesale in order to distribute their endowments among courtiers. There were probably more schools in proportion to the population at the end of the fifteenth century than there were in the middle of the nineteenth. 'These endowments were confiscated

by the State and many still line the pockets of the descendants of the statesmen of the day...King Edward VI's Grammar Schools are the schools which King Edward VI did not destroy.'[5]

Unfortunately, this is a continuing argument. Lawson[6] was even unkind enough to suggest that A.F. Leach, the author of *English Schools at the Reformation 1546–8*, was only guessing at the numbers. What seems clear is that by the fifteenth century monastic schools were not making any considerable contribution to education; chantry schools were much more important, and Edward VI was guilty of abolishing some of them. According to Lawson[7] many of them were replaced by local, rather than royal, endowments. More will be said about the relation between the Reformation and schools in the next chapter. Meanwhile, it will suffice to report that the number of schools was inadequate for Renaissance requirements and that the Reformation did not solve the problem. Educational ideas were in advance of provision both before and after the Reformation.

PHILOSOPHY, SCIENCE AND EDUCATION

Francis Bacon (1561–1626) is better known as a statesman, philosopher and scientist than for his writing on education. However, he was interested in education partly because he disliked scholasticism in the universities and wanted to replace it with scientific studies and subjects concerned with the real world. In many respects Bacon might be better discussed in Chapter 7 because he was very 'post-Reformation' in his thinking; on the other hand, he was also a splendid example of Renaissance man – statesman, lawyer, courtier, philosopher and writer on many subjects including science and education.

Bacon wanted to link science with experiences of the senses and recommended that the curriculum should include such practical subjects as modern languages and politics as well as history and literature. Above all he thought that science was neglected in schools and universities. One of his enduring beliefs was that science should harness nature for the benefit of mankind. Aristotle and scholastic education had exaggerated the value of the deductive method of logic and neglected the inductive. Bacon became the champion of the empirical method consisting of systematic observation, testing by experimentation and then generalising from particular examples to principles or laws of nature – in other words, the inductive process.

He believed that this kind of scientific method should be applied to human beings as well as to the world of nature, for which reason he has sometimes been regarded as a forerunner of sociology. One of the ways in which he suggested we could benefit by looking more closely at human behaviour was his work on what he referred to as the four 'idols'. These idols, Bacon claimed, hindered the mind in its search for truth. He began with 'idols of the tribe' (traditional thought or local superstitions) which were shared by the whole of humanity in various ways: they were human limitations of reasoning which made all human beings prone to error, for example, a tendency to seek greater order in the world than really exists or to generalise on the basis of inadequate observation. At the other extreme, Bacon discussed 'idols of the cave', an individual's distorted perception because he thinks his 'cave' is the whole world, by which he meant individual bad habits of thinking and reasoning, personal prejudices which encouraged individuals to make bad judgements or reach false conclusions; a tendency for human beings to make generalisations from their own point of view, ignoring more general evidence. In between the universal and the individual idols were two other kinds. 'Idols of the market-place', language and social interaction, referred to the misunderstandings which arose out of using language, for example, using words and phrases carelessly, and words which were invented for the non-existent. Finally, Bacon spoke of idols of the theatre (dogmatic 'fairy-stories' used to explain the world), fallacious modes of thinking perhaps derived from false philosophies, such as scholasticism.

Bacon also thought that the educational experiences of the young should be geared to their future status: schools should educate future statesmen and men of action as well as clerics and scholars. Bacon condemned many of the writers discussed earlier in this chapter. Whilst he criticised scholasticism and the version of Aristotle's logic still being taught in universities, he was equally dismissive of the learned debates about the new theology which only led to further argument. He also disliked the 'new learning' of humanism because it failed in something which Bacon regarded as all-important – the advancement of learning – by concentrating on the past rather than the future. Bacon was convinced that progress in education depended on much greater attention being paid to scientific observation and experimentation, and correspondingly less time being spent on classical texts and theological disputes. Some of his ideas were taken up, as we shall see in Chapter 7, by post-Reformation educationists.

CONCLUSION

The term 'Renaissance man' or 'Renaissance woman' is still used to convey the idea of a well-balanced individual whose knowledge is wide but not too specialised. In practice, however, there has been a growing tendency, especially in England, to encourage young people to specialise early and to think of themselves as 'arts' or 'science'. This may be only a temporary deviation from the Renaissance ideal or a reformulated version of it.

One generalisation which has surfaced several times in this chapter was the tendency for writers on education to prefer understanding and critical thinking to mere memorisation of canonical texts. Such ideas did not originate in the Renaissance but, as we have seen in earlier chapters, went back at least as far as Quintilian. These ideas would continue to be advocated, and challenged, throughout the next five centuries. Another recurring theme was the need for teachers to treat their pupils as individuals: a precept that was easier to preach than to practise in schools where there was always a tendency to teach the whole class using the same method and expecting all pupils to learn at more or less the same speed. Finally, especially with Bacon, we see education being placed in a much wider context: not just the preparation of monks, priests and clerks, but the intellectual and practical education of a much greater proportion of the population.

REFERENCES

1. R. Tarnas, *The Passion of the Western Mind* (Random House, 1991), p. 225.
2. G. Procacci, *History of the Italian People* (Pelican, 1973), p. 102.
3. J.H. Plumb, *The Penguin Book of the Renaissance* (Penguin, 1964), p. 25.
4. Ibid., pp. 46–7.
5. R.H. Tawney, *Religion and the Rise of Capitalism* (Pelican, 1926), p. 136.
6. J. Lawson, *Medieval Education and the Reformation* (Routledge & Kegan Paul, 1967), p. 70.
7. Ibid., p. 81.

Further Reading

Compayré, G., *The History of Pedagogy* (Swann, Sonnenschein, 1905).
Eby, F., *The Development of Modern Education* (Prentice-Hall, New York, 1952).
Hale, J.R., *Renaissance Europe* (Fontana, 1971).
Leach, A.F., *English Schools at the Reformation 1546–8* (Russell, New York, 1968).
Simon, J., *The Social Origins of English Education* (Routledge & Kegan Paul, 1970).

7

The Reformation and the Counter-Reformation to the End of the Seventeenth Century

INTRODUCTION

We have divided the Renaissance (Chapter 6) from the Reformation rather artificially by putting them into separate chapters, but they overlap both in time and in ideas. Humanists such as Erasmus played a major part in both accounts. The Reformation is a complex term. It is accepted that a series of events in Europe in the sixteenth century caused the division of the Christian church into Roman Catholics and Protestants. That much is not controversial; but the causes of the Reformation and the relative importance of those causes are much more open to debate. Aspects of the Catholic church had been under criticism for many years: corruption, nepotism, the sale of ecclesiastical offices, the exploitation of superstitions by such practices as indulgences and pardons; some put the doctrine of transubstantiation into the same category as superstitions and ignored papal instructions about such beliefs. All of these problems might have been put right by internal reform, but there were political pressures in Germany, and later in Henry VIII's England, which eventually ended the idea of a single, united Christian church led by the Pope. Henry VIII's children, the future King Edward VI, Queen Mary and Queen Elizabeth, were educated in ways that caused them to have quite different attitudes to the Reformation, ranging from the extreme Protestantism of Edward to Mary's inclination to burn Protestant heretics. However, they all experienced some key aspects of Renaissance education.

William Tyndale (1494–1536) believed that the Protestant Reformation was God's way of bestowing 'grace' upon the English people, but it was bestowed on condition that the Church purged itself of Popish idolatry. Tyndale wanted Christians to regard the Bible as the source of religious belief and doctrine, rather than the Church, which he regarded as corrupt. There was a strong element of reformist thinking in England before Luther, Calvin and others became vocal on the Continent.

We shall also look briefly at the way the Catholic Church reacted to the Reformation in a movement which has been generalised as the Counter-

Reformation. Both the Reformation and the Counter-Reformation had interesting influences on educational thinking throughout Europe.

LUTHER AND MELANCHTHON: THE REFORMATION AND EDUCATIONAL CHANGE IN GERMANY

Martin Luther (1483–1546) was born in Eisleben, the son of a reasonably prosperous copper miner. He became an Augustinian monk and, later, professor of Scripture at the University of Wittenberg. In 1517 he achieved fame by denouncing the Dominican monk Tetzel for selling indulgences. Later in the same year, on 31 October, Luther extended his list of complaints about corruption within the church and nailed his 95 theses to the door of Wittenberg Church. For this attack on the sale of Indulgences and other criticisms of the Pope, Luther was summoned to the Vatican to defend himself. Instead of going to Rome, in 1520, Luther publicly burned the Papal Bull which had condemned 41 of his propositions as heretical. The specific argument about Indulgences was avoided by the Pope's advocates who preferred to regard Luther's attack as a challenge to papal authority. This encouraged Martin Luther to broaden his attack: away from a theological debate about indulgences and the lack of scriptural authority for them, to a condemnation of Papal infallibility and the authority of the traditional Church. Luther soon took the next step: denying the authority not only of the Pope but of the Councils of the Church, he was left only with the Scriptures through which God communicated directly with individual Christians. This elevation of the individual had profound effects both on the history of Christianity and, indirectly, on the history of education. He had moved from trying to purify the Church to creating a very different one. Luther and his followers eventually depicted the Pope as Anti-Christ and Rome as the Whore of Babylon.

In 1521 Luther was excommunicated, and Charles V, King of Spain and Holy Roman Emperor, opened a Diet (or Assembly) in Worms. Martin Luther would not recant, and at this point in history politics rather than religious conviction influenced the next stage of the conflict. Elector Frederick of Saxony, seeing the advantage of a German Church independent from Rome, but unwilling to provoke a split in the Church, arranged for Luther to be 'kidnapped' and hidden away safe from assassination in the Castle of Wartbürg. Luther spent some of his exile translating the New Testament into German: an essential requirement if the laity were to do without priests.

Most of the population, however, were unable to read the Bible, even in the vernacular, hence the link between the Protestant reforms and popular education. Luther's German Bible was revised by his friend Philip Melanchthon who was to take on the leading role in Protestant educational reform. By then (1524), however, Luther had antagonised many humanists who might have supported him, such as Erasmus, who wanted reform but not a separate church.

Philip Melanchthon (1497–1560)

Educating the people was part of a programme of liberating the masses from the domination of 'corrupt' priests and bishops. 'Reformed' priests would become teachers and preachers, and the ritual of the Mass would become available to all in their own language. However, more than this was required. Each individual needed to be able to read the Bible, and this was to become part of Melanchthon's educational mission.

In 1529 Luther had written his *Greater and Little Catechisms*, one for the clergy, the other for the laity and their children. Together with the German Bible, and the German Mass, the *Little Catechism* became a source of instruction for children. In 1530, Melanchthon presented a 'Confession of Faith' to the Diet of Augsburg. This 'Augsburg confession' became for a time the accepted doctrine of Lutheran churches. Melanchthon's preferred method of persuasion was reason rather than emotion, and he was very different from Luther in other respects – much less prone to violent and abusive language. For him, education reform was an essential part of systematic social and religious progress by means of which social order and authority could be preserved.

Melanchthon was faced with the enormous task of spreading literacy to the whole population. To a great extent he was assisted by the invention of printing and the spread of printing presses throughout Germany, meaning that thousands of Bibles could be produced every year. Never forgetting his Humanist principles, Melanchthon set about the task of reorganising the entire German education system, including the founding or reformation of many universities. In 1528 he published *Instructions for Visitors*, a set of instructions for commissioners visiting the reformed Imperial States and devising constitutions for the churches. These instructions included an educational outline for elementary schools: Saxony was the first state to establish a Protestant elementary school system. Melanchthon's plan was widely copied throughout Germany, and more than 50 cities sought his help in establishing schools. His plan also included the production of textbooks and the training of teachers. He never, of course, achieved anything like mass literacy, but he did succeed in making the Bible available to a much wider percentage of the population.

PURITANISM IN ENGLAND AND SCOTLAND

By steering a middle way between 'reform' and 'tradition', Queen Elizabeth I secured a lasting religious settlement; the Thirty Nine Articles were generally, though not universally, acceptable to her subjects. Among those who were not content with the settlement were those now referred to as Puritans. This was a term rarely used in the early seventeenth century and then usually as a term of abuse. Puritanism was a way of life as well as an ideology; their characteristics were thrift, sobriety, asceticism and sometimes hypocrisy, as in the case of Shakespeare's Malvolio.

The Puritans in Elizabethan and Stuart England wanted to purify the Church of England of any remaining 'Popish' practices such as statues of saints, kneeling for communion and anything that might be covered by the biblical condemnation of idolatry. Some of the ideas associated with Puritanism can be traced back to earlier times, for example, Wycliffe and the Lollards in the fourteenth century who wanted to be able to read the Bible in English. After John Calvin (1509–64), there was a shift of belief in the direction of predestination and the notion that there was an 'elect' group who were ordained by God to live a good life on this earth in preparation for a guaranteed place in heaven after death.

Another aspect of Puritan policy was simplicity of worship. This was, of course, potentially antagonistic to the desire of royalty for splendour and display in all public events, including religious ceremonies. Rather than the mass, particularly high mass with candles, crucifixes, incense and the veneration of the host, Puritans preferred long sermons, the explication of key Biblical texts, simple prayers and psalm-singing.

Nicholas Hans[1] made a very important distinction between two traditions of Puritanism that developed: one he described as 'intolerant and domineering', the other as 'liberal and conciliating'. Among the intolerant, Hans included Calvinists, the followers of John Knox (1514–72) and the English Presbyterians. The liberal Puritans emphasised individual responsibility, tolerance and freedom of conscience; they included the Huguenots, the Dissenters in England, and later, Comenius who was very critical of those whom he accused of debasing Puritanism by their intolerance and harshness.

Democratic Ideas and Education

There was a link between some aspects of Puritan belief and the growth of democratic theory and practice, although it should not be exaggerated. Puritans believed in direct communication between individuals and God;

they were opposed to Church hierarchies and aristocracies (bishops and Popes); the predestined elect were not socially differentiated in this life, and inevitably such beliefs called into question the privileges of kings and the nobility. Some Puritans held the belief that everyone should be literate so that they could have direct access to the Bible, without priestly intervention. By the end of Elizabeth's reign, Puritanism had spread considerably and there were many in influential positions, for example in the University of Cambridge.

Other Puritan Ideas

In 1603 Puritan hopes were high. James had been brought up in Scotland by Calvinists, and when he arrived in England he was presented with the Millenary Petition setting out a list of Puritan grievances. In 1604 James called a Conference at Hampton Court, but he had no intention of moving the Church in the Puritan direction. He appeared to listen sympathetically to some aspects of the Puritan cause, but his Archbishop of Canterbury, Richard Bancroft, encouraged Convocation in 1604 to draw up *Constitutions and Canons* against the Nonconformists. James also antagonised Puritans by ordering that his *Book of Sports* be read in every church, listing recreations which were permitted on Sundays. In 1607 the emigration of Puritans began to increase, first to Holland and in 1620 the Mayflower took the celebrated group to Plymouth, Massachusetts.

FROM PURITAN DISSENT TO REVOLUTION

In 1625 James died and was succeeded by his son Charles I who in 1628 appointed William Laud to be Bishop of London. Laud embarked upon an anti-Puritan campaign in London, and when he became Archbishop of Canterbury in 1633, he extended the policy to the whole country and even – dangerously – to Scotland. This led to an uprising by the Scots which involved Charles in expensive military campaigns. The need for money obliged the King, very reluctantly, to call a Parliament (something he had carefully avoided up to that time). The Puritans in the Long Parliament (1640–53) made the most of their power, and the dispute between Charles and his Parliament was a direct cause of the Civil War and the execution of Charles I in January 1649.

Under Cromwell, the Puritan philosophy became dominant, and many variations of Puritanism flourished in England, including George Fox's Quakers, some of whom were persecuted by other Puritans. After

Cromwell's death the less extreme Puritans supported the restoration of the monarchy together with the return of the Church of England to a more traditional form. Charles II promised to tolerate Dissenters, but Puritans were generally disappointed both by the king and by the 'Cavalier' Parliament. A new Act of Uniformity (1662) enforced *The Book of Common Prayer* and about 2,000 Puritan ministers were expelled from their parishes. The Conventicle Act of 1664 punished adults who attended religious meetings which were not conducted in accordance with the Book of Common Prayer. Puritanism was by no means dead in England after the Restoration in 1660; although no longer either the dominant ideology or a powerful political force, it remained influential on educational thought and practice.

EDUCATION IN ENGLAND IN THE SIXTEENTH AND SEVENTEENTH
CENTURIES

There was a clear connection between Puritanism and education. Reading the Bible was an essential activity for any Protestant; it was important that all should be given the opportunity not only to learn to read but also to be educated more widely. During the Civil War when many institutions were being challenged or swept away, education was a frequent topic for debate. There were several individuals who were particularly concerned to promote educational reform. For example, the German-born English educationist, Samuel Hartlib (1600–62) combined a desire to unite the Protestant churches with the promotion of educational reform.

Hartlib and Education

Hartlib supported the ideas of the famous Czech educationist, Comenius, in *A Reformation of Schools* (1642), and translated several books and tracts by Comenius, including *Pansophiae*, which set out the purpose of education as understanding nature in all its forms through reason and the senses as well as divine revelation. Hartlib accepted Comenius's view that education should be available to all, and he encouraged Comenius to visit England in 1641. It was also Hartlib who persuaded Milton to write *On Education*. Hartlib's own plan for reforming education was outlined in *Considerations Tending to the Happy Accomplishment of England's Reformation in Church and State* (1647). In this book, Hartlib not only made the radical suggestion of education for all, but also suggested many other radical social reforms. He failed to get some of these ideas into legislation during the Long

Parliament but was rewarded by Oliver Cromwell with a pension of £300. In many of his efforts he was associated with John Dury (1596–1680), a Scottish philosopher and educational reformer, who advocated universal education as well as nursery and infant schools.

John Milton on Education

Milton (1608–74) is, of course, best known as a poet – author of *Paradise Lost, L'Allegro* and many others; but he was also a brilliant prose writer. One of his lesser-known prose pamphlets is *On Education* (1644) which was composed in the form of a letter to his friend Samuel Hartlib.

The Reformation might have been expected to have extended the numbers of pupils attending schools; there were some schools established during the Tudor and early Stuart years, partly to enable more young people to become readers of the Bible, but the rate of increase in literacy was slow, and education was generally available only to a privileged minority. While Hartlib and his friends were concerned to increase the provision of school places, they were also interested in reforming the content of education, the curriculum and pedagogy.

Charles I was not executed until 1649; part of the background to Milton's essay was the idea of encouraging those on the side of Parliament to continue vigorously to oppose the King and to secure further social reforms, including education reform. Milton had received a relatively privileged education under the old regime: he had attended St Paul's School, one of the best grammar schools in the country, following Colet's enlightened ideas, and then Christ's College, Cambridge. He had even copied the aristocratic practice of a grand tour of Europe before settling back into London, where for a few years he ran a school, probably for sons of his friends, of about 12 pupils. In this practical experience and in his essay, Milton attempted to combine Humanist ideas on education with Puritan principles.

The Royalists tended to oppose these Puritan views on education, preferring the Elyot and Ascham tradition of the education of the gentleman. This tradition continued into the seventeenth century; for example James Cleland (1607) *The Institution of a Young Nobleman;* or Henry Peacham (1622) *The Compleat Gentleman*; or later in the century, John Gailhard (1678) *The Compleat Gentleman.* For these Royalist authors, the curriculum looked back to the fifteenth and sixteenth centuries and consisted of traditional subjects: cosmography, geometry, poetry, music, sculpture, drawing, painting and heraldry as well as gentlemanly sports and martial arts:

'All the people which be in our country be either gentlemen or of the commonality', wrote Mulcaster in 1581. This was the fundamental cleavage in Elizabethan and Stuart society – between those who were gentry and those who were not, a difference not only of birth and family but also of deference and privilege. The division was now accentuated by the changes in grammar school and university education. At all times the gentry were an ill-defined group, especially at the lower end. Wealth from land and a Coat of Arms were the usual criteria, but there were others, for example gentlemen did not work with their hands; now they all had the same sort of classical education and common ties with the same few educational institutions imparting the same elitist social values. The dichotomy between liberal and mechanical arts became the most striking feature of the educational system: Latin and Greek were subjects for gentlemen, merely useful or practical subjects were for tradesmen and artificers. As Kearney says, 'A classical education ... served to mark off the ruling elite from those below it. The classical tag was a class shibboleth of unerring simplicity'.[2]

This traditional curriculum, along with the teaching methods of grammar schools and universities, was attacked by the radicals of the seventeenth century, including Gerrard Winstanley, a notable 'Leveller', who said that the traditional learning contained in books was 'no knowledge, but a show of knowledge, like a parrot who speaks words, but he knows not what he saith'.[3]

EDUCATION IN EUROPE

In some parts of Europe, education had changed considerably as a result of the Reformation, but there was a good deal of social disorder during the seventeenth century, particularly the events associated with the Thirty Years War. Later in this chapter we shall discuss the Catholic reaction to the Reformation, and in particular the educational policies that were part of the Counter-Reformation. Meanwhile, it will be useful to look at the educational ideas of one of the thinkers who had a permanent effect on educational theory, Comenius, and who personally suffered as a result of the disturbances in the Thirty Years War.

John Amos Comenius (1592–1670)

Comenius's father was a member of the Protestant group, the Bohemian

Brethren. His parents died when he was 12 years old, but he continued to be part of a strongly Protestant community and was influenced at Heidelberg University by the Protestant Millennialists who believed in salvation on earth, and therefore in social reforms, including education reform. Comenius was also influenced by the writings of Francis Bacon and was attracted by Bacon's emphasis on reason and science.

The Thirty Years War broke out in 1618. Ferdinand II wanted to reconvert Bohemia to Catholicism. This forced Comenius and many other Protestants to flee to Poland. By now, Comenius believed that universal education could be a means of promoting peace and co-operation. For him, education reform would require two very different changes. First, there would have to be extensive reforms in teaching methods to ensure that while children's learning would be rapid and a pleasant experience, it would also be very thorough. He said that teachers should follow nature, that is, understand the mind of the child and make the most of it. His second requirement for educational reform was that European culture should be made available to all by improving Latin texts. He was to spend many years of his life on that task.

His key idea of universal education was a mixture of Moravian religious beliefs, which stressed reason as well as faith; Humanist thought; and the beliefs of those who advocated enlightened pedagogy, including using the senses to appreciate nature and to collect evidence, as well as practical activities. This programme amounted to the education of the whole person; and for all people. It was a harmonious integration of intellectual, moral and spiritual 'illumination'. In *The Great Didactic* he emphasised that education was not an individual matter but concerned the moral health of the whole society which depended on good education for all its citizens. The idea of a universal school, for pupils aged 6–12, included a wide-ranging curriculum for all. He disagreed, for example, with his friend J.H. Alsted who advocated a form of streaming according to social status. For Comenius, the curriculum should be ordered, deep, wide-ranging but coherent; and the emphasis should be on access to knowledge not detailed coverage of content. The vision of the reform of human society through education was a view he shared with Samuel Hartlib who invited him to England in 1641. Unfortunately, Hartlib's plan to start a college in England headed by Comenius was prevented by the Civil War, which broke out in 1642, and Comenius went instead to Sweden.

When the Thirty Years War ended with the Peace of Westphalia in 1648, Comenius was very disappointed that he still could not return to his native Bohemia. Instead he was invited to Hungary to open a school based on his own pedagogical ideas. The school opened in 1650 with 100 pupils but the teachers failed to understand the system. Comenius was frustrated and spent his final years in Amsterdam working on another book, *Consultation*, the manuscript of which was lost until 1939. Although Comenius was recognised during his lifetime as an enlightened educationist, it was many years before his ideas were accepted as part of mainstream educational theory. More will be said about Comenius and pedagogy in Chapter 16.

EDUCATION AFTER THE RESTORATION OF THE MONARCHY IN ENGLAND

From about 1640 onwards, the Renaissance educational ideal was superseded by the universalist ideas of Hartlib, Comenius, Dury and others who had a vision of education as what we might now call part of a grand scheme of social engineering. These ideas were not put into practice during the Commonwealth (i.e. the period of rule without a king, 1649–60) and discussion tended to fade away after the Restoration. Unfortunately, the reforming principles were not replaced by anything like a new model of education. Instead there was a half-hearted revival of some aspects of Renaissance education, but often they were the wrong aspects, a shallow version of the education of gentlemen concentrating on manners and etiquette rather than deeper insights into the human condition. This is not to deny that many schools flourished after the Restoration: grammar schools such as Westminster continued to be important for a minority but they were, on the whole, almost completely untouched by science, despite the remarkable scientific progress made in seventeenth-century England. Private tutors continued to be the norm for aristocratic families and, significantly, there was also a marked decline in standards at the English universities.

THE COUNTER-REFORMATION

It took some time for the Catholic Church to react in a positive way to the Reformation, particularly in the field of education. The Council of Trent (1545–63) was a prolonged discussion, held over three sessions (1545–47, 1551–52 and 1562–63) by the Popes and their senior advisors about what the Roman Catholic Church should do, partly by way of internal reforms and clarification of doctrinal beliefs and later through vigorous educational activities. Many of the abuses that had provoked Protestant criticisms were removed. Some areas of Europe, such as Comenius's Bohemia, were reclaimed for Catholicism; the authority of the Church was restored and discipline tightened; from that time a high priority was to establish a much better educated priesthood.

The Jesuits

In 1534, Ignatius Loyola (1491–1556), a Spanish aristocrat, had founded the Society of Jesus. Originally it was not intended as a teaching order as missionary work was always a high priority, but soon, and especially after the Council of Trent, educational activities were encouraged by the Pope and by Catholic rulers throughout Europe.

The major educational outcome of the Council of Trent was to plan for the clergy to be sufficiently well educated to be able to react convincingly against the doctrinal innovations from the Lutherans, Calvinists and others. The first Jesuit College was opened in Sicily in 1548. By 1615 there were 372 Jesuit Colleges and by the mid eighteenth century there were over 700. The education of the clergy was a major aim but future leading lay members of the Church were now targeted as well as priests. This was a considerable change in policy from the pre-Reformation idea that the Scriptures and other teachings of the Church should always be mediated by the clergy.

In 1599 the Jesuits published *Ratio Studiorum*, a detailed prescription for a course of studies designed to provide guidance for their colleges. The full course was spread over 13 years in three stages, but it was only intended that those studying for the clergy should complete all three stages. The first stage, lasting six years, concentrated on grammar and rhetoric, as well as on religious studies; the second three-year stage concentrated on philosophy; finally, there was a theology stage lasting four years. An important element of the *Ratio* was that the teacher was not only an academic instructor but also a moral educator and someone who would have general control over student behaviour, and competition was a feature of the teaching method. The Jesuit organisation was extremely efficient, not least in their training of teachers, and this partly accounted for the rapid spread of the Jesuit Colleges.

The *Ratio Studiorum* provided detailed guidance for the teacher on how to lecture so that students could take notes; the order in which authors should be studied; and how a text should be explained. In addition, there was advice on how a discussion should be conducted, as well as revision techniques.[4] The method recommended for classical texts was the *praelectio,* which had much in common with the methods of teaching in scholasticism: the professor began by carefully reading a passage from a text, probably in Latin. He would then outline or summarise the argument, examining each sentence and elucidating any difficulties of content or syntax. The students would eventually make a literal translation of the passage into the mother tongue. Finally, the master would revise the whole lesson, and at a later stage examine the students' note books to ensure neatness and accuracy. This was a very different regime from that which Ignatius had experienced at grammar school. If it now seems rigid or even mechanical, we should remember what it replaced. The *Ratio* was by far the most systematic regime of teaching and learning recorded. There were many admirable features, including the recommendation that one day a week should be devoted to revision. There may seem to be an element of military efficiency in the recommendations for teaching and learning, but the *Ratio* withstood the test of time: it remained as a requirement in all Jesuit Colleges until 1832.

Another interesting feature of Jesuit methods was the use of examinations and tests: these were regarded as very practical innovations in the sixteenth century, and were used competitively, pupil against pupil, group against group ('Romans' versus 'Carthaginians'), class against class. Again the military influence is obvious. There were other examples of extrinsic motivation, for example, marks, badges and prizes. (Could this be the origin of the 'gold stars' favoured by many primary school teachers today?) The *Ratio* also emphasised to teachers that they should win the affection of all their pupils.

One criticism of the *Ratio Studiorum* is that its emphasis on close supervision of students went too far, but we should view the Jesuit recommendations in the context of the general laxity of schools and universities in the sixteenth century. Ignatius considered that the lack of supervision in the schools and universities he had attended led to a lack of purpose and low standards. Clearly there is a happy medium between control and chaos: the Jesuits erred on the side of control. A second criticism is that the *Ratio* was a threat to teacher autonomy and deprived gifted masters of their freedom to innovate: no deviation from the *Ratio* was permitted. Again, there is some justice in this complaint, but we should also see the *Ratio* in the context of the sixteenth century where the main problem was inefficiency and low standards. At that time, the notion of setting minimum targets would have seemed very sensible to those who wished to raise the performance of students. Although the Jesuits had been expelled from many countries and have often been unpopular with Church and State authorities, the quality of education has been preserved, and even today Jesuit education has a reputation for high standards and efficiency.

It is important to emphasise that the Society of Jesus was not specifically founded as the educational wing of the Counter-Reformation. It was a conscious attempt by Ignatius and others to provide a reinvigorated sense of moral purpose in Catholic society. Education was the major instrument for achieving that sense of purpose which was clearly expressed by the motto *Omnia ad majoram Dei gloriam* (All for the greater glory of God). Everything in life and education was dedicated to God himself. Shoddy workmanship or lack of intellectual rigour was an insult to God. This could have been initiated even had Luther and Calvin never existed. The spirit of 'all for the greater glory of God' continued to inspire education for centuries after the death of Ignatius. It may be significant that in the twentieth century Jesuit schools were among the first in England to become comprehensive; and in South America, Jesuits became the champions of the poor and the oppressed, developing what became known as 'liberation theology' which influenced the radical educational work of Paulo Freire.

Other Educational Aspects of the Counter-Reformation

Seventeenth-Century Developments in France: In countries such as France which remained Catholic, there was official encouragement given to education as well as attempts to control it. In addition to the Jesuit initiatives, there were several other groups which endeavoured to improve education on behalf of the Catholic Church, specifically in France and owing much to René Descartes (1596–1650), particularly to the idea of faith based on reason.

The Oratory of France: This congregation was based on an earlier Italian association: the Italian Oratory founded by St Philip Neri (1515–95) as a free society of secular priests with the common purpose of improving the education of future clerics. The French association was founded by Pierre de Berulle (1575–1629) as the Oratory of France in 1611.

De Berulle's vision for a society was based on the power of prayer (*oratio*). Unlike the Jesuits, no new religious order was involved, instead the whole organisation was concerned with secular priests. Originally the schools admitted only future priests, but this was later relaxed to include other potential leaders of society. In many cases the Oratorians were invited by local communities to establish a college in their area in return for some funding. Such arrangements often involved inspection and a degree of official control. Instruction was based on Latin but everything was taught through the medium of French, and pupils under the age of 12 received lessons on French language and literature. Latin retained its central importance in the curriculum largely because priests needed to be able to understand and explain the liturgy, including the mass, in Latin. Greek was given a lower status, and Hebrew, where taught, came lower still. History was given unusual importance by the Oratorians: the subject included biblical and Church history, Greece and Rome, and finally, in the upper forms, the history of France. Geography was also taught; in both history and geography encouragement was given to keeping notes written in good French. There was no national policy for the Oratorian curriculum; local variation was encouraged and in some schools enlightened methods of teaching mathematics and science developed. There were eventually 36 Oratorian colleges in France before the decline began, partly due to the hostility of the Jesuits who criticised the Oratorians for alleged unorthodox theological beliefs, including a suspicion of Jansenism (see below). Before that the colleges had spread into Belgium and Spain.

The Little Schools of Port Royal: In 1636 Jean Duvergier de Hauranne, Abbot of St Cyran, took over the convent of Port Royal near Versailles and began a programme of education for boys. In ten years the school became a group of schools spread throughout France. Although Duvergier was a leading supporter of the Dutch theologian, Cornelius Jansen, the schools themselves were not officially Jansenist, but many assumed that they were. The curriculum was similar to that of the Oratorians: instruction was in French; students were encouraged to write about their own experiences and to read, in keeping with the theory that learning should start from what is familiar to the pupil. However, there was also strong emphasis on traditional philosophy and logic. When Jansenist theology was attacked, the schools were suspected of promulgating potentially heretical ideas and were all closed down by Louis XIV in 1660.

DEBATES ABOUT EDUCATION IN THE SEVENTEENTH CENTURY

England in the seventeenth century was dominated by political debates about the powers of King and Parliament. After the execution of Charles I, in 1649 there was then an Interregnum until 1660 when the monarchy was restored in the form of Charles II; on his death in 1685 the disputes became more acrimonious and culminated in the exile of another King, James II in 1688. John Locke was at the centre of much of this political conflict.

John Locke (1632–1704)

John Locke was still a child when the Civil War began. His father, a lawyer, fought on the side of Parliament against Charles I. In 1646, Locke went to Westminster School and later to Oxford University where he studied philosophy and science. He also qualified as a physician. Almost immediately he became involved in political activity: in 1667 Locke entered the household of the Earl of Shaftesbury who was opposed to the government of Charles II. From 1675 to 1679, Locke was in France where he added to his knowledge of philosophy. In 1681 Shaftesbury was tried for treason, and although he was found not guilty he decided he would be safer living in Holland. In 1683 Locke rejoined Shaftesbury and was soon involved in political intrigue, to replace the Stuart monarchy by William of Orange and Mary. He was also writing some of his most important philosophical works, for example *An Essay Concerning Human Understanding* which was not published until 1689. Meanwhile, Charles II had been succeeded by his brother James II in 1685, and the conspiracy to replace the Stuarts intensified. In 1689 William of Orange was invited to become King, and John Locke was given the task of escorting Mary, daughter of James II and wife of William of Orange, to England. In the same year Locke published *A Letter concerning Toleration.*

Locke was also interested, as a philosopher, in educational issues. The first part of his *An Essay Concerning Human Understanding* is a vigorous attack on the theory of innate ideas, as expounded by Descartes and others who believed that human beings are born with some mental functions. This was rejected by Locke who emphasised the importance of experience. This was of significance for education because teachers, instead of being required to draw out and shape ideas that already existed in the mind, should be concerned with providing appropriate experiences or sensations. Locke has been criticised for using the word 'idea' to cover all mental activities, and he probably overstated his case against 'innate ideas', but his work certainly encouraged teachers to move away from rote learning and other arid practices towards thinking of teaching as an opportunity to provide worthwhile experiences. On the other hand, Locke has also been criticised for promoting the notion of the mind as *tabula rasa*, or a blank slate waiting to be written upon. Locke was anxious that his ideas should not be oversimplified: 'I do not say to be a good geographer that a man should visit every mountain, river, promontary and creek upon the face of the earth'.

Some Thoughts Concerning Education: It is likely that Locke had been influenced directly or indirectly by the ideas of Comenius. Locke emphasised the importance of 'environment' rather than 'heredity' in education, a revolutionary idea shared by Comenius, Hartlib and others earlier in the century. He provided philosophical justification for this democratic belief, and said that because minds can develop in different ways it is essential to expose them only to experiences of a worthy kind. Developing good habits was important for similar reasons, and, like Comenius, he made practical recommendations for the physical well-being of children: plenty of exercise, regular patterns of sleep, simple food and the avoidance of regular dosing with medicines.; habits of discipline and self-restraint were also stressed. Children should be trained to be well-mannered and courteous; they should be treated firmly but not harshly; children should be neither too submissive nor too sheltered – balance was the secret. Play was also important, but should be controlled.

Locke was critical of schools for their evident inability to follow his precepts. This view may have been based on his personal experience of Westminster School where he was certainly unhappy. He wanted better teachers, but he was also critical of many parents who either mistreated or spoilt their own children.

Locke's Other Publications on Education: Locke reflected the seventeenth-century view of social segregation in education in his writings. On the one hand, he gave advice to the upper classes in *Instructions for the Conduct of a Young Gentleman*, and *Thoughts concerning Reading and Study for a Gentleman*; on the other hand, he reflected on what should be provided (compulsorily) for the children of the poorer classes on relief in *Working Schools*. Children over three years old should attend schools and be fed on the diet they were used to, bread and water plus a little warm gruel in winter. They would be taught useful skills such as knitting and would be educated in morality and made to attend church on Sundays. The products of their labour would help pay for the rest of the scheme, which also involved boys being apprenticed at the age of 14. Locke has been criticised for advocating a regime which seemed to conflict with his *Treatise on Civil Government* which advocated a system of constitutional government based on liberty and equality.

CONCLUSION

The results of the Reformation should not be thought of simply in terms of increasing literacy but also as a profound influence for change in attitudes to the nature of education and who should be educated. Similarly, the Counter-Reformation was not an attempt to resist the educational ideas of the Protestants but rather the implementation of a policy to adopt the best of the educational reforms and to improve upon them. The link between religion, education and democracy should not be exaggerated, but the move towards greater educational participation was, in the long run, very significant. Equally important was the gradual development of the idea of the individual, with individual rights and responsibilities, including the right of access to education.

One part of Reformation thinking was that all Christians should be able to read and discuss the Bible. This became a tremendous impetus towards mass literacy. This trend was both dependent on and facilitated by printing. The idea of a Bible being printed cheaply enough to encourage the aim of having one in every household would have been impossible without the kind of printing presses used by Gutenberg and Caxton. The educational importance of printing in the sixteenth and seventeenth centuries cannot be exaggerated. There was also an important link between printing, mass literacy and democratic ideas. Especially after the execution of Charles I there were many radical ideas about a better, less hierarchical society, which would be, to some extent, dependent upon a better distribution of educational chances. Comenius was well aware of these connections and proposed innovations in curriculum and pedagogy much in advance of his time.

It is also interesting that in terms of education, the Catholic Counter-Reformation did not attempt to revert to the situation that had existed prior to the Reformation. The Jesuits and others saw the need to move with the times: the organisation that Ignatius had seen primarily as a Catholic missionary force became famous for efficient teaching methods, especially the systematic organisation of curriculum and encouraging competitive motivation. This has survived into the twenty-first century. David Hamilton[5] makes the claim that the concept of curriculum as we now use it was a sixteenth-century invention designed to cope with new educational needs and demands. The concept has survived remarkably well.

REFERENCES

1. N. Hans, *Comparative Education* (Routledge & Kegan Paul, 1967), p. 152.
2. J. Lawson and H. Silver, *A Social History of Education in England* (Methuen, 1973), pp. 144–5.
3. Quoted by Lawson and Silver, op.cit., p. 155.
4. S.J. Curtis, and M.E.A. Boultwood, *A Short History of Educational Ideas* (University Tutorial Press, 1953, 4th edn, 1965), p. 156.

5. D. Hamilton, *Towards a Theory of Schooling* (Falmer, 1989), p. 43.

Further Reading

Chadwick, O., *The Reformation* (Pelican, 1964).
Murphy, D., *Comenius* (Irish Academic Press, 1995).

8
The Eighteenth Century: The Enlightenment

INTRODUCTION

Post-Reformation Protestant attitudes and beliefs, including the growth of individualism, had profound effects not only on religious institutions and practices, but also on social, political and economic ideas and ways of thinking, including educational thought. Scientific advances, especially those of Isaac Newton, impressed an increasing number of people throughout the seventeenth century; by the beginning of the eighteenth century a combination of scientific and philosophical thinking was beginning to produce a different world view, partly as a reaction against the Counter-Reformation which we discussed in Chapter 7.

The eighteenth century has sometimes been referred to as the Age of Reason. Intellectual ideas, stemming directly from the Renaissance and Reformation were encapsulated in the term 'Enlightenment'. Unlike words such as Renaissance or Gothic, which were much later inventions, the notions of light and enlightenment became current during the eighteenth century in several languages: the French *Le Siècle des Lumieres* became *Aufklarüng* in German from about 1780.[1] The English word Enlightenment did not become current until the nineteenth century but the idea of the light of knowledge shining through the darkness of ignorance was popular during the eighteenth century:

> Nature and Nature's laws lay hid in night.
> God said, let Newton be! and all was light.
>
> (Alexander Pope, *Essay on Man*)

Significant advances in science continued from the seventeenth century into the eighteenth. The illumination, or Enlightenment, provided by science was gradually but consciously extended to political, social and economic issues. On both sides of the Atlantic questioning the political *status quo* contributed to the causes of the War of Independence in

America and the Revolution in France. It is always dangerous to make causal links between intellectual theories and political events, and later in this chapter we shall attempt to describe a much more complex set of interactions between ideas and actions, including those in the field of education, but it is difficult not to be impressed by the power of ideas in the eighteenth century.

There is another important strand running through eighteenth-century history which also interrelates with the world of ideas: the continuing process of technological development which is conventionally, but somewhat misleadingly, labelled 'The Industrial Revolution'. The title is misleading because the process had started long before the eighteenth century and had continued steadily over many years rather than happening suddenly and dramatically. Yet the word 'revolution' does help to convey the tremendous impact that technological development was having on many aspects of life in the final quarter of the century.

Despite the drama of the two kinds of revolution in the second half of the eighteenth century, however, the general background of the first half of the century was largely peace and tranquility. In England the 'Glorious Revolution' or non-revolution of 1688–89 had led to the dull but comparatively stable reigns of William and Mary, and Queen Anne, and then the artistic and architectural harmony of the Georgian era which can still be seen in such buildings as the Bath Crescent and Carlton House Terrace in London. In France the long reigns of Louis XIV and Louis XV, extending over 130 years, almost gave the impression of a permanent regime with no imaginable alternative. There were occasional succession disputes and wars of rivalry between the great European powers, but on the whole the background could be described as peaceful and prosperous. There were, of course, danger signs: emerging nationalism, the gap between rich and poor; and the rapidly rising populations with food shortages and famines.

THE ENLIGHTENMENT

It is difficult and perhaps unwise to attempt to summarise the main features of an era as complex as the Enlightenment, but in a book of this kind we must attempt to pick out what seem to be the most important attitudes and beliefs, even at the risk of simplification. There are many problems in describing the Enlightenment. The first is that the process of Enlightenment thinking carried with it the seeds of its own destruction: early on in the application of critical thinking to traditional beliefs it became apparent that the Enlightenment itself would be subject to hostile attacks of a similar kind. For example, we shall see that Rousseau began as a supporter of Diderot and d'Alembert's great Encyclopaedia and other examples of advanced thinking, but soon reacted strongly against the Enlightenment. It is still difficult to decide whether Rousseau should be seen as one of the Enlightenment thinkers or as an early exponent of Romanticism, or both. The second difficulty is that although Enlightenment is generally accepted as a useful term to describe an important process in history, there have been endless debates about exactly what should be included and also what is the most appropriate date for the beginning of the Enlightenment.[2] It is not difficult for historians to identify early signs of the Enlightenment long before the eighteenth century; nevertheless we use the Enlightenment as an appropriate term for the eighteenth century.

We select five major features of the Enlightenment for discussion in slightly more detail: belief in the power of scientific reasoning; faith in progress; human rights; freedom of thought and enquiry; and finally, the desire to promote education as a means of furthering the 'Enlightenment project'.

Reason: As we saw in Chapter 7, seventeenth-century Europe was dominated by two kinds of 'authority', the Bible and the Greek and Roman Classics. Both involved looking back to a previous age for moral inspiration: a sort of Garden of Eden and Golden Age attitude. The Renaissance and Reformation had each reinforced that view: the Renaissance building up a fuller picture of classical antiquity, the Reformation reinterpreting the Bible and recommending individual attention to it rather than group acceptance of the authority of an abstract 'Church'. One of the intellectual triumphs of the later Middle Ages had been the fusion of classical philosophy – especially Aristotle – with Christian theology. We observed in Chapter 5 how Thomas Aquinas had succeeded in this task, but the Reformation tended to upset the balance.

Most early proponents of the Enlightenment were not opposed to religion but they were critical of many of the religious practices of traditional Christianity which they regarded as irrational superstitions. Many Enlightenment thinkers, such as Voltaire, were Deists who were greatly impressed by Newton's discoveries in physics which they took to be evidence of a supreme intelligence of some kind, a God, who created a universe which operated according to the physical laws discovered by Newton. They strongly objected to belief in miracles, shrines devoted to saints and doctrines such as the transubstantiation of the bread and water in the mass into Christ's body and blood. They saw their epoch as the age of reason and believed that the application of reason to personal and social life would lead to the perfectibility of human beings and of society itself: the ills of society such as injustice, crime and cruelty were due to unreasonable beliefs, institutions and practices. Most Enlightenment thinkers were rationalists in the non-atheistic sense of the word, but some wanted to dispense with the supernatural and metaphysical altogether.

Progress: Belief in progress was clearly connected with the idea that the application of science and reason would result in improvements of various kinds, but progress meant more than that. Whereas traditional Christianity had looked back to a golden age, and the Renaissance had recalled the glories of Greece and Rome, Enlightenment thinkers saw history as a relentless process of moving from superstition to science and from the supernatural to the natural as a sequence of linear development. Certain kinds of rationality would inevitably come, but could be speeded up or slowed down by human actions: there was a strong element of determinism or historicism in much Enlightenment thinking.

Rights: A quite separate line of development was a general humanitarian concern for human beings. Enlightenment thinkers tended to look back on the Middle Ages as a time of barbarity, cruelty and injustice. Most did not question the institution of property itself but questioned the exploitation of some human beings by their supposed superiors. Some went further and questioned the whole idea of the privilege of rank; others were satisfied with the notion that privileges included duties as well as rights. The Age of Reason was not an age of equality, but some questions of social justice were raised, including the whole issue of slavery.

Freedom: The question of freedom was seen as complex. Some limitation of individual freedom was accepted as the price paid for living in a society (Rousseau and others saw this as a kind of social contract). The freedom that was advocated was freedom of thought which was then extended to freedom of expression. Censorship was generally seen as part of traditional, irrational and repressive authority, and intellectuals tended to be clearer on what they disliked about traditional authority than on the acceptable limitations of individual freedom. They were sure that the practices of the Inquisition, by which unorthodoxy could be punished by torture and execution, were intolerable, as was the persecution of individuals for heretical beliefs, religious or otherwise. Some of them, no doubt, had in mind such examples as the fate of Galileo who was punished for his scientific enquiries, or at least for publishing his interpretation of the results. Others criticised the whole notion of inhibiting freedom of enquiry by 'authorities' who feared the consequences of allowing controversial ideas to be discussed.

Education: The Enlightenment not only changed traditional beliefs about what should be taught and the most effective ways of teaching the young, but also saw education as a means of encouraging greater progress on the road to reason. Ignorance and superstition were the twin evils which could be eliminated, it was hoped, by education. Fatalism, or the acceptance of one's lot in life, was to be replaced by the notion that much could be achieved by improved educational programmes, although the exact kind of education was open to debate, as was the question of the control of education: while most intellectuals wanted educational institutions removed from Church control, not all agreed that the State should take over that responsibility. We shall return to a fuller discussion of education later in this chapter.

Other Features of the Enlightenment

There were many other features of the Enlightenment view of a good society which were interesting and which, in the much longer run, affected educational thought. For example, while many historians have pointed to the rise of nationalism as a characteristic of the nineteenth century with its origins in the eighteenth, most Enlightenment thinkers were universalistic in their outlook. Many explicitly proclaimed that they were European rather than French or German; others saw human progress in terms of world-wide peace.

Another characteristic of the Enlightenment *philosophes* was that they advocated toleration, for example, toleration of the Jews and of other faiths and ways of life. Not only did they dislike persecution for humanitarian reasons, but they saw toleration as a positive virtue in its own right: our reason should enable us to understand and to respect other cultures and other individuals.

EDUCATIONAL IDEAS BEFORE AND AFTER ROUSSEAU

We saw in Chapter 7 that some significant educational ideas were developing in the seventeenth century. For example, Hartlib's views on education for the whole of society; the contribution made by Comenius to educational theory and practice; the philosophical thinking of Locke which, as we shall see in a later chapter, led to some aspects of the development of psychology. All of these trends were to make further progress during the eighteenth century, but at the beginning of the century educational practices were generally extremely backward and lagging behind the needs of rapidly developing societies such as that in England. Schools in general were unenlightened places in most respects; universities were generally not much better, but were less oppressive.

SALONS, SOCIETIES AND ACADEMIES

Salons in the eighteenth century, essentially groups of like-minded friends meeting together to discuss important issues, had developed from the kind of salon which became famous during the reign of Louis XIV. Women were often at the centre of such informal groups: for example, Madame de Sevigny or Ninon de Lenclos had salons which became notorious meeting places for sceptics and free thinkers. During the 1760s, Encyclopaedists, including d'Alembert, met at the house of Mademoiselle de Lespinaire.[3] Salons also existed outside France – in Vienna and Berlin, for example, and particularly in London where they tended to be much more political.

A slightly more formal organisation might be called a literary society or a reading society. Some of these were established specifically to disseminate Enlightenment ideas; others indulged in practical, moral activities such as raising funds for a school or poor relief; many were purely for the enlightened entertainment of its members. One of the earliest was the Dublin Society, founded in 1724 to provide relief for a famine, but which continued to exist well into the twentieth century with a much wider agenda. In 1754, London copied Dublin with the Society for the Encouragement of Arts, Manufactures and Commerce, later known as the Royal Society of Arts. Many societies were also founded about that time in Spain and Latin America.

Other societies were modelled on Plato's Academy in Athens. Many of these were devoted exclusively to discussions about science. The Royal Society in London, which was founded before the beginning of the eighteenth century, was of this kind and was copied in many parts of Europe. Some societies and academies were ephemeral; others still exist.

The reasons for discussing these groups in the context of the Enlightenment are two-fold: first, they indicate the great thirst for knowledge and discussion in the eighteenth century; second, they were important because they stimulated the development of intellectual activities, including reading and writing about science, reform and education. They also helped to promote the idea that discussion itself could be an educational activity, even in schools.

THE ENCYCLOPAEDIA (*ENCYCLOPÉDIE OU DICTIONNAIRE RAISONNÉ DES SCIENCES, DES ARTS ET DES MÉTIERS*)

Another name that was given to the eighteenth century was 'The Philosophical Age'. Then, as now, philosophical could be used loosely to mean the general pursuit of wisdom, or in a more restricted way to indicate a more rigorous intellectual discipline, as studied at universities. In France the word *philosophe* could have either meaning, and it was also used to refer to the group of intellectuals who contributed to the great Encyclopaedia edited by Diderot, assisted by d'Alembert.

Diderot and d'Alembert's Encyclopaedia, a central publication of the Enlightenment, was itself an ambitious educational project, intended not only to wage war upon superstition and ignorance but also to provide a new map of knowledge and an outline of all existing knowledge. It was a tremendous task which took 21 years and 28 massive volumes to accomplish. Denis Diderot (1723–84) devoted much of his adult life to the Encyclopaedia, which had begun as a translation of Chambers' English Cyclopaedia, but developed into a much more ambitious project: Diderot's vision was a definitive text on all known scientific and technical knowledge which would provide a basis for further enquiries and discoveries. It also became a collection of Enlightened opinions on politics, economics, philosophy and religion. It was not anti-religious but it was anti-clerical. It was sold on a subscription basis and became an almost immediate success not only in terms of critical acclaim but also commercially: the print run of 4,000 copies sold out quite quickly, despite the high cost.

The Encyclopaedia was attacked by traditionalists of various kinds, was subjected to censorship by the Jesuits and repressed completely in some countries. Diderot was advised to leave France but he stayed to complete his task. The first volume appeared in 1751 and the project was finished in 1772. A revised, enlarged edition, appeared in 1782 and work continued throughout the Revolution. Diderot died in 1784 and his last words were said to be 'The first step towards philosophy is scepticism.'

The Encyclopaedia was influential throughout Europe and also gave its name to a way of thinking about the place of knowledge in the curriculum. The word 'encyclopaedism' is derived from the Greek term meaning a whole system of learning. The encyclopaedist view of curriculum lasted much longer in France, but it was for a while fashionable in teacher education in England, and was parodied by Charles Dickens in *Hard Times*.

JEAN JACQUES ROUSSEAU (1712–78)

Rousseau soon became critical of both the Encyclopaedia and of the various activities of the Academies and Societies. He wrote an article on Political Economy for the Encyclopaedia in 1755 (and several items on music), but in 1761 he published *La Nouvelle Heloise* which is regarded as an early example of Romanticism. His own view of education is set out at length in *Emile*, which was published in 1762, the same year as *The Social Contract*. It was a remarkable, even sensational, book which was an immediate success and has featured in discussions of educational theory ever since. It preached an approach to education totally different from that of the Encyclopaedists. At the time, *Emile* was banned by the Catholic Church, partly because Rousseau made some explicit critical references to Catholic doctrine, but also because it was regarded as dangerously subversive; *Emile* was also seen as immoral and potentially revolutionary. It was, for example, debated and condemned by the Paris Parlement. Rousseau prudently left France and returned to his native Geneva, but there the Council also signalled its disapproval of the book. Rousseau left for England where he was helped by David Hume and other English sympathisers, until he quarrelled with them and returned to France in 1770.

Rousseau's Educational Ideas

It is important to see Rousseau's writings on education in the context of the kind of schools that he was familiar with, and also in the context of his social and political ideas. It would also be a mistake to ignore *La Nouvelle Heloise* which was written in the form of a novel before *Emile*. In the novel, Rousseau describes the education of children not in a school but at home, protected from the corrupting influences of society. It provides us with one of Rousseau's fundamental articles of faith: that children are born naturally good, but become infected by the evils of society unless measures are taken to keep the child away from them.

There is a problem here: a tension exists between Rousseau's desire for children to be free from the evils of society whilst accepting the notion of a 'contract' between people and society whereby individuals give up some liberty in return for the protection of the State. Nothing should be imposed by the State that was in conflict with 'the general will' of the people, but who was to decide what was the general will? This revolutionary aspect of Rousseau's political philosophy is difficult to reconcile with Rousseau's educational views which preached that children should be free from society's corrupting influence. We should also note that in one of Rousseau's later publications, *Considerations on the Government of Poland* (1772), he came to quite different conclusions: he argued for a State system of education on the grounds that the State had a right to form the character of its citizens so that their tastes and morals would be different from those of other nations. So much for individual freedom and education according to nature!

Many educationists have chosen to ignore this contradiction and move on to Rousseau's major educational principle: that it is more important to understand the nature of the child than to be concerned with what knowledge to inculcate. This principle has given rise to two kinds of debate about the education of young children: the first recognising that children are not miniature adults but develop by going through a sequence of stages of development. This was not a new idea in education – we have in earlier chapters referred to Quintilian and Erasmus in this connection; but Rousseau took the idea of stages in a different direction, as we shall see later in this chapter. The second debate provoked by Rousseau concerns the idea of children's 'needs'. In *Emile,* Rousseau advocated a child-centred approach to education rather than a teacher-centred or curriculum-centred programme. The teacher's task was to observe the child, identify needs and provide experiences to meet those needs. As we shall see, there are problems about this interpretation of needs: there is inevitably a social dimension to 'needs' – meeting needs is not simply a question of individual differences. It may be easier to accept Rousseau's emotional reaction against the harsh and repressive treatment of children during the eighteenth century than it is to accept *Emile* as a fully thought out systematic philosophy of education.

Emile (de l'Education): This book is Rousseau's attempt to square the circle: how to provide a good education for the innocent child and protect him from the evils of a corrupting society. Rousseau avoids the problem of presenting a logical philosophical argument by putting forward his ideas in the form of narrative, the story of an orphan, Emile, who is cared for by an ideal tutor. *Emile* is divided into five Books, each dealing with a stage of development:

Book I: Infancy (from birth to 2 years)

Book II: Boyhood (2–12 years)
Book III: Early adolescence (12–15)
Book IV: Later adolescence (15–20)
Book V: Adulthood and marriage (20+)

(There are some similarities with Rousseau's stages of development and those proposed by twentieth-century psychologists, including, as we shall see in Chapter 12, the stages postulated by Piaget and Bruner.)

We should also note that some of the terms used by Rousseau, for example, discovery, experience, readiness, child-centred, natural, have become sources of conflict between traditional and progressive educationists throughout the twentieth century. We must also remember that Rousseau was an admirer of Plato's *Republic*, but in *Emile* dismissed it as an impossible contemporary model because he thought that no such community as envisaged by Plato existed in the eighteenth century having been replaced by corrupt 'civilisations' such as eighteenth-century France. Yet in his later advice to Poland, Rousseau returned to a set of recommendations much more like Plato's *Republic* than his own *Emile*.

Rousseau's work on education was packed with brilliant insights into childhood and what was wrong with traditional education; it is, unfortunately, also scattered with false assumptions, ignorance of some aspects of children's behaviour as well as amazing internal contradictions. For example, he preached the doctrine of 'natural' freedom for children, but his writing is full of commands about what children must not be allowed to do. His method of exposition, fictional narrative, allowed him to assume that all his methods would be successful, and he therefore described the adolescent *Emile* as having grown up in just the way that Rousseau predicted. His writings show all the arrogance of someone who was certain the he was right; one of the problems is to distinguish the brilliant insights from the nonsense.

Our task in this book is not to evaluate all of Rousseau's life and ideas; it is merely to give him credit for the remarkable insights he had into some aspects of the process of educating the young. These include ideas about stages of human development, learning from discovery and personal experience, the danger of formal instruction, the idea of readiness, including reading readiness, and teacher–pupil contracts. Rousseau often overstated his case, but many of his ideas, stripped of exaggeration have withstood the test of time and will need to be discussed in several later chapters.

We have talked about giving Rousseau credit for ideas many of which have become part of the agenda for progressive education in the twentieth century. We can be sure, however, that even had Rousseau never existed these ideas would have emerged as part of the Enlightenment or post-Enlightenment debate on education. Some of them existed long before *Emile*; others were developed by writers such as Pestalozzi. What Rousseau certainly did was to express the ideas in a way that made them accessible to large numbers of readers from the 1760s onwards, but in the longer run, that may not have been an advantage.

Johann Heinrich Pestalozzi (1746–1827)

Pestalozzi was clearly influenced by *Emile* but the major difference between Pestalozzi and Rousseau was that Pestalozzi was a self-critical practitioner who developed his ideas experimentally rather than being satisfied with dogmatic assertions based on opinions or strong emotional reactions. As well as Pestalozzi there were others in the eighteenth century who felt strongly about the prevailing educational practices and who tried to find better alternatives. The enlightened educators included such names as David Manson (1726–92) who ran his own private school in Belfast which had no corporal punishment and used various 'play way' techniques to encourage the children of the poor to achieve. In Alsace, there was Jean Frederic Oberlin (1740–1826), a Protestant pastor who established a group of five schools for the poor in his large parish, trained teachers for them, and not only improved the level of education of the parents and their children but also raised the standards of agriculture. His life was occasionally threatened by opponents. As we have seen, those with progressive views on education ran the risk of being perceived as politically subversive, and this was sometimes true of Pestalozzi.

Pestalozzi was born in the prosperous city of Zurich in Switzerland which possessed some of the features later associated with a welfare state: some provision was made for the poor and the sick; libraries were maintained at public expense but schooling was comparatively neglected. Pestalozzi's family were middle-class Protestants of Italian origin; his father was a successful surgeon who died when Pestalozzi was young leaving insufficient funds to continue the family's lifestyle. Pestalozzi's early memories included genteel poverty and unhappy school days. At the age of 15, his high school provided a more satisfactory regime, but still one which Pestalozzi later criticised for its lack of concern for practical abilities. At this time Pestalozzi was developing political interests, and he gave up the idea of becoming a clergyman; instead when he left college he experimented with farming. In 1769 he married, and following the birth of his son, he developed his educational theories, combining this with observing his child's development. Later he also experimented with methods of teaching science and other subjects from practical experiences. He had read Rousseau and was initially impressed, but soon became critical of some aspects of the 'theory' in *Emile*: for example, he disagreed with Rousseau's extreme ideas on liberty, preferring a balance between freedom and obedience.

Pestalozzi defined education as the process or art of assisting natural development; his theory included the idea that the child's mind receives impressions from outside itself and makes sense of those impressions by trying to make them fit with previous learning. Pestalozzi saw education as a means of assisting this natural process in a variety of ways – the child learns to think by thinking and to speak through speaking – these are natural developments which can be assisted by a good teacher, or impeded by a bad one.

In *How Gertrude Teaches Her Children* (1801), Pestalozzi talks of assisting in the learning process in the development of language, observation and mental skills which proceed from the three elementary powers of making sounds, forming images and constructing concepts. From these fundamental principles Pestalozzi elaborated his theory of teaching and learning. He saw the mind as a natural sorting device, classifying new objects by number, shape and name. In terms of modern learning theories, this classification process would seem far too simplistic, but Pestalozzi was on the right lines, developing techniques of teaching that were advanced for the time and more 'scientific' than those of Rousseau, for example.

Among other advanced ideas were the importance of children working in groups for some purposes, proceeding from the familiar to the unfamiliar and devising a curriculum in accordance with the achievements and development of individual children. Pestalozzi also saw the political importance of educating the poor, as well as the humanitarian benefits. He divided his curricular aims into three: head, body and heart or intellectual, physical (including vocational training) and moral which he considered to be the most important. Although his educational programme was analysed in this three-fold way, he stressed that it should be taught as an integrated whole.

Pestalozzi's practical efforts to put his ideas into practice in classroom situations often met with difficulties: sometimes financial, sometimes lack of business acumen, sometimes local opposition. His most successful enterprise was the boarding school at Yverdon which kept going for about 20 years from 1805. This school was visited by many reformers interested in education, including Froebel, Herbart and Mayo who stayed three years and then started a school in England. By the twentieth century many of the ideas became part of teacher training orthodoxy. His influence was considerable in Prussia and Saxony but took longer to take hold in England. In Switzerland, his ideas continued to develop with his former pupil, Philippe de Fellenberg. In the longer run his influence was also seen in the work of such major theorists as John Dewey, Maria Montessori and Jean Piaget. In 1826 his *Swansong* was published which ends with a challenging idea for a teacher: 'Life itself educates.'

CONCLUSION

The Enlightenment was in many ways a reaction against certain aspects of the seventeenth-century world: religious intolerance, superstition and magic were replaced by humanitarian, scientific reasoning and a belief in progress. The implications for education were enormous, but before they really began, as we have seen, counter tendencies began to operate such as the Romanticism of Rousseau and others. This will be explored in Chapter 9.

The long-term effects of the Enlightenment on education were numerous and very important: apart from advocating a more humanitarian treatment of the young, the *philosophes* encouraged a more scientific attitude to the study of education – the development of child psychology, an interest in careful observation which influenced pedagogy, and an approach to curriculum which encouraged matching content with the developing abilities of individual pupils.

At the beginning of the eighteenth century, science was seen as a way of understanding how Nature worked. Nature included the human mind, and investigating that area was no longer forbidden territory, but rather a legitimate subject for enquiry. The key to answering such difficulties was Reason, and in particular scientific reasoning. It was inevitable that some enthusiasts for Reason would over-state their case: one of the reactions to this was Romanticism, not only in art, music and literature but also in education. A key figure in this was Rousseau who began by being a supporter of the Encyclopaedia but later made a highly emotional, but brilliant, response to the problem of education. In addition, the Industrial Revolution created a working class which would have to be educated and tamed. They would need to be literate and numerate as well as obedient. These requirements would in turn present further difficulties for the nineteenth century.

Above all, the Enlightenment virtually destroyed for ever the idea that education was primarily concerned with memorising sacred texts, or indeed any other books. The Age of Reason demanded that education should be concerned with developing the powers of the mind to criticise the *status quo* and to think rationally. In retrospect it is easy to parody the *philosophes* for their optimism about human reason and for under-estimating the power of emotions; but it was a very important lesson to be learned. Those responsible for planning national curricula are still trying to get the balance right between educating the intellect, moral education and educating the emotions.

REFERENCES

1. U. Im Hof, *The Enlightenment* (Blackwell, Oxford, 1994), p. 5.
2. Some writers would like to date the Enlightenment from the second half of the seventeenth century.
3. U. Im Hof, op.cit., pp. 114–15.

Further Reading

Hampson, N., *The Enlightenment* (Penguin, 1968).
Porter, R., *Enlightenment: Britain and the Creation of the Modern World* (Allen Lane, Penguin Press, 2000).

9
Romanticism

We have seen in the last chapter that the period of the Enlightenment was characterised by five main features: a belief in the power of scientific reasoning, faith in progress, human rights, freedom of thought and enquiry and the desire to promote education as a means of furthering the 'Enlightenment project'. The Enlightenment was followed by a radical change of values in the last part of the eighteenth century, what Isaiah Berlin has called 'the greatest single shift in the consciousness of the West that has occurred'.[1]

The difficulties of defining Romanticism have led to many different interpretations of the word. Some writers have in fact denied the legitimacy of the general term 'Romantic', stating that we can effectively examine only different romanticisms.[2] Broadly speaking, Romanticism can be said to be concerned with some aspects of the following: the modern in contrast to classicism; a union of love, religion and chivalry; an escape from the Industrial Revolution; a bourgeois revolt against the aristocracy; a desire to soar into the infinity; an emphasis on individuality and self-assertion; and the secret and inexpressible delight of the soul. Berlin would include in Romanticism the joy of every day Nature, novelty, revolutionary change, nostalgia, energy, force, and will, a sense of alienation, toleration of eccentricity, and the rejection of knowledge, past, present and future.[3] The Romantic movement was responsible for dramatic changes in art, literature, music and architecture both in form and content, resulting in new ways of looking at the world. Its influence on educational thought was also considerable.

The main difference between writers of the Enlightenment and those of the Romantic period was in their attitude towards Nature. The former saw Nature as a universal mechanism operating according to a set of natural laws. When these were discovered, man would be able to control his own destiny. The Romantics, on the other hand, believed that Nature could not be analysed but was to be accepted as a mysterious, brooding force whose moods were to be interpreted. More important for education was the contrast between the Enlightenment view, that man could control his destiny by the use of reason, and the Romantics, who stressed that the human condition was a much more complex process and that feelings rather than the intellect were of paramount importance. Rejecting the notion that man had progressed in history through the use of reason, they argued that man was linked to the past by an unbroken flow of experience.[4]

Whilst it may be useful to contrast the Enlightenment and Romantic views in order to illustrate their main differences, in practice the dividing line between the two philosophies is often blurred. For instance, if we examine the educational precepts of Rousseau which were dealt with in the previous chapter, we can see that his writings often consist of sentiments which belong at times to the old order and in other places to the new. This is not surprising in a figure such as Rousseau, who was a mass of contradictions in his personal life, and this was reflected in his writings. Perhaps his most memorable words which place him in the Romantic tradition occur at the opening of his *The Social Contract*, published in 1762, 'Man is born free and everywhere he is in chains.' In *Emile*, Rousseau exalts the 'noble savage' and advocates the 'Back to Nature' movement. Rousseau was also an early exponent of child-centred education and the notion of child development, both of which were taken up by the Romantics.

However, when we examine the term 'nature', we can see that there are at least three important meanings:

1. The nature that underlies individual things or concepts, that is, to understand what human nature is, we must include the different processes of development.
2. A different meaning is the natural as opposed to the artificial, the world as it is rather than a man-made environment.
3. The third meaning, an all-inclusive view of Nature, considers it as a process which assumes that humanity is in harmony with Nature. Man can study Nature's methods and apply the results to aid her in the process. This leads Rousseau, on the one hand, to use this argument to interfere with the course of a child's education at different stages in his life and, on the other, to advocate that we should follow Nature.

In his educational theory, Rousseau draws on all three meanings.[5] Furthermore, Rousseau's own five stages of education are somewhat prescriptive and at times positively unenlightened. Nevertheless, his advocacy of a revolt in education, from convention to nature, although not the first, was the most striking, inspiring later Romantics in formulating their views on education.

THE INFLUENCE OF GERMAN ROMANTICS

Although Rousseau's contribution to Romanticism deserves due acknowledgement, its true origins are to be found in Germany rather than in France. Unlike England and France, Germany in the late eighteenth century was not a unitary state and there were literally hundreds of princes with their own territories. Its culture was, compared with the rest of Europe, somewhat provincial, and its scholarship tended to be pedantic. Lutheranism had led to an examination of the relationship between man and God, stressing the individual suffering of the human soul. Pessimism was rife, as expressed in the *Sturm und Drang* (Storm and Stress) movement which prevailed in the 1760s and 1770s, typifying the philosophy of the time.

Perhaps the earliest and most influential philosopher who brought to bear revolutionary changes in outlook was Immanuel Kant (1724–1804). Kant, in his *Kritik der reinen Vernunft* (Critique of Pure Reason) (1781), challenged the Cartesian notion that all knowledge is innate, that knowledge of the world comes only from our senses, by experiencing things. Mathematical concepts, he stated, are not the result of the functioning of our senses any more than our sense of duty or of beauty. Our judgements about things and their relations to one another are made because of categories inherent in the structure of the mind. The senses supply the crude materials of knowledge but the mind itself completes the process by adding factors which come from elsewhere. The mind is unable to know the ultimate nature of things; we only know their outward appearance and how they act. The educational implications of Kant's philosophy are important. In contrast to Enlightenment thinkers, he saw that every individual is an end in him or herself and never a means for another's end: 'Be a person and respect all others as persons.' Individualism and humanity were two of the hallmarks of Romanticism.

An acquaintance of Kant, Johann Gottfried Herder (1744–1803), who made important contributions to the study and advancement of history, was one of the few Romantics who had a close personal experience of school teaching. When he was at Weimar between the years 1776 and 1788 as *Generalsuperintendent*, one of his duties was as inspector of schools. During this time he carried out a number of practical reforms, founded new educational institutions and outlined a plan for studies in his book *Ideen zur Philosophie der Geschichte der Menscheit* (Philosophy of Man) (1800). Herder stated that the development of human groups could best be described by reference to Nature, with its biological and botanical growth. All actions need to be understood in their historical context and the intentions of the participants examined. An object, he claimed, could not be described without reference to the purpose of its maker and it was therefore necessary to enquire into the maker's mind and motives. It would then be possible to understand why a particular society's art, philosophy, political system and geography developed. It could also help discern why different civilisations flourished or declined and why progress was made in some countries and not in others. In this view Herder thus anticipated both historicism and evolutionism.

He concluded that each human group has its own internal life and that each person belonging to it should speak the truth as he or she understands it. Such individuation of societies postulated the tolerance of differences in ideas, culture and traditions without seeking for unity, that is, individuals not having to fit into a given structure and with freedom of action. One of Herder's main contributions to educational theory was to develop naturalistic explanations for culture in such spheres as language, history, religion and the mind.[6]

Among the many early German Romantics, Friedrich Schiller (1759–1805) stands out as an educational thinker. He was primarily a dramatist who strongly believed that art had a beneficial and humanising effect. When he was 36, he published *Über die ästhetische Erziehung des Menschen in einer Reihe von Briefen* (Letters on the Aesthetic Education of Man) (1795) which influenced later educationists such as Pestalozzi, Herbart and Froebel. The major educational problems of his day raised five questions: was education to be controlled by the State for its own ends or should it be private and concerned with improving humanity; should education be directed towards the passive and receptive or towards the active and the creative; how to bring about the transition from sensory experience to abstract thinking; how to change people to act on moral principles and disinterested motives; and finally, how to educate man for freedom in a mechanically determined world.

Schiller's answers to these questions show his debt to Kant. Aware of the public debate then taking place in Germany on the matter of the relationship between the individual and the State, he deplored any attempts by the State to suppress individuality. Moral improvement, he believed, stemmed from individuals and would therefore lead to a better society. Spiritual freedom and freedom of the mind were essential.[7] However, he believed that the mind was passive and receptive and our desires and emotions the result of animal spirits. One of the problems confronting educationists, then, was how the mind could best become engaged in art, moral conduct and rational thinking. Schiller thought it could be achieved by imposing inner images on outer matter, as creativity is the chief function of the soul. It is the artistic impulse in man that unites a concept with sensory experience.

Schiller also expounded a theory of play which is not confined to children, but is also applied to the creative faculty in adults:

> Reason makes the following demand: there shall be interaction between the impulse-to-form and the material impulse – that is, there shall be a play instinct – because it is only by the unity with form, of the accidental with the necessary, of the passive state with freedom, that human nature is completed.

An important aspect of Schiller's thinking was his attention to the need for aesthetic education. He regarded the sublime as the peak of spiritual experience. The sublime was the feeling of awe when contemplating for the first time a scene of natural beauty, or contemplating some great event in history. The sublime, he argued, could be regarded in education as part of the process of emotional development and in elevating man to a higher plane of morality. In considering infinity, time and space, the individual can be both aware of his own insignificance and at the same time inspired to express his vision.

This leads to his theory of aesthetic education. To develop from the lower level of the sensuous to the moral, man must use imagination to create new images of art in order to transcend the laws of Nature. The highest point is reached when man can apply his art to his own personality. It was for this reason that Schiller advocated that dancing, poetry, music, drama and art should be taught from an early age. No worked-out system was adumbrated by Schiller, though he suggested three stages of development through which individuals must pass – the physical, the aesthetic and the moral. At the first stage, the child is still an animal in harmony with Nature; the aesthetic instinct of artistic interest may also develop towards the end of this stage. In youth and early manhood, he becomes aware of moral beauty and spiritual pleasure, and now looks towards a moral unity. In his theory, Schiller expressed the idea that the child recapitulates the cultural history of the species, the cultural epoch theory, which was widely accepted at the time.

Schiller's views, although in many respects flawed, proved to be a great stimulus to subsequent educators. He advanced Rousseau's advocacy for 'the harmonious development of all powers', a concept which was taken up by Pestalozzi in his work. Herbart's theory of education of taste and the development of sympathy were also derived from Schiller. Froebel's principles of creativity, self-realisation and socialisation were similarly inspired. In putting forward the doctrine of play as the chief means by which the child constructs an interpretation of reality,[8] Froebel wrote, 'Every person forms his world for himself', an almost exact quotation from Schiller's Thirteenth Letter in *Letters On the Aesthetic Education of Man*.

An exponent of what Isaiah Berlin terms as unbridled Romanticism was Friedrich Wilhelm Joseph von Schelling (1775–1854). At the age of 23, he was appointed professor of Philosophy at Jena University, then the main centre of the movement. He admired Kant, Fichte and Spinoza, and became acquainted with Goethe at Weimar where Schelling was also domiciled. The latter's studies of physical science led to his book *Ideen zur Philosophie der Nature* (Thoughts on the Philosophy of Nature) in 1797, and he developed his views on *Naturphilosphie* in subsequent writings. Briefly, Schelling applied to the philosophy of Nature insights gained from Kant and Fichte to propose a theory of three stages of knowledge, described as progressing from sensation to perception, from perception to reflection and from reflection to will.

Schelling also presented his views on higher education in his *Vorlesungen über die Methodie des akademischen Studiums* (Lectures on the Method of Academical Studies) (1804). His philosophy can be summed up in the phrase 'Nature is invisible mind, mind invisible nature.' Schelling regarded Nature as a living entity, starting with rocks which are the will in a state of total unconsciousness, through to plant life, then animals. Nature is striving to achieve some unknown purpose, whilst man is self-consciously aware of what he is striving for; through his efforts, the world is brought to a higher consciousness of itself. This doctrine was important in influencing the contemporary theory of art and aesthetics which stated that the only works of art which are valid are those depicting Nature as a living, though not wholly conscious, thing. Great works of art and music were the embodiment of the artist's infinite spirit which he is able to articulate through the operation of the unconscious. Schelling's interest in symbolism, mythology and the dualism between appearance and things in themselves contributed to his standing as one of the more influential of the Romantic thinkers.

August Schlegel, a contemporary writer on Romanticism, claimed that the movement was influenced by three main factors: the French Revolution, Fichte's theory of knowledge and Goethe's *Wilhelm Meister* novels.[9] Although Fichte's idealist philosophy will be dealt with in the next chapter, a brief reference to his educational ideas must be mentioned here. Before being appointed to a chair in Philosophy at Jena in 1794, Fichte had for several years been a tutor in various parts of Saxony and Switzerland, becoming friends with Pestalozzi and studying his writings. Schlegel was the author of a book *Die Problematik der aphoristichen Form* (Aphorisms on Education) (1804), written after Germany's defeat by Napoleon, where he attributed the defeat to the country's moral decay and the corruption of its citizens. He adopted Pestalozzi's notion that the educator's task is to motivate the child to learn, preferably through active rather than by passive means; if a child could become self-motivated, this would lead him from the realm of the selfish and sensuous to a pure and moral life. Moral education, he claimed, could best be achieved by surrounding the pupil with good examples. Young people should be taken away from their homes and educated in State-run institutions, staffed by carefully selected teachers, in order to train them in the ways of moral rightness. Much of Fichte's educational philosophy was based on his theory of knowledge. He believed that contemporary knowledge was ineffective, as knowledge is an instrument for the purpose of an effective life, of knowing how to live. 'We do not act because we know', he wrote, 'we know because we are called upon to act.' Unlike some of the early Romantics, Fichte saw an individual's freedom was to be obtained through action rather than by passive contemplation.

The writings of Goethe were influential, as we have seen, among the Romantics even though, as he himself admitted, 'For philosophy in the strict sense I had no organ.' Johann Wolfgang von Goethe (1749–1832) had studied law at Leipzig where he met Herder, who was to become his intellectual mentor. Goethe was a man of wide interests. He was employed by the Duke Karl August of Weimar at his Court, and apart from his official duties and his literary interests, he undertook research and published works on anatomy, geology, biology and optics. He was also director of the Weimar Theatre and was involved in the administration of Jena University. Goethe's biological studies, particularly the metamorphosis of plants, led him to believe that organisms were constructed on a uniform plan. His interest in science was based on a quest for a unifying law which would explain the diversity of forms and species in Nature.[10]

Goethe's own educational experience consisted of tutoring, when he was a young man, three children from humble backgrounds and he assumed responsibility for the education of the son of an aristocratic woman friend in Weimar. His success as a tutor was only modest. Goethe never formulated any theories on education, but it is through his novels that his views and convictions on the subject can be seen. Two of his major novels are *Wilhelm Meisters Lehrjahre* (Wilhelm Meister's Apprenticeship Years), published in 1795–96, and 20 years later, *Wilhelm Meisters Wanderjahre* (Wilhelm Meister's Wandering Years). The first book caused a sensation when it first appeared. It is to a large extent autobiographical, with Goethe himself as the hero, and gives an account of his own development, with reminiscences of books he has read, and it contains discussions on aesthetics. Goethe later told one of his disciples, 'Basically, the whole work seems only to be trying to say that, despite all the stupidity and confusion, man, led by a higher hand, eventually reaches a happy ending'.[11]

The first book, with its intricate plot interspersed with allegorical tales, depicts Wilhelm Meister's intellectual and cultural development. It is an account of Wilhelm's progress from the time when he leaves his parents' home to the point where, having completed his apprenticeship, he is entrusted with the education of his son. He advocates a view of education which was based on trial and error; only through searching and erring, through independent confrontation with the world, will the individual be able to discover his or her innate talents. The notion of the importance of the development of one specific skill in accordance with one's talents becomes central to *Wilhelm Meisters Lehrjahre*. Here the emphasis is on renunciation; Wilhelm has to relinquish his aim of cultivating his mind in an aristocratic society. The aim now is the acquisition of a practical skill in order to be a useful member of the community. Wilhelm entrusts his son to the 'education province', an educational Utopia, dedicated to practical activities and the inculcation of reverence: reverence to God, of one's fellow human beings and of Nature (the earth, suffering and death), leading to the highest form of reverence, self-reverence. There is a distinction between education (*Bildung*) and inner development, the latter a process capable of changing a character, leading him to a goal, unspecified, which society has set for him. By the end of the novel, Wilhelm has advanced towards that goal.[12] To Goethe, education was evolutionary, drawing forth from the individual that which was best , 'the realisation, as completely as possible, of the general type of the species'. His motto was 'In the beginning was action': he therefore urged 'Do, and by doing you will attain to your highest and best'. In the education of infants, as in the government of nations, he thought that repressive measures were futile. 'Man,' he said, 'is naturally active: open a way for action, and he will follow you.'

Goethe in many respects typifies the Romantic movement. Not all the thinkers mentioned in this section consistently subscribed to the idea characterising the movement. Goethe himself, towards the end of his long life, declared 'Romanticism is a disease, classics is health.' Others, such as Rousseau are difficult to classify under any one particular label with some describing their views which would at different times fit under either the Enlightenment or Romantic headings. Nevertheless, the influence of German Romanticism reached beyond that country and found ready roots in countries such as England.

BRITISH ROMANTICS

The outbreak of Rousseaumania between the 1760s and the 1790s had many manifestations, not least in Britain. Thomas Day's *Sandford and Merton* (1783–89) was but one example of a number of educational novels which highlighted the benefits of a natural as distinct from a formal education. Day's novel tells the story of how Tommy Merton, a corrupt and idle child, is transformed by a tutor, Mr Bob Henry Sandford, into a child of nature. David Williams, a radical deist, organised a school on principles described in *Emile*, and Richard and Marie Edgeworth's *Practical Education* (1798) argued that educational principles should be based on child nature. A wide range of people became interested in education at this time, including Joseph Priestley, the discoverer of oxygen, the philosopher and novelist William Godwin, Mary Wollstonecraft, and Erasmus Darwin, the scientist, who all wrote works influenced by Romanticism.[13]

Much more closely linked with the mainstream of the German Romantics was the writer and poet Samuel Taylor Coleridge (1772–1834). In early youth he had been a subscriber to the materialist philosophies and theories of human nature. At the age of 26, Coleridge went to Germany to study the works of Kant and Schelling at Göttingen. Shortly afterwards, in his own words, Kant took hold of him 'as with a giant's hand'.[14]

Coleridge's philosophical ambitions were to provide a new synthesis and 'reduce all knowledge into harmony'. This proved to be unrealisable, but his views on childhood and its educational implications are valuable. Some of these views were shared by some of his contemporaries, but Coleridge's expression of childhood displays an unusually superior intellect. It will be convenient to discuss them under four headings: innocence; morality; imagination; and language.

1. Innocence: As one writer has defined Coleridge's view, 'It included candour which has not yet come to acquiescence in the routine

corruption of the adult world, single-mindedness untainted by the hypocrisy of conventional valuation, spontaneity undrilled into the stock response, and a virtue of intense, fierce honesty.'[15] Therefore the education of the intellect should aim, at a gradual pace, at assisting the child in making 'pertinent connections.'

2. Morality: Because children have less power to express their meaning than adults, adults make the mistake of believing that a child's moral categories are different but this is misleading: 'They have less power to express their meaning than men, but their opinion of justice is nearly always the same; this we may prove by reference to our own experience.' As he wrote, 'All speculative truths begin with a postulate, even the truths of geometry. They all suppose an act of will, for in the moral being lies the source of the intellectual.'

3. Imagination: Coleridge believed that imagination was an important educative agency, for it assists in cultivating a sense of the aesthetic. ' The rules of the imagination are [themselves] the very powers of growth and production.' Schools should stimulate the child by bringing before him or her works of high quality imagination. This would include an introduction to science, which is a human achievement imaginatively initiated. Coleridge saw this process of childhood as a movement from the sensuous to a life in the idea.

4. Language: Coleridge lay great store in cultivating in the child a greater consciousness of the use of words:

> To emancipate the mind from the despotism of the eye is the first stop towards its emancipation from the influence and intrusions of the senses, sensations and passions generally. Thus most effectually is the power of an abstraction to be called forth, strengthened and familiarised, and it is this power of abstraction that chiefly distinguishes the human understanding from that of the higher animals – and in the different degrees in which this power is developed, the superiority of man over man mainly consists.

Coleridge wrote in his *Biographia Literaria*, 'I include in the meaning of a word not only its correspondent object, but likewise the character, mood and intentions of the person who is representing it.' For instance, in the 'eternal language' of Nature, as depicted in his poem 'Frost at Midnight', in a statement reminiscent of Schelling,

Coleridge affirmed that the child should perceive not just lakes and sandy shores, crags and clouds, but the 'processes and results of imagination by which these natural forms echo or reflect each other:

the clouds
Which image in their bulk both lakes and shores
And mountain crags.

Coleridge was conscious of the limitations of conventional language which militates against an all-encompassing 'eternal language'.[16] In attempting to make sense of his world at a time of revolution and intellectual moral confusion, Coleridge postulated a number of educational theories which still bear close examination.

The friendship between Coleridge and his contemporary, William Wordsworth (1770–1850), is well known. Coleridge once wrote to friend, 'Wordsworth is a Poet ... he will hereafter be admitted the first and greatest philosophical Poet – the only man who has effected compleat and constant synthesis of Thought and Feeling and accompanied them with Poetic Forms.'[17] After studying at Cambridge, Wordsworth paid two visits to France in the 1790s, becoming an enthusiastic supporter of the French Revolution in its early days. When Robespierre fell from power, he expressed his hopes in the Revolution that reform would be effected by education and reason. Coleridge visited Wordsworth in England in 1795 and, two years later, Wordsworth moved down to Somerset to be near Coleridge.

Wordsworth, like many others in the Romantic movement, never formulated a coherent theory of education. However, in his poems, particularly *The Prelude,* an autobiographical memoir, we can piece together his views. The writing and revision of the poem occupied Wordsworth for almost half a century, the first two parts appearing in 1799 and the final version in 1850. He had read *Emile* as a youth and was in sympathy with many of Rousseau' s views, but differed on some practical points. Unlike Rousseau, Wordsworth had enjoyed his childhood, being surrounded by family and schoolmates. As has been well said, 'Wordsworth's childhood had much in it which conformed not with Rousseau's extra vagaries or pedantries, but with his best mind.'[18]

It is interesting to note that the subtitle of *The Prelude* is 'Growth of a Poet's Mind', for as Wordsworth stated, ' The true standard of poetry is as high as the soul of a man has gone, or can go.' Wordsworth explored in this and later poems the growth of the human mind and its implications for the unfolding of human power. In infancy, Wordsworth believed, the mind is expressed and benefited by touch, which is, in some respects, the infant's first language, a genuinely human experience. As the child grows older, it is the experience of his senses and the interplay or sense activity and feeling that help him or her in accumulating experiences.

The well-known lines:

> The Child is father of the Man:
> And I wish my days to be
> Bound each to each by natural piety.

emphasise the importance Wordsworth places on childhood experience, for the adult cannot acquire full wisdom unless he has remained true to the first principles of his childhood. Knowledge can be acquired by storing up facts and reading books: true knowledge is not intellectual in nature but is absorbed organically from childhood onwards, and need not be a conscious process, as was summed up by Henry James: 'Small children have many more perceptions than they have terms to translate them; their vision is at any moment richer, their apprehension even constantly stronger than their prompt, their at all producible vocabulary.'

The second stage of a child's education was to place before him or her imaginative experiences. As the mind develops, the child should discover and analyse 'manifest distinctions' and 'the observation of affinities'. Wordsworth, like many of his contemporaries, was a supporter of analytical intelligence, though intellectual advance required an interplay with feeling, feeling with sensuality and sensibility with language.[19] Wordsworth's mysticism, which marks him out as a Christian pantheist, was based on a love of Nature and is reflected in his views of education:

> One impulse from a vernal wood
> May teach you more of man.
> Of moral evil and of good
> Than all the sages can.

His mystic vision of Nature was a further reason for regarding education as the mere imparting of information. Wordsworth was writing at a time when most grammar schools offered a rigid curriculum and when conservative forces were advocating the spread of only basic literacy in order to have a stabilising effect on the mass of the population.[20] Wordsworth opposed such an approach:

And – now convinced at heart
How little those formalities to which
With overweening trust alone we give
The name of Education, have to do
With real feeling and just sense.

True knowledge was to be developed and grown by the individual; the acquisition of knowledge was not an end in itself. One writer has claimed that Wordsworth's views led him to deny almost entirely man's right to authority over the child.[21] Unlike Rousseau, Wordsworth did not deny the child the study of books, except that it should occur at an appropriate stage. Nor did he approve of Rousseau's notion of a solitary Emile and a tutor, but preferred the social life of schooldays. Wordsworth's main achievement was to draw attention to the bond between child (as man) and Nature, to show that human nature is part of Nature, and to demonstrate the relationship between the development of the mind and experience.

CONCLUSION

Romanticism had its roots firmly in the Enlightenment but as a movement it was much more diffuse. French, German and British Romanticism each had their own individual characteristics. In Germany, the movement, as we have seen, was a reaction to French relativism and was linked to nationalism. The overlap between the Enlightenment and Romanticism was most clearly seen in France in the person of Rousseau. In Britain the movement drew heavily on the German tradition (Coleridge) and the French (Wordsworth).

In the sphere of educational thought, what the movement had in common in all countries was a view of Nature as a mysterious and unknown force which could not be analysed, but which man should engage with his emotions. If the Enlightenment believed that man's reason would enable him to control his life, the Romantic would regard this view as an oversimplification of man and society. Man was directed more by his feelings and emotion than by reason, though the intellect should be engaged by them. Whilst the Enlightenment looked towards a better life for the future, Romanticism looked back to the past in examining man's destiny, with an emphasis on traditions, folklore and nostalgia.

The contributions of Romanticism to educational theory and practice has been valuable. They include an emphasis on the use of play in childhood; the education of the emotions as well as the intellect; a new way of looking at aesthetic education and the arts; and the establishment of the first elements of modern child psychology. How far these aspects were accepted or ignored in the age of industrialisation which followed will be dealt with in Chapter 10.

REFERENCES

1. I. Berlin, *The Roots of Romanticism* (H. Hardy (ed.)), (Chatto & Windus, 1999), p. 1.
2. N.V. Riasanovsky, *The Emergence of Romanticism* (Oxford University Press, Oxford, 1992), p. 69.
3. Berlin, op. cit., pp. 16–18.
4. G.I. Gutek, *A History of Western Educational Experience* (Waveland Press Inc., Prospect Height, IL, 1972), p. 186.
5. J. Adams, *The Evolution of Educational Theory* (Macmillan, 1928), p. 274.
6. F. Beiser, 'Johann Gottfried Herder', in *Concise Routledge Encyclopaedia of Philosophy*, (Routledge, 2000), p. 348.
7. F. Eby, *The Development of Modern Education* (Prentice-Hall, 2nd edn, 1952), p. 418.
8. R.D. Miller, *Schiller and the Ideal of Freedom* (Clarendon Press, Oxford, 1970), pp. 112–14.
9. Berlin, op. cit., p. 93.
10. J.R. Williams, *The Life of Goethe. A Critical Biography* (Blackwell, Oxford, 1998), p. 49.
11. R. Friedenthal, *Goethe: His Life and Times* (Weidenfeld, 1993), p. 358.
12. S. Reiss, *Goethe's Novels* (Macmillan, 1969), p. 123.
13. W.A.C. Stewart. and W.P. McCann, *The Educational Innovators, 1750–1880*, vol. 3 (Macmillan, 1967), p. 31.
14. D. Jasper, 'Samuel Taylor Coleridge', in J. Raimond and J.R. Watson (eds), *A Handbook of English Romanticism* (Macmillan, 1992), p. 69.
15. W. Walsh, *The Use of Imagination: Educational Thought and the Literary Mind* (Chatto & Windus, 1959), p. 17.
16. A.W. Keech, 'Romanticism and Language', in S. Curran (ed.), *The Cambridge Companion to British Romanticism* (Cambridge University Press, Cambridge, 1993), p. 114.
17. T. McFarland, *Coleridge and the Pantheistic Tradition* (Clarendon Press, Oxford, 1960), pp. 115–16.
18. H. Wodehouse, *A Survey of the History of Education* (Edward Arnold, 1929), p. 114.
19. Walsh, op. cit., p. 49.
20. I. Britain, 'Education', in I. McCalman (ed.), *An Oxford Companion to the Romantic Age. British Culture 1776–1832* (Oxford University Press, Oxford, 1999), p. 162.
21. E. Legouis, (trans. J.W. Matthews), *The Early Life of William Wordsworth, 1770–1795* (Dent, 1897), pp. 60–1.

Further Reading

Harris, R.W., *Romanticism and the Social Order 1780–1830* (Blandford Press, 1969).
Hill, J.C. (ed.), *The Romantic Imagination* (Macmillan, 1977).
Menhennet, A., *The Romantic Movement 1785–1830* (Croom Helm, 1981).
Prichett, S. (ed.), *The Romantics* (Methuen, 1981).
Rust, L.R., *The Contours of European Romanticism* (Macmillan, 1979).

10
Industrialisation, Nationalism and the Cult of Efficiency

The coming of industrialisation to Europe in the late eighteenth and early nineteenth centuries had an enormous impact on attitudes towards religion, politics, economics, social problems and, not least, education. Another important aspect of this change was that it led to the formation of new social classes, the industrial and commercial middle classes and a large working class. The Industrial Revolution, which resulted in the establishment of factories employing labour in methods of mass production, relied heavily on children to carry out some of the more tedious processes. They were often apprentices, living in quarters under the supervision of the mill owners or, if still living with their families, were frequently herded into small and unhealthy dwellings in the new or expanding manufacturing towns. Britain is a good example of these changes.

Reformers began to pay serious attention to the physical, religious and moral well-being of the young and to the lack of provision of education to ameliorate the situation. The Sunday School movement, started by Robert Raikes in 1785, inspired evangelicals to address themselves to the problem. 'I cannot think,' wrote Mrs. Sarah Trimmer, the wife of a brick fields owner, 'of little children who work in manufactories, without the utmost commiseration.' She subsequently opened a school at Brentford, Middlesex, in the hope of civilising street Arabs, and publicised her work in a book, *The Oeconomy of Charity* (1787). Her views were by no means overly sentimental. When she was given a spinning wheel for a Sunday School, Mrs Trimmer had the idea of forming a spinning school, to be conducted on weekdays, in order to 'inure them (the children) early in life to industry'.[1] This notion, of linking work and education, spread, with the popularly held conviction that schools of industry in each parish, sustained by a parish rate, would provide a satisfactory means of combating possible evils. Attempts to make this possible by legislation were made by Samuel Whitbread in 1797 and Lord Brougham in 1820, but both were unsuccessful.

Apart from moral and religious considerations, there was a growing belief from the 1780s that the working classes should receive and benefit from some sort of education as a good in itself. G.H. Bantock has pointed out that the traditional technical arrangements brought about by the Industrial Revolution inevitably affected the whole culture. The comparative stability of a folk culture was transformed by industrialisation and involved considerable impoverishment in the texture of everyday existence. This led to a unique experiment, the setting up of a system of education intended to lead to universal literacy.[2]

Raymond Williams has described the growth of industry and of democracy which brought about a debate on the concept of education. It was seen that education was a good in itself but the industrial argument led to a definition of education in terms of future adult work, with teaching geared to the formation of social character, such as habits of regularity, self-discipline, obedience and trained effort.[3] These considerations were fired by the political, economic and social philosophy of the day. Jeremy Bentham (1748–1832), a leading proponent of Utilitarianism, in his *Fragment on Government* (1776) propounded the principle of the happiness of the greatest number. If this could not be achieved by individual effort, he argued, then governments and laws should be reformed. Bentham believed that morality was an exact science. As man is governed by the avoidance of pain and the maximisation of pleasure, the principle of utility could be employed in punishing wrong-doers. For this reason he became interested in prison reform. Bentham promoted and designed the building of a Panopticon, a circular prison where all the inmates could be supervised by a small body of warders. He extended this idea to schools, publishing a plan for a Chrestomathic School (1815–17), with pupils graded into different classes and with minimal staff. Fortunately, the building never materialised, but Bentham's principles were carried into practice by Bell and Lancaster.

A devoted follower of Bentham was James Mill (1773–1836). Mill's main contribution to Utilitarian psychology, which was to be of importance in educational thought and practice throughout the later nineteenth century, was his theory of the association of ideas. This theory will be discussed further in a later chapter of this book, but it may be noted here that it stresses the intellectual processes of a child rather than the emotional and was too mechanistic an approach. His son, John Stuart Mill (1806–73), although subscribing to Utilitariansm, differed from Bentham and his father in stating that some kinds of pleasure are more desirable

116

than others. He also distinguished between two aspects of education – whatever helps to make the individual what he or she is, or hinders him or her from being what he or she is not, is part of his education; and the other, that education consists of the culture which each generation gives to its successor, if possible raising the level of attainment.

Although there was a clash of viewpoints between Utilitarians on a range of issues, there was widespread agreement on the need to provide education. Adam Smith, in his *Wealth of Nations*, for example, had considered education as a profitable investment for society. Though the cost could be high, this would be rapidly repaid by the increase it would bring in production. Education was also seen as a social good, preventing crime, and it was essential, he believed, if people were to make intelligent political choices. Smith considered that the State should be responsible for 'the most essential part of education – namely, reading, writing and arithmetic'.[4]

The role of the State in providing education proved to be a contentious issue. Much less so was the means by which education should be conducted: this was seen broadly as the application of factory techniques to schools and the children. In 1796, Sir Thomas Bernard, one of the founders of the Society for Bettering the Conditions of the Poor, stated that the monitorial system was 'the division of labour applied to intellectual purposes. The principle in schools and manufactories is the same.' At the beginning of the nineteenth century this system was applied in day schools, sponsored by voluntary effort, by two rival bodies, the Institution for Promoting the British System for the Education of the Labouring and Manufacturing Classes of Society of Every Religious Persuasion, shortened in 1814 to the British and Foreign Schools Society, and one established by the Society for the Promotion of Christian Knowledge, the National Society for the Education of the Poor in the Principles of the Established Church, known as the National Society. Dr Andrew Bell (1753–1832) a former chaplain to five regiments in Madras, had employed a bright pupil to teach his colleagues to write and read in the sand. Bell was engaged by the National Society to carry out education on a mass scale in England. Joseph Lancaster (1758–1838), for the British and Foreign Schools Society, employing similar methods, claimed to educate 1,000 children with one teacher and the assistance of monitors. Bell wrote:

> The advantages of this system, in its political, moral, and religious tendency; in its economy of labour, time, expense and punishment; in the facilities and satisfaction it affords to the master and the

117

scholar; can only be ascertained by trial and experience, and can scarcely be comprehended or credited by those who have not witnessed its powers and marvellous effects.

Like the steam engine, or spinning machinery, it diminishes labour and multiplies work, but in a degree which does not admit of the same limits, and scarcely of the same calculations as they do. For, unlike mechanical powers, this intellectual and moral engine, the more work it has to perform, the greater is the facility and expedition with which it is performed, and the greater is the degree of perfection to which it is carried.[5]

The Lancasterian system, which was similar in many respects, represented the Nonconformist educational effort. The only reading material employed was extracts from the Scriptures, which served also for Scripture lessons. William Allen, the Treasurer of the Society and author of *Scripture Lessons for Schools on the British System for Mutual Instruction*, spelt out the aims of such teaching, which was to produce biddable dutiful pupils:

We have made them (the Scripture Lessons) to bear upon those duties in a very striking and prominent way without any comment whatever; but merely in the words of the Scripture; such as the duties of subjects to government in the words of Scripture; the duties of servants to masters in the words of Scripture; the relative duties of husbands and wives, and parents and children in the words of Scripture. They were most anxiously calculated to bring out those great and important duties, and to engrave them upon the minds of the children.

The work ethic was particularly emphasised on every possible occasion. For example, in one of Mrs Trimmer's texts for schools, published in 1824, a passage read:

Though this worthy woman had such pious thoughts, it was not her wish to be reading and praying all day long, because she knew that it was the duty of poor people to labour for their food and raiment: she therefore resolved to be industrious, and to go out washing and ironing, as she used to do.[6]

Another aspect of the school regime, common throughout the nineteenth century, was that little money should be expended on the schools. Dr Bell had declared, 'It is not proposed that the children of the poor should be educated in an expensive manner, or even taught to write and cipher.' The 'useful arts' and manual labour were to form the major part of the curriculum, but the factory analogy was seen at its best in the teaching methods used. The master would give a system of signals, by using a semaphore fixed to his desk, to the monitors who then transmitted the command to the pupils. The consequences of such a system was described by one inspector:

> Of the mechanical character of such teaching the following may serve as an illustration. On entering a large school, I requested that the instruction of the children might go on, according to its accustomed course – that I might judge of the means daily called into operation before I proceeded to inquire into the results. Astonished to find that some time elapsed before the machinery could be put into motion, I proceeded to inquire into the cause, and found that the monitors were in the act of placing the finger of each individual boy upon the first word of the lesson to be read. This accomplished, and the monitor having read one word of the lesson, and the boys simultaneously after him, each boy advanced his finger one word, and the process was repeated.[7]

Criticism of such an education was voiced by Radicals, especially those associated with the Society for the Diffusion of Useful Knowledge. Only slow progress had been made towards universal provision, but two small steps were taken to ameliorate the situation in 1833. A Factory Act stipulated that factory children should receive two hours of instruction daily; in the same year, the first government financial assistance towards the building of schools was made. Even at the highest level, this minimal provision of education was viewed with scepticism. In a conversation with the young Queen Victoria which she recorded, Lord Melbourne, then prime minister, stated:

> I don't believe there's anybody who doesn't know what is wrong and what is right. He doubts education will ever do any good; says all Government has to do 'is to prevent and punish crime, and to preserve contracts.' He is FOR labour and does not think the factory children are too much worked; and thinks it very wrong that parents should not be allowed to send their children who are under a certain age to work.[8]

Nevertheless, there was a growing awareness both within the British and Foreign and National Societies and generally, that an education based on the Bible alone was an inadequate preparation for a future work force. Moral education, for instance, was hardly taught. With the introduction of secular readers from the early 1840s, it was realised that the poor could be introduced to the newly fashioned science of economics. Lessons in thrift, better health, the avoidance of the pawnbroker and economical shopping could be conveyed through appropriate text books. Official bodies eagerly embraced an education which could reflect these desiderata. By 1861, the Newcastle Commission on the State of Popular Education in England was able to pronounce that 'the knowledge most important to a labouring man is that of the causes which regulate the amount of his wages, the hours of his work, the regularity of his employment and the price of what he consumes.'[9]

ROBERT LOWE AND PAYMENT BY RESULTS

A good illustration of the effects of industrialisation on educational thought and practice can be seen in the life and work of Robert Lowe (1811-92). Born at a time when the experience of the French Revolution was still fresh in the minds of his contemporaries, Lowe had, at an early stage in his career, developed a dislike of 'mobocracy'. He was hostile to trade unions and 'to any violation of economic laws to the inevitable detriment of society, by whatever means'. He had entered the House of Commons in 1852 and became vice-president of the Committee of Council for Education seven years later.

His speech in the Commons on the First Reading of the Representation of the People Bill in March 1866 displayed his contempt for the lower classes:

> Let any gentleman consider – I have had such unhappy experiences and many of us have – let any gentleman consider the constituencies he has had the honour to be concerned with. If you want venality, if you want ignorance, if you want drunkenness and facility for being intimidated; or if, on the other hand, you want impulsive, unreflecting and violent people, where do you look for them in the constituencies? Do you go to the top or to the bottom?[10]

In an address given in Edinburgh in the following year, *Primary and Classical Education*, Lowe dealt more centrally with the education of the working classes:

> The lower classes ought to be educated to discharge the duties cast upon them. They should also be educated that they may appreciate and defer to a higher cultivation when they meet it; and the higher classes ought to be educated in a very different manner, in order that they may exhibit to the lower classes that higher education to which, if it were shown to them, would bow down and defer.[11]

It is not surprising, given Lowe's philosophy, that when the Newcastle Commission was appointed to 'consider and report what measures, if any, are required for the extension of sound and cheap elementary education instruction to all classes of the people', he agreed with the underlying premiss in the Commission's remit that costs should be kept to a minimum. The details of the scheme known as 'Payment by Results' which Lowe implemented after the Commission's report are not important here so much as the philosophy underlying it. Briefly, the system made the schoolmaster's salary dependent on the performance of each pupil at an annual examination in a range of subjects. It fitted in well with the *laissez-faire* climate where competition brought out the best in both individuals and in business and industry. Examinations similarly would have a stimulating effect which would produce the best efforts in pupils. Thirdly, as certain standards were set in ability for the 3Rs and other subjects, comparability could be achieved and targets set. Finally, the factory analogy was complete with the insistence on measurable output, with its emphasis on quantity and, hopefully, quality. One of the most perspicacious criticisms of the system came from Palmerston, who was prime minister at the time. In a letter to Lord John Russell he wrote:

> It is easy to say that Payment is to be regulated by the number of children who on Examination shall be found able to read, write and cypher well. But the attainment of a child in writing, reading and arithmetic cannot be measured by a fixed and certain standard like his height and weight, and besides the objection with respect to the time which such examination will take, will not each examiner find it difficult to draw the line which is to separate sufficient from insufficient attainment, and is it not likely or indeed certain, that different examiners will apply different standards, and that thus inequalities will arise which will cause complaint.[12]

These arguments are pertinent to the present time, where a similar system of virtual payment by results for teachers is about to be introduced and where league tables of attainment and examination performance exist.

NATIONALISM

We have seen the effects of industrialisation on educational thought and practice. An equally potent source for change was the rise of nationalism in the later part of the eighteenth century and the early part of the nineteenth. The starting point was the French revolutionary and the Napoleonic wars which were closely allied to liberal conceptions of political rights. Other countries, inspired by the spirit of French nationalism, followed suit. Nationalism also brought with it calls for democracy in growing industrial societies. Universal education was a necessity for individuals if the full military and economic strength of a nation was to be realised. Prussia was an example of the extreme development of nationalism in education with its heavily centralised system. France displayed a type of accommodation between the demands of nationalism and those of democracy, whilst in Britain there was a more conservative response.[13] The existence of the British Empire up to the middle of the nineteenth century was not unduly emphasised in schools. When entry to the Indian Civil Service was by public examination after the Northcote–Trevelyan Report of 1853, public schools changed their curriculum to accommodate subjects which would prepare their students for such professions. The French invasion scares in 1859 and 1860 led to the establishment of the Volunteer Movement to repel any possible attacks on this country. Among the Volunteers were such figures as W.E. Forster and A.J. Mundella, both future vice-presidents of the Committee of Council on Education in the 1870s and 1880s. The latter, in advocating more technical education in England, compared the working men of England to 'badly drilled soldiers fighting with antiquated weapons'.[14]

The link between nationalism, imperialism and education became clearer after 1870 when the great European powers, England, Germany, France and Italy, indulged in large-scale imperial expansion. The creation of Queen Victoria as Empress of India and the purchase of the Suez Canal were manifestations of this new situation. The historian J.A. Froude, writing in 1871, sought to justify the need for an Empire:

> When we consider the increasing populousness of other nations, their imperial energy, and their vast political development, when we contrast the enormous area of territory which belongs to Russia, to the United States, or to Germany, with the puny dimensions of our own island home, prejudice itself cannot hide from us that our place as a nation is gone among such rivals unless we can identify the Colonies with ourselves, and multiply the English soil by spreading the English race over them.

Disraeli, in his speeches from 1872 onwards, stressed the need to develop a strong link between Britain and her colonies. Schools were encouraged to promote a knowledge of and pride in the Empire. An important example of this attitude can be seen in the Education Code of 1878 issued to Her Majesty's Inspectors of Schools by Viscount Sandon, Disraeli's vice-president of the Committee of Council on Education. Called by the inspectors 'Sandon's Sermon', it stated:

> As regards history and geography, you will encourage, as far as you can, such teaching as is likely to awaken the sympathies of the children, to the lives of noble characters and to incidents which tend to create a patriotic feeling of regard for their country and its position in the world; and while they should be acquainted with the leading historical incidents that have taken place in their own neighbourhood, and with its special geographical features, an interest should be excited in the colonial and foreign possessions of the British Crown.[15]

A typical school text book of the time, *The British Possessions* (1882), translated these sentiments into words. One chapter begins:

> We have said that our possessions in the Mediterranean are chiefly important as holding the keys to India ... One of the most remarkable facts in English history is the conquest and possession by the little island of Britain of all the great countries that make up India.

To reinforce the links between Britain and the Empire, emigration societies such as the British Women's Emigration Association were established. Working-class girls, particularly unmarried women, were encouraged to settle in the colonies and provide partners for men already working there. The Girls' Friendly Society, an association of Christian women concerned with the moral and religious welfare of the young, was involved at home and overseas in preparing members of the Society for their future role. As late as 1913, the Society's president, the Honourable Mrs Ellen Joyce, speaking at the Society's Imperial Conference, declared:

> The two points that I want to press today are, first, that the true aspect of GFS makes for Patriotism – and its larger interpretation, Imperialism. Secondly, that those who care most for purity, for country, for King, for God, have an enormous organisation in their

123

hands for developing, deepening, expanding, these influences, and that it is of vital importance they should use it in the right direction. The genius which the world admits to belong to the English, is the genius of Colonisation; this genius carries with it the privilege, the intention, the responsibility of evangelisation.[16]

Another initiative which reflected the growing campaign for the inculcation of patriotism in the young was the Empire Day Movement. At the beginning of the twentieth century, Reginald Brabazon, Earl of Meath, a former diplomat, put forward the idea of celebrating Empire Day on St George's Day, 23 April, each year, by holding ceremonies in Britain and in self-governing and Crown colonies around the world. Meath described its aim as 'the subordination of selfish or class interests to those of the State and the community, and the inculcation in the minds of all British subjects of the honourable obligation which rests upon them of preparing themselves, each in his or her sphere, for the due fulfilment of the duties and responsibilities attached to the high privilege of being subjects of the mightiest Empire the world has ever known'. Meath argued that as the Empire constituted one-fifth of the world's population, it should make its influence felt throughout the other four-fifths of the earth's inhabitants. There was another country whose education system provided an appropriate model to follow – Japan:

> The virtues of loyalty, of patriotism, of obedience to authority, and of self-sacrifice in the public interest since 1867 have, by order of the State, been daily taught in the schools of Japan under the name of 'Bushido'. Some credit for the extraordinary united, lofty, patriotic, and self-sacrificing spirit of the people must therefore be given to the schoolmasters of Japan, who for years have been at work systematically and daily teaching their school-children to reverence their Emperor, to love their country , and to remember that the greater the sacrifice made by the State of the individual, the greater the honour. The Empire Day movement proposes to breathe into the soul of the subjects of the King-Emperor a spirit conceived on lines we hope shall be of equal and even of greater power to inspire to noble deeds – both in peace as well as war – than that of 'Bushido'.[17]

The movement was widely adopted. Union flags were hoisted on public buildings but schools became the main focus for the activities connected with the Day. A school manager of a rural school at Badby,

Northamptonshire, Lady Knightley, described one such ceremony in 1907:

> Went down to Badby and had a little ceremonial to celebrate the day. The movement, inaugurated by Lord Meath, has spread wonderfully. The children marched in, saluted the flag, and sang Rudyard Kipling's *Song of the Children*:
>
> Land of our birth, we pledge to thee
> Our love and toil in the years to be,
> When we are grown and take our place
> As men and women with our race
>
> Mrs Scratton (the vicar's wife) and I made little speeches. We sang God Save the King and I distributed buns. The children have been learning the Empire Catechism all the winter and took up my points in several places.[18]

In addition to Empire Day and school lessons, there was a growing volume of literature, novels and poems for children with Imperialist themes, such as the books of G.H. Henty and the works of Sir Henry Newbolt and Kipling.

The nationalist philosophy which prevailed from the last quarter of the nineteenth century made an impact on educational thought and practice through official pronouncements, administrative memoranda, textbooks and popular literature aimed at the young, and pageants and displays on appropriate national occasions, such as Empire Day, which promoted imperialism.

MILITARISM

Closely bound with the spread of Imperialism was militarism. The nineteenth century was a period of expansion of the British Empire through the use of force, for example the Maori Wars, the conquest of the Sind, the two Sikh Wars, the intervention following the Indian Mutiny, the Ashanti War and the Zulu War. In addition, the Crimean War had demonstrated the need for an efficient fighting army. Although the public schools had set up their own rifle corps in the 1860s, the impetus for introducing drill into the elementary schools came after the Education Act of 1870 and the founding of school boards.

The notion of Christian manliness which underlay this aspect of the curriculum served two purposes. One was that drill provide a suitable physical exercise which would improve the boys' (and to a lesser extent, girls') physique. The second was to instil compliance and obedience and co-operation as preparation for soldiering, to maintain a military force for the Empire. However, it is significant that from 1872, schools offering girls drill did not receive grants for this activity.

A matter for much debate was the form which such drill should take, that is, whether ordinary or military drill. The latter became popular with teachers in elementary schools. The War Office approved Militia and Volunteer sergeants drilling boys in nearby schools and publications such as *The Schoolmaster's Drill Assistant. A Manual for Elementary Schools* (1874), were popular. The drillmaster of the Home and Colonial Society, W.S. Glover, produced a widely used manual, *School Drill*, which had gone through three editions by 1877; this included a chapter on military drill for boys, and sections on marching, the formation of squads, wheeling and company and battalion drill.[19]

There was opposition to military drill from a number of quarters. The Trades Union Congress in 1885 expressed its concern that military drill was a 'cunningly devised scheme by which military authorities and a number of Board schools have been, step by step, preparing the way for the pernicious Continental system of conscription'. It urged working-class ratepayers to frustrate the design of the promoters and leave school boards to their proper task, 'to develop the intellectual and moral faculties of children committed to their care'.[20]

Whilst most schools offered physical exercises rather than military drill, by the late 1890s, the Boer War brought the issue once more to the fore. Organisations based on semi-military lines, such as the Boys' Brigade, the Church Lads' Brigade and the Lads' Drill Association had been formed to develop conservative, conformist attitudes and attracted many recruits.[21] After the War had ended, the Interdepartmental Committee on Physical Deterioration (1904), a body set up to examine the causes of physical deficiencies in the male population, encouraged the military training of the young. Pressure came for universal military training for youths, and senior military figures encouraged rifle practice in the elementary school curriculum. The newly formed Board of Education took a stand against this activity and political opposition from the Labour Party prevented legislation on the matter. The only success of the campaign was a scheme, in 1910, for a national cadet force, to be called the Officer Training Corps, with military and financial support from the War Office. This vestige of militarism survived until well after the Second

World War in secondary grammar and public schools; gradually, alternatives, such as social service work, were introduced as the ethos of militarism in schools diminished.

EFFICIENCY

The expansion of industrialism and nationalism in Britain during the nineteenth century gave rise to a third element which had an impact on educational thought, namely, the quest for efficiency.

By mid-Victorian times in the 1850s and 1860s, it became clear to reformers and politicians that there were many areas of public life which needed investigating. Parliamentary reform in 1832, the Municipal Corporation Act of 1835, the Poor Law Amendment Act of 1836 and the creation of County Courts in 1846 had been early indications of this desire for change. The professions also came under scrutiny; for example, the Medical Act of 1858 which laid down strict rules for qualification to practice. Social issues, such as prostitution and workplace conditions were also subjected to close examination. Centralisation, with the creation of new bodies or departments, was a major feature. The change from patronage to merit in public life was seen in the reorganisation of the Civil Service, which opened the way to promotion through competitive examinations. Such change had many critics. One, Sir James Stephen, a high-ranking, retired official, told the Northcote–Trevelyan Commission that he opposed the new system as 'In every age, and land, and calling, a large share of success has hitherto been awarded to the possession of interest, of connexion, of favour, and of what we call good luck.' Regulation was not the only path pursued. Samuel Smiles' *Self Help*, which was published in 1859 and became an immediate success, summed up the spirit of the time: that it was not beyond the bounds of possibility for individuals to succeed by their own efforts. In the same year, Darwin's *On the Origin of Species* appeared. Its message, summed up in Herbert Spencer's phrase, the survival of the fittest, neatly complemented those of Smiles. The mid-Victorian era, therefore, was characterised by a collectivist tendency alongside a regard for *laissez-faire* principles, a balance which the historian W.L. Burn has called 'The Age of Equipoise'.[22]

These elements are well-illustrated in attitudes towards education. We have already seen that the Newcastle Commission on Popular Education, reporting in 1861, had recommended the provision of 'sound and cheap elementary education' by the State. Herbert Spencer, in his *Social*

Statistics (1851), had earlier condemned such provision by the State as a totalitarian attempt to mould children into a moral and intellectual pattern:

> Legislators exhibit to us the design and specification of a state-machine, made up of masters, ushers, inspectors and councils, to be worked by a due proportion of taxes, and to be plentifully supplied with raw material in the shape of little boys and girls, out of which it is to grind a population of well-trained men and women who shall be 'useful members of society'.[23]

On the other hand, Matthew Arnold, in his survey *Popular Education of France, with notice of that of Holland and Switzerland* (1861), believed that the State's greatest service was ensuring that schools were respected as well as inspected. This, he said, was particularly necessary at a time when there was a massive explosion in the population rate and a diminution in the use of child labour in factories.

Efficiency in education was by no means confined to the elementary sector. There was a Royal Commission on the Universities (1850–52) which brought about reforms at Oxford and Cambridge. From 1861 to 1864, the Clarendon Commission investigated the nine leading public schools; it favoured a more liberal approach to the education of the élite, denouncing the exclusiveness of classics in the curriculum and recommended that more time should be devoted to modern languages, mathematics and natural science. Although the Public Schools Act of 1868 encouraged modern studies and recast governing bodies and the antiquated statutes of these institutions, change was slow in coming.

An even more root-and-branch reforming body followed with the Taunton Commission (1864–68), which investigated over 800 endowed grammar schools. Unlike the elementary schools, there was no central authority responsible for the oversight of secondary education, and the commissioners, appointed by a Liberal government, revealed the corruption of masters and the misappropriation of endowments. New schemes were drawn up, often in the face of fierce local opposition, and the schools were placed on a new footing, both financially and academically. The effect was undermined by the subsequent failure to introduce legislation, because of the lobbying of a group of public school headmasters, which would have set up a Central Board to supervise and inspect endowed schools. The Taunton Report was also weakened by the educational philosophy of the Commission itself, which declared:

> The education of the gentry has gradually separated itself from that of the class below them, and it is but natural that this class in their

turn should be unwilling to be confounded with the labourers they employ.

These class differences were reflected in the system of efficient schools which were created by the Endowed Schools Act of 1868; the first grade, the classical schools, would prepare boys for an élite education; the second grade schools were for boys leaving at the age of 16 with more general curriculum, and the third grade was for future artisans leaving school at the age of 14.

The educational thinking underlying the work of the Education Commissions arose from a combination of factors, particularly the need for a more bureaucratic approach if efficiency were to be obtained for a population who needed to be educated, and given the skills required in an industrialised nation. From the last quarter of the nineteenth century, there emerged an 'efficiency' group, consisting of academics, politicians, administrators and writers who set out, in the their own words on 'the quest for National Efficiency'.

There were a number of reasons for this renewed interest in efficiency. Until the 1860s, Britain's natural leadership in Europe was unquestioned. The rise of Bismarck, the Dual Alliance between France and Russia and the re-armament race which followed, raised questions of national security and the need to provide an efficient fighting force. Naval construction, the basis of sea power, was dramatically increased in the 1880s. Observers noted the technological superiority of German shipyards and an acceleration in their naval output. The birth rate in England suffered a comparatively greater decline than in other European countries in the last quarter of the nineteenth century and the Great Depression in agriculture and industry raised public alarm. Britain's industrial supremacy was now in doubt, being overtaken by America and Germany in particular, especially in the science-based industries.

At the same time, in politics there was a growing disillusionment with Liberalism. There was a reaction away from a neutral Civil Service, the prevailing belief in a liberal education and a higher education system which did not prepare undergraduates for the world. The ideology of efficiency brought together three separate strands of thought. Imperialism, especially the example of India, had demonstrated the necessity of central autocratic administration in order to carry on successful government – no such opportunity existed in Britain. The second strand lay in the Broad Church tradition of social philosophy which was antagonistic to atomistic and mechanisitic modes of thought; a more acceptable mode would be for a National Church, which would make known its views on issues with authority. The third strand was the firm belief in science which was so crucial in a modern nation and which would be disseminated through a well-planned, centralised education system.[24]

If education was to be the cornerstone of a policy to halt England's economic decline, there was much work to be done. A Royal Commission on Scientific Instruction and the Advancement of Science, chaired by the Duke of Devonshire, had reported in 1875. It recommended more science teaching in elementary schools, and suggested the training of more teachers to carry out the work. It also highlighted the need for the Education Department and the Science and Art Department, both of whom provided for the subject, to co-ordinate their activities. The scientist Thomas Huxley, giving evidence before the Commission, stated, 'I must confess that I think the present state of affairs is an anomaly which could only exist in our country. Separating the teaching of science from education is like cutting education in half'.[25]

Similarly, a Royal Commission on Technical Instruction (Samuelson), set up seven years later as a result of worries about foreign competition, drew attention to the variety of bodies offering this subject and the lack of co-ordination between them. More science and art teaching was recommended and it was suggested that local authorities should be given powers to establish technical and secondary schools for the study of natural science, drawing, mathematics and modern languages. It was left to the Royal Commission on Secondary Education, chaired by James Bryce in 1895, to recommend a central authority for secondary education under a Minister of Education and with responsibility for elementary education. This led to the Act of 1899 which established a Board of Education, with is own president, to co-ordinate the education system.

The setbacks suffered by the British forces during the Boer War and the subsequent national inquest as to its causes have already been mentioned. The War confirmed the worst fears of the national efficiency group. The word 'group' is perhaps misleading as indicating a number of people sharing a homogeneous political ideology. In fact at the turn of the twentieth century there were various groupings, such as the Liberal Imperialists and the Liberal League, both consisting largely of politicians. There was also an informal group, the Co-Efficient Club, begun by the Webbs in 1902 to work out a programme for a 'Party of Efficiency', which brought together 12 distinguished individuals, all men, from different fields, politicians, academics, administrators and social theorists; these included Sydney Webb, L.S. Amery, R.B. Haldane, Edward Grey, Halford Mackinder, Bertrand Russell and H.G. Wells.[26]

The Education Bill of 1902 was seen by these different groups as an attempt to educate the Liberal Party in using the criterion of efficiency in its judgement of policy. They argued that educational reform would transform the economy and the same time help to produce a new class structure, based on achievement in education:

> The elementary school raises our people to the level at which they may become skilled workers. The secondary school assists to develop a much smaller but still large class of well-educated citizens. But for the production of that limited body of men and women whose calling requires high talent, the University or its equivalent alone suffices.[27]

The subsequent Education Act of 1902 sorted out the administrative muddle of the education system, sweeping away the School Boards and replacing them with county and county borough councils which were responsible for both elementary and secondary education, working through the newly formed Local Education Authorities. Each LEA was required to 'consider the educational needs of their area and to take such steps as seem to them desirable, and after consultation with the Board of Education to supply or aid the supply of education other than elementary, and to promote the general co-ordination of all forms of education'. They were also 'to have regard to any existing supply of efficient schools and colleges and to any steps already taken for the purposes of higher education'. The Act was an impressive triumph for the efficiency group; a national system could now be formed which would, it was hoped, help to re-establish Britain's economic and technological superiority once more. Furthermore, a ladder of opportunity was made available with links between the elementary and the grammar schools for talented youths which was the beginnings of a meritocracy in education.

The belief, during the century considered in this chapter, that the failure in British industrial efficiency and performance could be directly attributed to an inadequate educational system is now seen as too simplistic. There are complicated cultural, political and economic factors which are of considerable importance and it cannot be assumed that education and training are the main influences. Nor is it clear that earlier educational ideas of schools as providers of vocational preparation are valid – the question 'Preparation for what?' requires an answer. To many, a liberal/humane education is perhaps equally valid as a preparation for good citizenship.

131

REFERENCES

1. W.H.G. Armytage, *Four Hundred Years of English Education* (Cambridge University Press, Cambridge, 1964), p. 76.
2. G.H. Bantock, *Culture, Industrialisation and Education* (Routledge & Kegan Paul, 1968), pp. 11–12.
3. R. Williams, *The Long Revolution* (Penguin Books, 1961), p. 162.
4. A. Smith, *An Inquiry into the Nature and Causes of the Wealth of Nations* (London, 1875 edn), p. 621.
5. P.H.J.H. Gosden, *How They Were Taught* (Blackwell, Oxford, 1969), pp. 6–7.
6. J.M. Goldstrom, 'The Content of Education and the Socialization of the Working-Class Child, 1830–1860', in P. McCann (ed.), *Popular Education and Socialization in the Nineteenth Century* (Methuen, 1977), p. 97.
7. Minutes of the Committee of Council on Education, PP 1844, xxxviii, vol. 2, p. 511.
8. Viscount Esher (ed.), *The Girlhood of Queen Victoria* (Murray, 1912), vol. 1, p. 148.
9. Newcastle Commission on the State of Popular Education in England, PP 1861, xxi, Report, p. 127.
10. Hansard, 3, 182, 13 March 1866, cols. 147-8.
11. R. Lowe, *Primary and Classical Education* (Edmonston and Douglas, Edinburgh, 1867), p. 32.
12. D.W. Sylvester, *Robert Lowe and Education* (Cambridge University Press, Cambridge, 1974), p. 48.
13. E.H. Reisner, *Nationalism and Education since 1870* (Macmillan, 1922), p. 37.
14. W.H.G. Armytage, 'Battles for the Best: Some Educational Aspects of The Welfare-Warfare State in England', in P. Nash (ed.), *History and Education. The Educational Uses of the Past* (Random House, New York, 1970), p. 296.
15. Education Code, 1878, Viscount Sandon's Instructions to Her Majesty's Inspectorate, 16 January 1879, reprinted in PP 1881, lxxii, p. 217.
16. E. Joyce, 'The Imperial Aspect of Girls' Friendly Society Emigration', *Imperial Colonist*, August 1913, pp. 123–4.
17. Earl of Meath, 'The Empire Day Movement, *Imperial Colonist*, May 1906, pp. 63–4.
18. P. Gordon (ed.), *Politics and Society: The Journals of Lady Knightley of Fawsley, 1885 to 1913* (Northamptonshire Record Society, Northampton, 1999), p. 429.
19. A. Penn, *Targeting Schools. Drill, Militarism and Imperialism* (Woburn Press, 1999), p. 23.
20. Ibid., p. 34.
21. J. Springhall, *Youth, Empire and Society. British Youth Movements, 1883–1940* (Croom Helm, 1977), p. 18.
22. W.L. Burn, *The Age of Equipoise* (Unwin, 1964, 1968 edn), p. 17.
23. D. Wiltshire, *The Social and Political Thought of Herbert Spencer* (Oxford University Press, Oxford, 1978), p. 143.
24. G.R. Searle, *The Quest for National Efficiency. A Study in British Political Thought, 1899–1914* (Blackwell, Oxford, 1971), pp. 30–2.
25. Devonshire Commission on the Scientific Instruction and the Advancement of Science. Minutes of Evidence, PP 1872, xxv, p. 26.
26. W.A.S. Hewins, *The Apologia of an Imperialist* (Constable, 1929), vol. 2, p. 65.
27. H.C.G. Matthew, *The Liberal Imperialists. The Ideas and Politics of a Post-Gladstonian Elite* (Oxford University Press, Oxford, 1973), p. 230.

Further Reading

Mangan, J.A., *The Games Ethic and Imperialism* (Frank Cass, 1998).
Morris, P., *Industrialisation and Education* (Industrial Welfare Society, 1954).
Open University, *Education and Production* E353, Block 3 (Open University Press, 1972).
Ploscataska, L.M., 'Geographical Education, Empire and Citizenship' (PhD thesis, University of London, 1996).
Simpson, L.M., 'Education, Imperialism and National Efficiency in England 1895–1905' (PhD thesis, Glasgow University, 1979).

11
The Idealist Tradition

THE NINETEENTH-CENTURY PRUSSIAN SCHOOL OF IDEALISTS

Although philosophical idealism can be traced back to Plato, its main proponents, Kant, Fichte and Hegel, all lived in late eighteenth- and early nineteenth-century Prussia. The idealists wished to combine the lessons learned from this period (see Chapter 8) with the Greek concept of reality as an organic whole. A distinguished predecessor, Gottfried Wilhelm von Leibnitz (1646–1716), drawing on the writers of the British and French Enlightenment, set out the principles of importance in determining human knowledge and proposed a plan of universal harmony.

Immanuel Kant (1724–1804) was professor of Logic and Metaphysics at the University of Königsberg and is best known for his *Kritik der reinen Vernunft* (Critique of Pure Reason) (1781) which subsequently permeated much of the philosophy of the British Idealists. Kant was greatly influenced by the writings of Locke, Hume and Rousseau in his search for a secular morality. All perception, he believed, was interpreted in terms of mental concepts, though without being applied to experience they would be useless. On the one hand was the natural world of phenomena perceived by man's senses and on the other, a transcendental reality that is the basis of this reality but which is not accessible to the senses. Knowledge of ideas, therefore, can be achieved by pure reason independent of sense experience.

Kant's theory of education drew heavily on those of Rousseau though he did not share the latter's belief in the 'noble savage'. In a collection of lectures entitled *Pädagogik* (On Education) published in 1803, a year before his death, Kant set out his beliefs. The rational nature of man was important in bringing up the child. Moral and cognitive aspects of education and discipline were the two important features. A child's experiences should be controlled in order to shape his or her organic growth. Discipline would restrain the animal nature and by giving appropriate knowledge, lead to good social conduct. Moral education was essential as part of the educational process, as the child is born morally neutral and it was only through education that the child would develop his or her humanity. 'Is man by nature morally good or bad?' asked Kant. 'He is neither, for he is not by nature a moral being. He only becomes a moral being when his reason has developed ideas of duty and law.'

The mental faculties were to be developed by *intellectual learning*; at the same time Kant believed that this should be balanced by *physical education*, which would help the mental faculties by developing quickness and self-confidence as well as presenting opportunities to learn co-operation. A third element was *practical education* which should follow formal education and which would fit the person for a vocation in life, training in the arts and citizenship and character training. The end product would be a person of temperance, cleanliness and truthfulness; reverence and respect for fellow citizens would be the main duties. Kant wrote:

> Children will understand – without abstract ideas of duty, of obligation of good and bad conduct – that there is a law of duty which is not the same as ease, utility or other considerations of the kind, but something universal, which is not governed by the caprice of man.

The ultimate aim of education, according to Kant, is a moral and socially better world which leads to the perfectibility of man.

Johann Gottlieb Fichte (1762–1814) had been dismissed from his post as professor of Philosophy at Jena University in 1799 because of his alleged sympathy with atheism. Like his contemporaries, he had been deeply influenced by the humiliation which Prussia had experienced after the Battle of Jena (1806) during the Napoleonic Wars. In his *Reden an die deutsche Nation* (Addresses to the German Nation), delivered in Berlin in 1807 and 1808, he envisaged a corporate state based on a new moral order with individuals acting as agencies for the 'sublime Will' to achieve its purpose. Education was seen as the main vehicle for achieving this end. It was to be made available to the whole of society and taught to a high standard. As Fichte wrote, 'By means of the new education, we want to mould the Germans into a corporate body which shall be stimulated and animated in all its individuals and members by the same interests.' His aim was to develop a moral order and produce citizens who would promote the good of the whole community. Teachers were to be an important element in the system and were seen by Fichte as advisers of individuals on moral and ethical problems.

Fichte was influenced by the ideas of Rousseau, particularly the view that society is corrupt whilst man is innately good. Following Plato, he advocated that as well as promoting universal education, the State should select from the system those of high intellectual ability for more scholarly study; they would, in due course, become the leaders of the new State though still subordinate to the central moral purpose. Fichte's idealist philosophy sprang from the need for a stronger Germany in which the citizen would bend his or her free will to the greater good of the State. Fichte, unlike Hegel and Kant, propounded a fully worked out theory of education which profoundly influenced his famous pupil, Johann Friedrich Herbart. However, the latter went further than Fichte in addressing the pedagogical and psychological aspects of how students learn.

Perhaps the most influential of the three idealist philosophers discussed here was Georg Wilhelm Friedrich Hegel (1770–1831) who at one time was professor of Philosophy at Heidelberg University. Hegel wished to combine the Greek concept of an organic whole with the idea of individual autonomy as expressed in Kant's ethics. If the Enlightenment programme of freeing the individual was taken to it ultimate point, Hegel stated, society would dissolve into a series of atoms with the destruction of institutions and customs – the French Revolution provided an excellent and recent example. In his posthumously published Lectures *Philosophie der Geschichte* (Philosophy of History (1837)), Hegel posed the question of the ultimate purpose of the world. He concluded that it was necessary, in order to obviate injustice and violence, to impose a corporate state as the best expression of a moral whole. The study of history showed that it was a cumulative record of the spiritual development of mankind ; the freedom of the spirit can only be assured when the State has reached its highest point, that is, when political and social conflict is eliminated and harmony exists.[1]

Hegel developed Plato's concept of dialectic. The study of the history of different civilisations showed that there were high and low points in their development which led to success or at their worst, disappearance. In every situation (thesis) there is conflict (antithesis), and progress is only ultimately achieved in synthesis. Hegel's view was that the State should, as an instrument of divine will, be the driving force towards dialectical progress. The individual's task was to assist in that development of the *Geist* (spirit) by understanding the metaphysical view of history and as a result becoming free. Education should be directed to this end by studies which included the scriptures, classics and literature and philosophy.

Although Hegel's writings are dense and difficult to understand, some interesting points for educational theory emerge. Hegel postulated the notion of education as the science of the ideal development of the spirit. By showing that the individual is part of a larger social whole which is in itself part of a wider metaphysical reality, the spirit can make mankind realise its power of creative thought in art, religion and in particular philosophy. His philosophy, in which the rational whole had greater claim to reality than its separate parts and the group was more important than the individual, was subsequently used to justify totalitarian regimes of both right and left. Karl

Marx, for example, using a dialectical approach, stood Hegelianism on its head by making matter, rather than reason or spirit, the ultimate reality. Ironically, Marx's version was directly evolved from idealism.

T.H. GREEN AND THE ENGLISH IDEALISTS

An attempt to translate into action some of these principles can be found in England from about 1870 onwards. The movement can be said to have centred round the philosopher T.H. Green and a group of men from Balliol College, Oxford, most of whom were teachers in the University of Oxford. It included individuals such as A.C. Bradley and his brother, F.H., Bernard Bosanquet, D.G. Ritchie, Arnold Toynbee, Edward Caird and William Wallace. Not all stayed within the confines of the university. Some entered politics, as Liberals, such as James Bryce, A.H.D. Acland, and R.B. Haldane, and others into the Church, such as William Temple, later Archbishop of Canterbury.

Thomas Hill Green's own short life – he died when he was only 46 – (1836–82) was spent at Oxford, the last five years of which he was professor of Moral Philosophy, the first recognised lecturer in this subject at the University. His own writings bore a strong Hegelian imprint, though it has been said of him, as the son of an evangelical clergyman, that he 'preached Hegel with the accent of a Puritan.' His main writings are contained in his two posthumous works, *Prolegomena to Ethics* (1883) and *Lectures on the Principles of Political Obligation* (1895).

Briefly, it can be said that this version of Idealism was a reaction to Utilitarianism. Green and his followers were convinced that Utilitarianism was barren as a political creed and that no further progress could be made in an understanding of politics until a new philosophic basis was found for Liberalism. If democracy was to grapple successfully with the many new problems which were rising, a way had to be found for reconciling a true individualism with the new functions which were being given to the State. But before an adequate political theory could be constructed, a proper conception of human nature and action was required In fact, politics were to be the outcome as a view of human nature and of the world.[2]

Two characteristics of Green's philosophy emerge from this. First, it is an amalgam of Hegel and Kant. From Hegel, he took the notion that individuals cannot be what they are, have their moral and spiritual qualities, independently of their existence as a nation. From Kant, Green incorporated the insistence on autonomy:

> The moral duty to obey a positive law, whether a law of the State or church, is imposed not by the author or enforcer of the positive law, but by that spirit of man which sets before him the ideal of a perfect life.

An individual's good cannot be treated as something apart from the good of others within his community. And the 'good' therefore cannot be identified with pleasure, as the Utilitarians believed: it is nothing less than the spiritual perfection of man.

Green argued that one index of the moral progress made by humanity is the gradual extension of the range of persons to whom the common good is conceived as 'common.' This was an important part of Green's philosophy, and stressed the need to mediate communities between the individual and the larger social wholes – in particular, the family, the town one lives in, and the nation-state. How should the spiritual capacities of all the members of one's community be best developed? The Church was not particularly favoured by Green. Social reform, working for the good of the community and extending the benefits of citizenship, was a noble pursuit.[3]

Here we come to the second characteristic of Green's philosophy, which differentiates him from other Idealists: his worked-out general philosophy included a philosophy of education, which, as we shall see, also had considerable influence on the development of educational practice. Green's concept of God, like others of his school, is equatable with Thought or Reason. The more an individual's consciousness is raised above the animal level, the more he becomes a vehicle of God. So as men become educated, as their minds expand and grow, reality is progressively infused with reason and the divine end becomes realised. Green believed that it is the individual's moral duty to raise human consciousness, not in isolation from one another but to promote consciousness-raising in general within his or her community. Education was an obvious vehicle for such a programme.

Green, like others of his followers, became involved in everyday matters which would promote the aims of Idealist philosophy. He became a member of the Oxford School Board, promoted secondary education in the town, started a coffee house and evening school in the poorer part of Oxford and successfully stood for election to the City Council in 1875. In his election address he proposed greater expenditure of rates on health and education and greater opportunities for poor boys to go to grammar schools. Green realised the awesome task he was setting himself and his followers. 'No one doubts,' he wrote, 'that a man who improves the current morality of his time must be something of an Idealist.' R.G.

Collingwood, a philosopher himself, stated that Green's former students, convinced of the philosophy, felt that it was their vocation to put it into practice, in brief, simple, religious citizenship.[4] Some aspects of this movement will now be considered.

Co-operation

Arnold Toynbee, the economic historian, who arrived at Oxford in 1873 and became a close friend of Green, argued that if true citizenship was to be achieved, a start could be made with existing voluntary associations. He saw in the co-operative movement of the time the spirit of the medieval guilds, which aimed at ending competition and possessing high ideals. To this movement should be given the task of the education of the citizen, which included knowledge of political, industrial and sanitary education, that is, the laws of health. Toynbee hoped that teachers could be recruited from the ranks of co-operators themselves, but he added that there were many from the universities who had studied political and social questions and had reached practical conclusions.[5] He looked to Oxford for assistance and drew together an informal society of young contemporaries, each of whom selected a special study. In January 1880, Toynbee delivered the first of a series of popular addresses in Yorkshire and during the following years, lectured on political economy to classes of working men in Oxford.

Toynbee's early death at the age of 30 in 1883 inspired others to respond to the call for continuing his work. Among the notable followers were Arthur Acland, later to become Gladstone's education minister. He in turn formed a small club called the Inner Ring where discussions of important issues of the day took place. Members included Cosmo Lang, later Archbishop of Canterbury, J.A. Spender, Michael Sadler and Anthony Hope Hawkins, better known as Anthony Hope, the novelist.

From his own experience of teaching co-operative classes, Acland advocated life-long education. In addressing a conference of working men he said:

> I speak to those who feel more and more assured every day they live, that while the period of *instruction* may cease before we are 20 years of age, the work of *education* is the work of our lives, and that education in the true sense ends when our lives end. All I can say is that if young men come to us and go back in any sense ashamed of that from which they came, we in the universities ought to be ashamed of ourselves.[6]

138

Acland, like Toynbee, believed that the practical and systematic education of co-operators as English citizens should be open equally to men and women if future generations were to become reasonably and rationally educated.

University extension

The co-operative movement with its aim of adult education was only one channel into which some of the followers of Green and Toynbee expended their energies. Another, which had wider implications, was the field of university extension. It was envisaged that as it was impossible in the mid-nineteenth century to bring the masses requiring education to the university it was therefore a good plan to try to carry the university to the people. A 'peripatetic university' for the working classes in large towns was conceived. Both Green and Acland were concerned with such a scheme at Oxford, the former saw that the dissemination of knowledge would act both as a unifying force for all grades of society and as a means to the moralisation of the people. Michael Sadler became secretary in place of Acland in 1885 and led a distinguished team of tutors including W.A.S. Hewins, who became the first director of the London School of Economics, William Ashley, the economic historian, H.J. Mackinder, the geographer, R.G. Collingwood, the philosopher and Cosmo Lang, the theologian. John Marriott, a politics tutor at Oxford, calculated that he had delivered over 10,000 lectures for the movement over a career spanning 53 years.

Another related scheme was suggested by another of Green's followers, Samuel Barnett, an East End vicar, with whom Toynbee often stayed. Barnett suggested a settlement of university men in the midst of a great industrial centre, with the director being a teacher who would supervise the work of the settlement. It excited the attention of many young men, leading in 1885 to the establishment of Toynbee Hall in Whitechapel. Generations of educationists were among those who participated in the work of the settlement, including Cyril Jackson, Robert Morant, Acland, Sadler, Sir John Gorst, J.A. Spender and later, Clement Attlee, R.H, Tawney and his brother-in-law, William Beveridge.

Though the movement rapidly spread and was a success not all academics were satisfied with what had been achieved. A.E. Zimmern, an early New College, Oxford, recruit, writing at the end of the First World War on 'The Evolution of the Citizen', considered that more adult education of itself was not a sufficient answer:

> The two spheres, that of education and that of religion, not only

overlap but interpenetrate one another. The tendency to divide them, to classify our moral and intellectual life into separate and watertight compartments, is precisely one of the curses of our present dissatisfaction and *malaise*. The life of the spirit is a seamless garment, not a miscellaneous patchwork composed of Sunday services and week-night committees, of sermons and lectures and evening classes, spiced with a dash of 'advanced' sociology and fiction. This incoherence, this undiscriminating and irregular appetite, this insensitiveness of the intellectual palate, constitutes a substantial aggravation of our condition.[7]

However, Zimmern's pessimism was unfounded at the time, though not in the long run. These organisations fitted well into the framework of Idealist thought. They provided exceptional opportunities for breaking down barriers between universities and the cities in which they were located. They also enabled many young men in the Balliol–Toynbee Hall tradition to combine effectively the political and scholarly aspects of their moral commitments.

University Reform

We have already noted that Green and a number of his contemporaries stressed the importance of forging links between the university and the local community. The growing demand for higher education in the 1860s and 1870s provided an opportunity to re-examine this issue. Green told a Royal Commission on Oxford University in 1877 that there was a need to democratise the election of Fellows and to appoint more Readers to promote the attainment of a higher standard of learning; the study of new subjects would thus be facilitated.

The admission of women on an equal footing with men was another reform which was sought. James Bryce, then professor of Law at Oxford, had played an active part in the founding of Girton College, Cambridge in 1873 and John Percival, headmaster of Clifton, was one of the prime movers in the establishment of Somerville College, Oxford. The main campaign, however, was fought in Scotland by a group of Idealists at Glasgow University. Edward Caird, shortly after his appointment to the chair of Moral Philosophy, campaigned in 1868 for the full admission of women to degree courses. Nine years later, he presented the University Senate with a petition from the recently formed Association of the Higher Education of Women, asking for the institution of examinations. In 1892, a year before Caird left Glasgow for Oxford, women were for the first time admitted as matriculated students to the university.[8]

140

New colleges followed the spread of extension teaching, such as those at Exeter, Reading, Leicester and Southampton and more ambitiously, at Sheffield, Nottingham, Manchester and Liverpool. One of the more interesting ones was Reading, whose first Principal was Halford Mackinder. Mackinder, a close friend of Sadler, was a keen exponent of the 'new geography' and a former Oxford extension lecturer.[9] He condemned the teaching at the new university colleges, stating that it was based on that of the old universities, and was not directed towards the education of citizens. The success of Reading College was due largely to Mackinder's far-sightedness in providing an institution which was, in Mackinder's words, 'the focus of local patriotism'. It provided facilities for adults as well as for students fresh from secondary schools, and a training college was established for student-teachers. The university extension system which had flourished in the town for five years was combined with science and art classes. This co-ordination of educational agencies within a town was especially praised by the Bryce Commission on Secondary Education which reported in 1895.

A much more thorough and philosophical approach to the question of higher education was successfully implemented by Richard Burdon Haldane (1856–1928). Haldane studied at Göttingen University in Germany, completed his studies at Edinburgh University and came to know Hutchison Stirling, the author of the *Secret of Hegel*. Inspired by the writings of Green, he edited and contributed to *Essays in Philosophical Criticism* (1883), which he dedicated to Green's memory.[10] A second book, containing his lectures, *The Pathway to Reality* (1903), contains an exposition of Hegel's doctrine of God and man as well as his own philosophy.

Taking Germany as the model on which educational reform should be based, Haldane believed that State-controlled elementary, secondary and technical schools and universities, should be brought into close relationship to each other by the State. Universities, he believed, ought to be permeating our education system in *Geist*, 'I mean the larger intelligence and culture without which education not only can be interesting, but can be sufficiently comprehensive to take on practical business'.[11] Educational reform would break down class barriers and create a new class structure founded on achievement. Another way of influencing events was by entering politics. Later, Haldane did this to good effect, becoming secretary of state for war and eventually Lord Chancellor in Liberal and Labour ministries.

With the Webbs, he was responsible for setting up the London School of Economics in 1895 in order to advance the study of social sciences. He also cultivated Robert Morant, the influential permanent secretary of the Board of Education for his most ambitious scheme – to launch a higher technological institute in London, a 'British Charlottenberg'. This culminated in the establishment of the Imperial College of Science and Technology. Besides becoming chairman of two Royal Commissions on University Education in London (1909–13) and in Wales (1916–18), he headed a small group whose deliberations eventually led to the creation of the University Grants Committee, a national body which recommended the allocation of money to universities.

Haldane's achievements were impressive. He followed Green's precept of entering wholeheartedly in serving society in order to attain self-realisation. Perhaps his view of society and it educational needs was oversimplified; his vision of the world as objectified reason and of knowledge as the remedy of societal ills proved to be over optimistic. The Hegelian strain of Idealism is seen in Haldane in a purer form than in many of his English contemporaries.

THE DECLINE OF IDEALIST INFLUENCE

Between the two World Wars, the influence of Idealism on British educational thought and practice diminished. It is important to try and account for this decline.

The first main reason was Idealism's decline as an educational force following its removal from the dominant position it had earlier held in academic philosophy. In 1903 G.E. Moore wrote an influential article in the journal *Mind* entitled 'The Refutation of Idealism' and realists, such as his fellow Cambridge philosopher, Bertrand Russell, grew rapidly to philosophical prominence towards the end of the nineteenth century. Oxford Idealism had appealed to religious young men who were perplexed by the influence of science, especially Darwinism, on their beliefs. To an increasing number of philosophers, the metaphysical foundations of Idealism were now less than compelling. New philosophical systems more congenial to empirical science, such as pragmatism, logical positivism and linguistic philosophy, emerged in the first half of the twentieth century to challenge Idealist assumptions.

The second reason was that from the First World War onwards, Idealism was closely linked with Hegelian or post-Hegel philosophy. L.T. Hobhouse's book, published in 1918, *The Metaphysical Theory of the State*, was an attack on the view that individuals only realise themselves as members of a state, which itself is seen as a supra-personality.

Individuals, Hobhouse argues, would thus be powerless to attempt to remodel society under such a system. The philosophy was linked with hatred of all things German, and the rise of Hitler ensured that Hegelian influence remained an object of intellectual and moral contempt until long after the Second World War. This can be seen clearly in Karl Popper's *The Open Society and its Enemies* (1945) and other attacks on historicism.

A third reason for the decline was the reaction to the Idealist's call for a cohesive, organically related, national system of education. Attempts were made to demarcate more clearly different kinds of schools, their objectives, the ladders and paths connecting each to each. Green and his followers also envisaged a national network of universities and associated network of adult education institutions, both of which were to be interconnected with the schools below them, providing for wider needs of the communities and regions which they served. After the First World War, interest in systematisation waned with the move towards institutional autonomy. Universities began to insist on academic freedom, university extension classes gradually lost their function as an instrument of working-class education and became centres of culture in middle-class suburbs. Educational theory in schools, especially the primary sector, looked more towards child-centred approaches and methods. Educational theory and practice under the European totalitarian states spelt out a message which deterred others from following the same path.[12]

CONCLUSION

Given this reaction to Idealist philosophy, it might be asked what, if any, was its contribution to educational thought today. There are several interesting legacies of this tradition to be found. We are constantly reminded that the whole ethos of a society and its institutions is an educative force. Schools and universities have their own social ethos which could and can be harnessed to educational ends. The Idealists hoped to be as practical as possible, such as the commitment to change within universities through breaking down social exclusiveness by encouraging links with the working classes, and the campaign to break down sexual exclusiveness by campaigning for the better education of women.

It is taken for granted now that schools and colleges teach by institutional example as well as by direct instruction; concern for the ethos of an institution is now an important aspect of education. The ideology behind comprehensive education, for instance, is that by learning together, children from different social classes will see themselves as belonging to the same co-operative community, all very much in line with the thinking of the Idealist reformers. Another example is the post-war interest in strengthening the links between schools and the local community, not least by the introduction of community schools which serve and cater for the wider needs and interests of an area. There have also been new ways of extending adult learning opportunities, through institutions such as the Open University and the University of the Third Age as well as new methods of distance learning. Idealists such as Green would no doubt applaud such examples of communitarianism.

At a different level, the education system itself, once visualised by the idealists as a rationally interlocking whole, has in recent times, changed from a series of theoretically autonomous parts into a more organic whole. From the mid 1970s, when the so-called 'Great Debate' took place, questions about the schools' autonomy over aims and curricula were raised and the need for an integrated national system gradually took shape. The introduction of a national curriculum might be seen as a recognition of this change. Similarly, in higher education there has been a move away from autonomy of institutions to a much greater central control over, and interference in, many aspects of their day-to-day working on the grounds of national need.

As the pendulum swings back from autonomy to accountability, the work of the Idealist reformers, it could be claimed, acquires new relevance. It brings up in an acute form the question, given that we require a more cohesive educational system, what role should the State play in providing this cohesion? There is always the fear that State direction is a form of totalitarianism. So far as the Idealist philosophers were concerned, their interest in the State was the reverse of totalitarianism. The idea that all intiatives should come from the centre and that other institutions should simply carry out orders from above was anathema to them. They conceived of the State not as something imposed on and in conflict with, free institutions, but as developing and remaining in harmony with them. It was important that such institutions should work with each other but to ensure that this happens, the State, representing the desire to promote the good of the whole society, must necessarily be something standing above these separate institutions. Though this raises questions such as the need for having a political community activated by a common desire to promote the good of the whole society; to what extent the State represents the whole of the political community; and whether the 'State' itself is undeniably an ideal, it may be claimed that the Idealist legacy is an important element in modern educational thought.

REFERENCES

1. J. Bowen, *A History of Western Education. Vol. 3. The Modern West: Europe and the New World* (Methuen, 1981), p. 263.
2. A.D. 'Lindsay, T.H. Green and the Idealists', in F.J.C. Hearnshaw (ed.), *The Social and Political Ideas of some Representative Thinkers of the Victorian Age* (Harrap, 1933), pp. 155–6.
3. M. Richter, *The Politics of Conscience. T.H. Green and His Age* (Weidenfeld & Nicolson, 1964), p. 14.
4. R.G. Collingwood, *An Autobiography* (Oxford University Press, Oxford, 1944), p. 17.
5. A. Toynbee, *'Progress and Poverty.' A Criticism of Mr Henry George. Being two lectures delivered in St Andrew's Hall, Newman Street, London* (Kegan Paul, 1883), p. 53.
6. A.H.D. Acland, *The Education of Citizens* (Central Co-operative Board, Manchester, 1883), p. 8.
7. A.E. Zimmern, 'The Evolution of the Citizen,' in O. Stanley (ed.), *The Way Out: Essays on the Meaning and Purpose of Adult Education* (Oxford University Press, Oxford, 1923), pp.33–4.
8. B. Bosanquet, *'Edward Caird, 1835–1908'* (Proceedings of the British Academy, 1908), p. 8.
9. E.W. Gilbert, 'Sir John Halford Mackinder', *Dictionary of National Biography* (Oxford University Press, Oxford, 1959), p. 556.
10. R.B. Haldane, *An Autobiography* (Hodder & Stoughton, 1929), p. 7.
11. E. Ashby and M. Anderson, *Portrait of Haldane at Work on Education* (Macmillan, 1974), p. 163.
12. P. Gordon and J. White, *Philosophers as Educational Reformers. The Influence of Idealism on British Educational Thought and Practice* (Routledge & Kegan Paul, 1979), pp. 201–6.

Further Reading

Butler, J.D., *Idealism in Education* (Harper, New York, 1966).
Cacoullos, A.R., *Thomas Hill Green: Philosopher of Rights* (Twayne, New York, 1974).
Goldman, L., *Dons and Workers: Oxford and Adult Education since 1850* (Clarendon Press, Oxford, 1995).
Mackenzie, M., *Hegel's Educational Thought and Practice* (Swann Sonnenschein, 1909).
Turnbull, G. H., *The Educational Theory of J. G. Fichte: A Critical Account Together with Translations* (Liverpool University Press, Liverpool, 1926).

12

The Development of the Social Sciences in the Nineteenth Century and their Influence on Education

INTRODUCTION

As we have seen, nineteenth-century ideas were influenced by the two great 'revolutions' of the eighteenth century: the Industrial Revolution which spread outwards from England, and the French Revolution which changed the social, political and economic map of the West forever. In this chapter we will need to refer back to Chapter 8 which discussed eighteenth-century ideas which bear directly upon the development of social science. A third 'revolution' of ideas was Darwin's Theory of Evolution which was more important than any other until Freud's ideas on sexuality appeared to cast further doubt on the supremacy of human rationality. Both theories tended to focus on human beings as a unique kind of animal with powerful instincts as well as limited rationality.

The social sciences emerged out of the Enlightenment and from reactions to it. The so-called Enlightenment project of the eighteenth century was concerned to provide rational explanations not only for the physical universe but also for humanity itself. In Chapters 8 and 9 we summarised Enlightenment thinking as five propositions: a belief in the power of scientific reasoning; faith in progress; human rights; freedom of thought and enquiry; and finally, a desire to promote education as a means of furthering the Enlightenment project. Enlightenment thinkers such as the editors of the Encyclopaedia, Diderot and d'Alembert were, generally, optimistic. Some of them were also over-enthusiastic, even fanatical: critics of the Enlightenment sometimes blamed the excesses of the French Revolution on a mixture of exaggerated faith in human reason and too little respect for traditions which they saw as the inherited wisdom or culture of their society. Clearly, the physical sciences were more advanced in the eighteenth century than the social or human sciences. One of the ambitions of some Enlightenment thinkers was to apply the lessons of physics and chemistry to human society. However, after the French Revolution, or at least after the defeat of Napoleon, the European political scene was dominated by conservative or reactionary regimes, and, equally important from our point of view, by conservative writers, for example, Francois René, Vicomte de Chateaubriand (1760–1848) or Joseph Marie, Comte de Maistre (1753–1821). These writers looked back in horror not only at the Revolution but at the Enlightenment itself. Felicité Robert de Lamennais (1782–1854), a Catholic priest and philosopher who attempted to bridge the gap between religious and political thought, expressed the problem eloquently:

> From equality is born independence, and from independence isolation. As each man is circumscribed, so to speak, in his individual life, he no longer has more than his individual strength for defending himself…[1]

It was not until the 1830s that what we might now recognise as the beginnings of social science emerged, by which time the Industrial Revolution had spread from England to other parts of Europe and to America.

THE IDEAS OF SOCIAL SCIENCE

It is not easy to know where to begin the history of social science. There is a plausible case for beginning with Aristotle who attempted to deal philosophically with many of the questions now considered to be social science. Others have suggested that Francis Bacon was also dealing with social science issues in *Novum_Organum* (1620), but there is a qualitative difference between the brilliant speculations of Aristotle, Bacon, Montesquieu and others, and the beginnings of the systematic theories of society and empirical studies that characterised the work of such nineteenth-century writers as Auguste Comte, Ferdinand Tonnies and Emile Durkheim.

SOCIOLOGY AND ITS INFLUENCE ON EDUCATION

Auguste Comte (1798–1857) and Sociology

Comte not only invented the word 'sociologie' (in 1830), he also developed the tradition in social science known as positivism which became influential in Latin American educational ideas as well as European, providing a secular, 'scientific' alternative to Christian dogma as a value system. Comte stressed the scientific treatment of society in his *Cours de Philosophie Positive*,[2] a huge work about the science of man in which Comte wanted sociology to explain human social life in the same way that biology had accounted for humans as biological animals. We should also note a strong evolutionary strand in Comte's thinking. Darwin's *On the Origin of Species* was not published until 1859 but evolutionary ideas were current much earlier in the nineteenth century; Herbert Spencer (1820–1903) and Karl Marx (1818–83) were, for example, essentially evolutionary thinkers. One further point about Comte and sociology: what he had in mind for his 'science' was that sociology would not be just one of many social sciences, separating politics, anthropology, economics and psychology from each other, but he envisaged sociology as a unified approach to the science of human life.

His ambition was to provide a means of explaining the whole of human life, past, present and future. He divided his science into social statics (permanent features of social life) and social dynamics (close to what we would now call social change). He was a great innovator but, of course, underestimated the problem of applying the methods of natural science to human beings. Essentially, Comte and other early sociologists were concerned with understanding and explaining the conflicts between medieval (or traditional) ideas and those of 'modern' society. The emergence of the individual in the post-Reformation, Protestant world, had changed social thinking in a number of remarkable ways.

Nisbet, in one of his many books on the history of sociological ideas suggested that while all social sciences were concerned with the individual and society, the sociological approach, which developed from about 1830, should be seen in terms of five unit ideas, words which were either invented or significantly changed in meaning between 1830 and 1900: community; authority; status; the sacred; and alienation. Each one of these five unit ideas has clear implications for education. We will take each of Nisbet's five ideas and extend them into the domain of educational ideas.

Community: One of the major themes for sociologists and the conservative writers who preceded them was loss of community in the modern world. In some respects the apparently irrational forces of traditional community had been replaced by the rational contract. In other respects, face-to-face relations were being replaced by the more abstract 'society'. Such changes caused problems as well as opportunities. The modern individual was in danger of lacking both a sense of commitment and an unconscious feeling of belonging to a community through family, religion, work and other aspects of social life. Durkheim, Tonnies, Weber and Marx all wrote extensively about community. For example, Tonnies contrasted *Gemeinschaft* (or community) with *Gesellschaft* (translated as association or society). Tonnies asserted, with many illustrations, that the medieval world and contemporary traditional societies were characterised by strong feelings of identification with their 'community' in which individualism was insignificant or even regarded as deviant.

It is worth noting as was mentioned in Chapter 11, that in education in recent years there has been renewed interest in community. 'The school in the community' and 'the school as a community' are frequent topics for discussion. In addition, the importance of the ethos of the school and analyses of school culture has been reasserted in the search for more efficient and more humane learning institutions.

Authority: The collapse of the order of the *ancien régime* caused much discussion about the loss of traditional authority, and again, there were advantages as well as disadvantages. Whereas in traditional society authority was taken for granted, deeply embedded in the family, the community and traditional hierarchy, in modern society it was necessary to rationalise and explain authority in order to make it acceptable. We have already referred to Weber's work on authority. One of his interests was the nature of order in society, and why it broke down. Order is connected with power, the probability that an actor will be able to realise his own objectives (get his own way) even against the opposition of others. Military or physical force is one way but astute rulers learn to adopt more subtle methods – authority. Weber postulated three 'ideal types' of authority: traditional; legal-rational (bureaucratic organisations); and charismatic leadership (Jesus, Hitler, Ghandi, Mao). We return to the question of authority in education later in this chapter.

Status: Various ideas connected with status such as hierarchy, the great chain of being, rank and degree have a long history, but it was the Enlightenment that mounted a systematic critique of the prevailing social order in Europe, the *ancien régime* and the French Revolution resulted in a temporary abolition of the French aristocracy and monarchy. Meanwhile, the Industrial Revolution was challenging the feudal hierarchy by the rise in importance of the bourgeoisie: money was beginning to supersede rank so that eventually social class would become more important than the 'vestiges of feudalism', the hereditary status of the landed class.

It is now generally agreed by historians and sociologists that the concept of class was a product of the economic and social changes of the late eighteenth and early nineteenth centuries. For Marx, class and class conflict were dominant features of his theory of dialectical materialism and, he believed, would lead inevitably to revolution. His prediction was not to be fulfilled, although some like Wheen[3] have quoted the 1848 uprisings throughout Europe as evidence that Marx was not entirely wrong. Nevertheless, many of his ideas have become accepted as part of the methodology of both history and sociology. The history of educational ideas could not possibly ignore Marx although he had little to say directly on the subject of education.

Marx examined the problem of industrial society – capitalist society – and was so appalled by the poverty, exploitation and human misery that he was convinced that capitalism was too full of contradictions to survive; he predicted a post-capitalist society in which workers would not be oppressed. He was so 'evolutionary', however, that he was criticised for his economic determinism or historicism which was later condemned by Karl Popper[4] and others.

Our ideas of social class have, of course, changed greatly since Marx, and class conflict has not gone in the direction Marx predicted, but the power of 'class' remains a dominant concept in the sociology of modern society and especially in the sociology of education. One of the unsolved problems of twentieth-century democratic societies is inequality of educational opportunity. Attempts have been made to solve problems of inequality by invoking motivational differences and sub-cultural variations in attitude towards learning, as well as more subtle cultural differences such as Bourdieu's[5] 'cultural capital' and the linguistic differences which form part of Bernstein's[6] theories. However, no country has yet solved the problem of eliminating class differences in educational opportunity, and even less so in performance and achievement.

Marx summed up the position:

> The modern bourgeois society that has sprouted from the ruins of feudal society has not done away with class antagonisms. It has but established new classes, new conditions of oppression, new forms of struggle in place of the old ones.[7]

Education forms part of the struggle. According to Marx, the bourgeois view of knowledge had become the educational view. His colleague, Engels, once described teachers as 'the hired lackeys of the bourgeoisie'. They were employed to pass on the ideology of the ruling class as well as inculcating habits of industry such as obedience and punctuality. This pessimistic view of schooling was revived several times in the twentieth century and we shall return to it in later chapters.

The Sacred: Most sociologists agree that one of the most important features of modern society compared with the traditional world is a dramatic move away from 'the sacred' to the secular, the profane or the utilitarian. This shift in values has been of particular importance in education. We have seen in earlier chapters that up to the time of the Enlightenment a major purpose of schools and universities was religious. The rational, secular values of the nineteenth and twentieth centuries greatly influenced school curricula and related educational ideas, but the sociological concern was much more than that. Nisbet states:

> I use this word [sacred] to refer to the totality of myth, ritual, sacrament, dogma and the mores in human behaviour; to the whole area of individual motivation and social organisation that transcends the utilitarian or rational and draws its vitality from what Weber called charisma.[8]

Educationists have been slow to recognise the importance of ritual and custom in modern schools. Only towards the end of the twentieth century did sociologists focus their attention on such intangible aspects as school ethos or the culture of the school. Just as a community needs social solidarity, common beliefs and practices to hold it together, so does a school, which may be why it is easier for a school to work well if it has some system of values and beliefs beyond the school curriculum, for example, in some Roman Catholic and some independent schools.

Weber's enormous contribution to this topic includes his development of the concept 'charisma'. Unfortunately the word has crept into common usage in a diluted form to mean any kind of outward show of rank or even competence. Needless to say, Weber meant something much more complex. One aspect of his concept was the type of authority manifested by national leaders such as Moses, Napoleon or Hitler who possessed a form of leadership of a non-rational kind. Weber was much concerned with the question of leadership and in his studies he often encountered a 'sacred' element, but there is another aspect of charisma. Weber made a detailed analysis of the 'routinisation' of charisma, by which he meant that the charisma of a great leader is often taken on by his family (for example, Napoleon I was followed by his nephew, Napoleon III, and many other 'royal' dynasties were founded in this way). Charisma may also be attached to an office – Popes, bishops and, to some extent, priests and teachers.

The relevance of all this for modern education may not be obvious. Once again we have to emphasise the contrast between traditional and modern. Education in a traditional context is encapsulated in the sacred or the charismatic and is thus supported by non-rational elements or factors; modern education, from the Enlightenment onwards but particularly in the twentieth century, relied on rational methods and explanations, but in many cases assumed that the school was still in some way a superior (but not sacred) place. Similarly, it was assumed that the teacher was entitled to respect and obedience by virtue of his office. The philosopher, Richard Peters,[9] attempted to square that circle by distinguishing between being 'in authority' and being 'an authority'. Thus the teacher was doubly blessed: he was in authority as someone properly appointed to be a teacher and could expect obedience by virtue of his office, and he was also an authority by virtue of his knowledge, superior – we hope – to that of his students.

As some modern (or postmodern) educationists have pointed out, however, teachers can no longer take for granted the deference, respect and obedience of their pupils – that was for another age. Is there some way by which charisma, of the second kind, can be restored in schools? For Weber, charisma was being replaced by the rationality of bureaucracy, and he feared the consequences. Durkheim was also equally concerned for the future, and believed that even in modern society there was a need for the sacred: thus for him the teacher had to be a kind of secular priest, concerned not only with knowledge, but with society's values and beliefs.

Alienation: One of Marx's key concepts was alienation: man is alienated from the product of his labour; he is alienated from himself because his relationship to work has made him a slave or animal rather than a rational being; and finally, he is alienated from his fellows. His life is dominated by the wishes of his capitalist masters. Their ideas are the ruling ideas of society; the ruling group controls not only the productive forces within society but also the ways of thought, including education. Nisbet's use of alienation includes Marx's well-known use of the word but extends it much wider associating it with both 'progress' and 'individualism', which Comte saw as the disease of the modern world. Other sociologists also had ideas on this subject without necessarily using the word alienation. Comte hoped that his positivism would provide a cure; Marx thought the solution was the abolition of private property; Spencer advocated the extension of education. Weber and Durkheim saw the problem as too great for simple, one-dimensional solutions.

Nisbet defines alienation in the following broad terms:

> Alienation is, quite as much as community, one of the major perspectives in nineteenth-century thought – in literature, philosophy, religion, as well as sociology. Tocqueville, Burckhardt, Dostoievsky, Kierkegaard, Weber – to draw from a wide range – all saw past, present and future in ways that would have been generally incomprehensible to the Enlightenment.[10]

Alienation is used to express not one but two perspectives. The first is concerned with individual alienation; the second is a perspective on alienated society. Alienation was seen to be the inevitable result of faith in progress and also of the exclusive rationality of the Enlightenment. In this sense Nisbet is relating the sociological thinking of Durkheim and Weber with the despair expressed by such post-revolution writers as Chateaubriand, as well as Lamennais who was quoted earlier in this chapter.

Alexis de Tocqueville's (1805–59) analysis is, however, far from optimistic. He took as his exemplar of modern society America, seen from a French point of view, and he was not impressed. His *Democracy in America* (1835–40), painted a picture of a society based on egalitarian ideology operating in a way which diminished rather than enhanced man. Human life was impoverished as a result of secularisation, of loss of community and loss of meaning in the workplace. We should perhaps beware of accepting too readily a French aristocrat's view of democratic society. It contains valuable insights but is by no means free from bias.

Durkheim's writings, on the other hand, represent a more optimistic view, yet Nisbet asserts that: 'The spectre of modern man's isolation from traditional society hovers over all of Durkheim's work.'[11] Emile Durkheim (1858–1917) was French and Jewish, and originally destined to be a rabbi until he lost his faith. This apparently irrelevant piece of biographical data is not unimportant: like many other nineteenth-century sociologists, Durkheim was concerned with the problem of order. The medieval world had possessed the order of religious belief, status, the paternalist family, traditional authority and social cohesion. This had passed away or was rapidly disappearing, and Durkheim's problem was finding a form of order that could replace the traditional. One of his main contributions to social science was to see that there are certain 'social facts', that is behaviour that cannot be explained by the psychology of individuals but must be considered as group behaviour. Another of Durkheim's contributions was his attempt to explain the transition from medieval to modern, or rural to urban–industrial, by distinguishing between two kinds of social solidarity: in traditional social life, the community is held together by essential similarities of interest (mechanical solidarity) as in the family or among neighbours in a simple community; in modern society, on the other hand, in industry, the army or other complex organisations we experience organic solidarity based on the complementary differences of the tasks we have to perform.

This view of social solidarity and order can be interpreted in a reactionary way – everyone has his part to play in a functioning social structure so we should not try to change it. It would be unfair to exaggerate this tendency in Durkheim's thinking, but it is true that he was extremely concerned about the problem of lack of stability in modern society. He was particularly worried about the condition of France at the end of the nineteenth century, when much of the traditional French way of life had gone and the values of the Catholic Church were being weakened by the growth of secularism. He thought the only hope for twentieth century France was education – teachers would pass on moral values as well as worthwhile aspects of traditional national culture. For Durkheim, individualism had separated man from the norms and communities which had provided spiritual life, and the resulting condition he termed *anomie*. However, he did have an answer: our modern institutions must have secure social bases, and he had faith in education as a means to this end as well as being an end in itself; education for Durkheim was essentially moral and social.

Weber was also obsessed with the problems created in the West by the move from traditional to modern society. In particular, he saw the main pressures of modern society as bureaucracy, the rationalisation of values and the alienation of individuals from community and culture. He did not directly apply these ideas to education but the implications are clear. For Weber, one of the dangers of bureaucratisation was that everything would be taken over. Today, a major complaint about mass education and modern schooling is precisely that. Large impersonal institutions which we still call schools and universities are often said to be in danger of being knowledge-factories or child-processing conveyer belts. They have, it is alleged, lost their spirituality, and possibly their humanity; students are alienated.

Durkheim was also concerned about the loss of moral norms in France and in industrial society generally. The concept of *anomie* was invented to convey the idea of normlessness which included excessive individualism, personal greed and lack of concern for community. What Durkheim, Weber and other sociologists were demonstrating was that the

Enlightenment view of humanity as potentially completely rational was mistaken, but educationists have tended to remain faithful to Enlightenment optimism, despite much evidence to the contrary. The end of the twentieth century was characterised by increased concern about values in education.

PSYCHOLOGICAL IDEAS AND THEIR INFLUENCE ON EDUCATION

Although psychology as a subject or discipline is relatively new, attempts to explain human behaviour, as we saw in Chapter 2, memory and some aspects of learning go back at least as far as fourth-century BC Athens. Aristotle invented the notion of the mind as *tabula rasa* or empty space to be filled by 'sensations'; he speculated about what we might now categorise as 'association', proposing three forms – similarity, contrast and contiguity. His ideas were accepted for hundreds of years, until they were refined by such philosophers as Locke in *An Essay Concerning Human Understanding* (1690) and Hume in *A Treatise of Human Nature* (1739). In the nineteenth century such philosophical ideas gradually developed into a separate field and became known as psychology.

Even so, many whom we now think of as psychologists started their professional lives as philosophers. For example, Wilhelm Wundt (1832–1920) began in philosophy but was drawn to spend more and more time on matters of the mind; and believing that there were some questions that needed careful empirical investigation, he established, in Leipzig in 1879, what was probably the first psychological laboratory, thus giving the subject a certain scientific status. From the outset, the subject was controversial and fraught with disputes about what the subject was and what methodologies should be employed. As the history of psychological ideas has progressed through various stages and paradigms, the disputes have continued. There was always a hope among teachers and education theorists that the science of psychology might provide some answers to educational problems, particularly those associated with the curriculum and teaching methods. Psychological terms that have been seized on for conversion into educational practice have included perception, thinking, cognition or learning, memory and personality. As we shall see, the word 'behaviour' has been as problematic in education as in psychology itself.

No attempt will be made here to trace the whole history of psychology. We are confining ourselves to a small number of psychological ideas that became educational issues or terms. The question of how human beings learned (learning theory) should have been crucial; unfortunately, but perhaps inevitably, it became entangled in a methodology issue: to what extent can animal experiments be used when the real question is how humans learn? Educationists have often expressed annoyance that so much psychological experimentation has been concerned with rats and mice rather than children. Part of the problem has been the concern of psychologists – some would say their obsession – to be seen as scientists. Ivan Pavlov (1849–1936), for example, wanted to study psychology in the same way as he experimented in physiology. If psychology were to be scientific the barrier between psychology and physiology would disappear. Pavlov's work with dogs on conditioning, although immensely important in the history of psychology has thrown little light on such human problems as learning or the acquisition of language. Nevertheless, one strand of psychological research extended from Pavlov to J.B. Watson (1878–1958) and eventually to Skinner and behaviourism. It is important to say at this stage that some psychological ideas, of which behaviourism is one, have had a clearly adverse effect on educational practice.

Without the benefit of a psychological equivalent to Nisbet, we intend to discuss five ideas in psychology that have become influential in education: behaviourism; human development; language acquisition; human nature and theories of personality; and finally, intelligence and learning.

Behaviourism (and Behavioural Objectives)

In our review of sociology we noted that one early movement, positivism, encouraged social scientists to benefit from the successes of the physical sciences by adopting or imitating their methodology. It did not wholly succeed, partly because the behaviour of human beings is so much more complex than the objects studied in physics and chemistry; and human beings complicate the methodology problem because they change the situation simply by being part of it. The same kind of problem has existed in psychology, but the urge to acquire 'scientific' status has been even stronger and has lasted longer, and there is another complication. As we have seen, one kind of psychology has remained close to physiology and this has encouraged some psychologists to concentrate their attention on what can be seen and physically observed, deliberately ignoring anything 'unseen' such as 'the mind'.

Although the roots of behaviourism may be detected much earlier, it was an American, J.B. Watson, who first outlined a systematic version of behaviouristic psychology which restricted its subject matter to the actions of organisms (including human beings) that could be observed objectively. This limited the field of psychology to organisms responding to stimuli (the stimulus–response or S–R theory derived from Pavlov). Introspection of any kind was forbidden. The advantage of this view was seen to be that records could be kept by independent scientific observers about the same events, just like physicists and chemists. In this way Watson expected that psychology would take its place as one of the natural sciences. The period from 1913 to about 1930 is often regarded as the period of 'classical behaviourism'; later, during the 1930s and 1940s, C.L. Hull and others developed the theory by taking on some of the philosophical precepts of logical positivism which declared that unless propositions could be tested empirically they were meaningless; thus ideas from religion and aesthetics were automatically dismissed as not worthy of discussion or rational consideration. (The use of the word 'positivism' in this context was significant.) This period is sometimes described as the period of 'neo-behaviourism'.

During the 1940s and 1950s the American psychologist B.F. Skinner[12] (1904–90) developed behaviourism in ways that brought it closer to educational theory. During the Second World War, he trained pigeons to perform intricate tasks such as piloting torpedoes, and after the war he developed the Air-Crib, a germ-free, sound-proofed, air-conditioned container for a baby for its first two years of life.[13] Skinner's experiments with animals which included, for example, training pigeons to play table tennis, led to the development of step-by-step, S–R learning into a theory of 'programmed learning' and then to teaching-machines for humans. He spelt out the application of behaviourism to human learning in *Science and Human Behaviour* and to the acquisition of language in *Verbal Behaviour*.[14]

The critics of Skinnerian psychology accuse the behaviourists of eliminating from their study all the most interesting features of human behaviour and social interaction. The American Noam Chomsky (1928–)[15] pointed out that the human capacity for language is different *in kind* from, say, pigeons' ability to learn table tennis. The relationship between language, thought and behaviour makes the study of human mental activities and thought processes essentially different from the methodology of natural science or of training animals.

During the 1950s and 1960s in the USA, behaviouristic psychology was combined with industrial theories of factory management to produce a curriculum theory which demanded that educational programmes should be planned on the basis of a series of behavioural objectives. This was intended to shift the focus of planning away from teachers' intentions to student outcomes. The only objectives that were acceptable were those that could be pre-specified and eventually measured. In the United

Kingdom, Lawrence Stenhouse (1927–82)[16] pointed out that the behavioural objectives (BO) model assumed that teachers could always predict what response would be appropriate for every pupil in the class. This was a very doubtful assumption both about the human mind and the nature of knowledge. How could a teacher predict, for example, a 'correct' response to a speech from *Hamlet*? Ambiguity and uncertainty are essential features of literature and indeed other subjects. Educationists have criticised Skinner's psychology and the whole school of curriculum planning by objectives for reducing pupils to mechanical objects and also for deprofessionalising teachers. Skinner described the teacher's role as a purely mechanical one: the teacher was one who 'arranges the contingencies of reinforcement' by which pupils were conditioned for specified behavioural changes.

Most educationists would now agree that the arguments against curriculum planning by BO have prevailed, but in practice the model seems to survive and behavioural objectives have appeared under different names in many recent curriculum plans – such as outcomes or performance-based curricula. This is one example where the influence of psychology has not been beneficial. Techniques of training which work well for animals and even for some lower level human skills do not apply to the whole of human learning. It is an error to try to force all human learning into the artificial behaviourist mould or to mistake a narrow training model as suitable for higher forms of human learning.

Human Development (and Stages of Development)

We have noted in earlier chapters that many writers on education, at least as far back as Quintilian in Rome, have speculated about the relations between the development of the human mind at various ages and how that might affect both what is taught and how it should be taught. Erasmus emphasised the importance of this factor, and Rousseau went much further and specified a series of stages of development for Emile's curriculum which would correspond with the child's natural sequence of understanding and ability to learn. He was most anxious that the child should be treated as a child rather than as a small adult. Rousseau prescribed this without seeing any need for empirical evidence to support his assumptions or speculations.

The tradition of ages and stages continued into the twentieth century. The philosopher A.N. Whitehead (1861–1947)[17] made assumptions about three stages of development: romance, precision and generalisation. The first to collect empirical data along these lines was, however, Jean Piaget (1896–1980).[18] On the basis of his studies with children, Piaget postulated four stages: sensory-motor (approximately 0–2 years); pre-operational (approximately 2–7 years); concrete operation (7–11 years); and formal operations (11–15 years). Piaget's ideas have been criticised, revised in the light of more data and refined by later psychologists, but few have challenged the concept of development or the existence of stages provided that they are not regarded as rigid or too closely related to chronological age. Later studies have certainly shown that there are important differences between cultures and that even within Western European cultures environmental factors will influence the stages. Piaget was also criticised by the Russian, Lev Semenovich Vygotsky (1896–1934),[19] for paying too much attention to the negative aspect of stages rather than concentrating on what children do know and planning progress from that point on. Vygotsky himself spoke about the zone of proximal development (ZPD) and many educationists have built on that concept to develop a view of children's learning that is referred to as 'constructivism'.

In that context the American psychologist and educationist, Jerome Bruner[20] (1915–), has also been responsible for a good deal of empirical work and theoretical thinking about human development and the learning process. Bruner preferred a framework consisting of three main stages that he called enactive, iconic and symbolic. Although Bruner's most frequently quoted remark that 'Anything can be taught to any child at any stage of development in some intellectually honest form' may appear to contradict Piaget, Bruner was most anxious to demonstrate that this was not so:

> We and the generations that follow us will be grateful for his pioneering work. Piaget, however, is often interpreted in the wrong way by those who think that his principal mission is psychological … He is deeply concerned with the nature of knowledge *per se,* knowledge as it exists at different points in the development of the child. He is considerably less interested in the processes that make growth possible … But in no sense does this formal description constitute an explanation or a psychological description of the processes of growth.[21]

Piaget was a genetic epistemologist rather than a psychologist. Bruner is a psychologist fascinated by human learning and he saw development in terms of evolution: he considered man's technological progress as having produced three systems which act as 'amplifiers of human capacities': human motor capacities (for example, a knife or weapon or other mechanical devices); amplifiers of human sensory capacities (from smoke signals to radio and television); and finally, amplifiers of human thought processes (from language to myth and to scientific theory and explanation). There is a clear relationship between Bruner's evolutionary idea and his defining developmental levels of knowing as 'enactive, iconic and symbolic'.

All theories of development have in common the concept of 'readiness' which suggests that effective teaching should always take into account the stage of development of the pupil. Bruner referred to the concept of readiness as a 'mischievous half-truth'. There are many studies to show that if 'readiness' is interpreted in a passive way to mean that teachers should wait until children are ready to learn, they may wait a very long time, and may miss important opportunities for encouraging growth and development. Teachers can stimulate children into readiness: the child is not a mechanical object which automatically becomes ready for new learning; the learning process can be speeded up or slowed down by appropriate or inappropriate learning or pre-learning situations as Vygotsky showed and others have built upon. Teachers are still often criticised for being too willing to wait for 'readiness' rather than to attempt to stimulate development.

Language Acquisition (and Language Learning)

One of the features that distinguishes human beings from other animals is the ability to communicate by means of language. We are language-using animals. But how does a child learn to use language and to what extent is it an educational problem? Linguists and psychologists tend to agree that learning ones own mother tongue as a young child is the most complex set of skills that anyone has to learn. Yet most children seem to acquire language 'naturally' with or without parental instruction and become reasonably competent speakers before beginning school. This is only partly true: most children have an aptitude for language acquisition, but they need models to listen to and imitate, and some adults are certainly better models than others. Children also benefit from help. Later on, when those children are older some will display much greater linguistic skills than others, especially when reading and writing are added to speaking as educational aims.

In Chapter 3 we noted that Cato was concerned that good linguistic models should be provided for young Romans: he was worried about the growing practice of affluent Roman parents hiring foreign nurses and servants. When discussing behaviourism earlier in this chapter we pointed out that one area on which psychologists are divided was how children learn to speak. Psychologists have produced an immense number of studies on this subject, only some of which have been regarded as relevant or useful by educationists. Part of the reason for teachers' lack of interest in some kinds of psychological research is that they become responsible for children at the age of four or five, or even later, by which time most children are already accomplished language users. This is deceptive, and may account for the fact that teachers have in the past tended to concentrate on teaching reading and writing rather than oral skills, literacy rather than oracy.

What psychological theories and studies might be of use to teachers? There are interesting studies of deprived children in very extreme circumstances who have been brought up without linguistic models; there are studies of institutionalised children; studies of twins whose linguistic behaviour is sometimes puzzling; and there are many studies of differences in verbal behaviour which are related to scores on intelligence tests. Teachers need to be familiar with such empirical studies as well as underlying theories about language.

In England, when the national curriculum was planned in 1988, there was a heated debate about language learning and how the subject 'English' should be interpreted. When it came to making decisions about the curriculum, psychological theories about learning were less influential than political prejudices. One aspect of the debate centred on the claim that standards in speech, reading and writing had declined because grammar was no longer taught in schools. There was a psychological issue here: would teaching grammar really help young people to use their mother tongue more effectively? One psychologist who had written extensively on issues relevant to that question was Noam Chomsky[22] whose research had been in the field of the structure of language as well as about how children learn. His field, psycholinguistics, was relevant to the debate about grammar, but was not always at the forefront of the arguments.

Part of the problem was that there were disputes not only about how children learn to speak but also about how they learned to read and write. Traditionalists tended to argue that only by providing children with knowledge about 'correct' English, including grammar, could they be expected to learn. Progressivists claimed that children learn to talk quite easily without the assistance of teachers (most speaking adequately before they enter schools) and the task of mother-tongue teaching should be to introduce pupils to interesting models of language which they could convert from passive understanding into their own active language use. Some extended the argument to the teaching of reading: the best way to learn to read, they asserted, was to be exposed to interesting 'real books'.

The opposite point of view, sometimes reinforced by psychological research owing something to behaviourism, was that children needed to be taught 'phonics' in order to crack the reading code – in other words, reading was assisted by the ability to split newly encountered words into consonants and vowels rather than relying on whole word recognition. The battle raged with almost religious intensity, and in the end the official policy in England was declared in favour of phonics, and this policy was converted into almost universal practice by the institution, in 1998, of the literacy strategy and 'literacy hour' which incorporated some phonic techniques.

Those who advocated phonics tended to believe in the explicit teaching of grammar, but after a good deal of semi-political acrimony a reasonable settlement was achieved. The psycholinguists generally agreed that teaching traditional Latinate grammar was of limited value, if any. On the other hand they could demonstrate the effectiveness of pupils being taught 'knowledge about language' including some simplified modern grammar based on the linguistic and psycholinguistic studies of Chomsky and others. A settlement was reached after two national reports on language learning, the Kingman Report (1988)[23] and the Cox Report (1989).[24] A programme, Language in the National Curriculum (LINC) was set up by the Conservative government and directed by Professor Ronald Carter.[25] For a long time the recommendations of this group were regarded by the government as too radical and remained unpublished until Carter defied his political masters and published his findings and recommendations commercially. A strange result for a government dedicated to the free market! It was, however, left to the Labour government in 1998 to incorporate some psycholinguistic ideas into the revised national curriculum and the literacy strategy for primary schools. Teachers were now expected to have some theoretical understanding about language and language learning, and this was incorporated into initial teacher training programmes.[26]

Human Nature and Theories of Personality (Teaching and Learning Styles)

One of the earliest ideas in education was the observation that individual children differed in temperament and learned in different ways. During the Middle Ages and Renaissance times, for example, the theory of 'humours' was used to explain differences: human beings were categorised as choleric or melancholic, for instance, according to their supposed physical constitution. Differential learning was acknowledged by Renaissance theorists such as Erasmus and Colet, but most schools tended to treat children with little regard for their differences, apart from the fact that some were slower learners than others and needed more time to learn skills and acquire knowledge. The tendency for schools to organise children into 'classes' reinforced the practice of associating achievement with age and treating all pupils in a class as more or less the same. When education for a minority was replaced by 'mass education' in the eighteenth century in some European countries, and the nineteenth century in others, there was a tendency for schools to imitate the model of mass production in factories as we saw in Chapter 10. Monitorial systems, whereby one teacher could delegate some instruction to senior pupils, were developed by Andrew Bell and Joseph Lancaster in England and by others elsewhere. Variations of the factory model were widespread and even when abolished left their mark in the form of organisational conventions and teacher attitudes.

Psychologists were not to blame for factory-model practices, but their work often did little to challenge the uniformity of teaching. In fact, the work of Piaget and others on stages of development tended to justify the linking of age to class in a rigid way. In some places, as we shall see, educational psychologists moved in the direction of mental testing, dividing children into ability groups on the basis of one-dimensional models of intelligence. Children classified by their intelligence quotient (IQ) could be put into different classes (or even different schools) according to their supposed ability and be taught on the assumption that all pupils in a class were equally able. In many, but not all, countries this strand of psychology was more influential than work on personality and learning styles. H.J. Eysenck (1916–98)[27] produced a good deal of evidence to justify categorising human beings as extrovert or introvert associated with many different personality characteristics. His work on IQ was, however, much more influential in the world of schooling.

Brian Simon[28] commented on this strange neglect in an essay 'Why No Pedagogy in England?' (It applies to many other countries as well.) Simon argued that educational psychology had mainly concentrated on IQ testing and classifying children into ability groups rather than attempting the more interesting, and important task of ensuring that all pupils could benefit from teaching. This psychological tradition was made official in England by important policy documents such as the Spens Report on Secondary Education (1938) and the Norwood Report on Secondary Curriculum and Examinations (1943) both of which were illuminated by 'authoritative' evidence from eminent psychologists such as Cyril Burt (1883–1971), whose work emphasised the importance of heredity rather than environment. The result was that on the basis of dubious evidence schools were organised in terms of supposed ability. This development was not coincidental in England and elsewhere: it fitted in well with elitist traditions which fostered the assumption that only a minority were capable of real education, the majority being better served by training for work and civic obedience. It was also assumed that the majority of pupils needed strong discipline and physical punishment to make them work and to prevent delinquency.

There were always theorists and practitioners who argued against such assumptions, invoking the greater importance of environmental influences. From Rousseau to Pestalozzi to progressives such as Edmond Holmes (1850–1936) and A.S. Neill (1883–1973) there have been voices calling for more humane and more efficient teaching methods. They were sometimes supported by psychology. In the case of Neill, the psychological support came from Freud – perhaps an over-simplification of Freud. The effect of that Neill–Freud alliance (or misalliance) was to associate psychology, in the popular mind, with extreme permissiveness and 'progressive' schools. This was unfair, particularly at a time when S-R psychology was influential. There were, however, by this time, many educational psychologists working within schools whose task was to diagnose individual difficulties and to find individual, personal solutions. In some respects their task was to put right problems that had arisen because schools had failed to treat children as individuals, but remained trapped within the nineteenth-century factory model.

The trend in recent research[29] has been to move away from single-factor personality theories such as learning styles and to concentrate more on individual choices. This kind of research indicates that it might be just as much a mistake to label students as 'convergent' and 'divergent'[30] or 'field-dependents and independent'[31] or 'holists and serialists'[32] as it would be to separate them into 'academic' and 'non-academic' groups. Ultimately every individual has to be expected to behave as a unique, unpredictable individual, not as a type, which does not, of course, mean that we ignore work on learning styles. Unfortunately, at just the time when lessons from both psychology and sociology might have been applied to the classroom, theory of any kind was criticised by politicians. Despite this, in the long run, teachers will again be able to profit from social science ideas.

Intelligence and Learning (and the IQ Problem)

In the previous section we observed that in some countries educational psychology had been dominated by psychometrics or mental measurement. The origins of that specialism are reasonably well known.

In France in 1904, Alfred Binet (1857–1911) was entrusted by the Ministry of Public Instruction with the task of devising tests that would diagnose at an early stage those pupils who would have difficulty in coping with normal classroom learning later on, the mentally retarded. He was reasonably successful in setting problems which could predict future success or failure at school subjects.

However, the origin of mental measurement can be traced in a different way. Mental differences can be seen as biological differences determined by heredity. Charles Darwin's *On the Origin of Species* (1859) and *Descent of Man* (1871) contained notions about evolution which were among the most important in the whole history of ideas. Some of those ideas have been used, or misused, ever since to support arguments that nature is more important than nurture, or that heredity is more important than environment, including teaching. Darwin's theory that the process of 'natural selection' had been responsible for the superiority of human beings, was extended to support the view that natural selection had also determined the fact that some humans were superior to others. Francis Galton (1822–1911), much influenced by Darwin, his cousin, wrote *Hereditary Genius* (1869) and undertook a genealogical study of scientific families which claimed to demonstrate that 'genius' was inborn and found in significant numbers in those families (including his own). He was concerned to ensure that the process of natural selection should not be impeded in an artificial civilisation where the average level of ability might be in danger of declining as a result of the below average 'over breeding'. He invented the word and the ideology of 'eugenics'. These views were taken up again by the Social Darwinists who, as late as the Thatcher years (1979–90), were ridiculing the ideal of equality, partly on the argument that inequality was 'natural' and should be accepted as part of the *status quo*.

Meanwhile, at the beginning of the twentieth century, before Galton died in 1911, Binet was involved in the practical task of testing and selecting. He improved his 1905 test in 1908 and again in 1911. The tests could not only identify the mentally retarded but also those who were above average and bright. Other psychologists on both sides of the Atlantic joined in this kind of research and in 1916 the Stanford-Binet test was devised purporting to predict future ability on the basis of present scores. A further refinement was the concept of Intelligence Quotient which was an expression of the relation between ability and chronological age, translated into a simple number by the following formula: IQ equals Mental Age divided by Chronological Age multiplied by 100. Thus an IQ of 100 was, by definition, the norm or average score, and marks above or below 100 indicated above or below average intelligence. Such tests were used during both World Wars for selecting personnel and allocating them to suitable jobs. Tests were also used, especially but not exclusively in England, to allocate children at about the age of 11 to attend grammar schools if they were in the top 15 per cent or so of the ability range.

Apart from questions about the fairness or validity of the tests, it was also alleged that by allocating a minority to 'academic' schools for able children, the other 85 per cent were regarded as failures. Tests which some psychologists supported as a means of selecting bright but poor children to receive an appropriate education, resulted in 'education for all' becoming a failure system for the majority. This criticism, combined with other evidence that accumulated during the 1950s and 1960s, resulted in IQ testing becoming discredited. The other evidence included the fact that tests were never 100 per cent valid and reliable and, argued Professor Philip Vernon (1905–87),[33] and other psychologists, never would predict with complete accuracy. Once again, human beings had demonstrated that they were more complex than animals or robots. Much later the simple, one-dimensional concept of intelligence was itself challenged. Howard Gardner of Harvard University, following the collection of an enormous amount of empirical data, has criticised conventional IQ tests and the theory of intelligence behind them. He recently wrote about 'multiple intelligence' and showed that the notion of intelligence that had emerged out of the Stanford-Binet tradition was only one narrow kind of ability, largely associated with what has become known as 'verbal reasoning'. Gardner[34] found it more useful to talk in terms of seven kinds of intelligence.

This psychological research had implications not only for classifying children, but also for school curricula since it was argued that the traditional curriculum concentrated far too narrowly on a limited range of academic knowledge and skills. It was suggested that a broader curriculum was needed and that children should be encouraged to use whatever kind of intelligence or ability they possessed. Three years later, in 1996, another psychologist, D. Golman,[35] claimed that even more important than traditional intelligence or any of the multiple intelligences was 'emotional intelligence' which included, for example, the ability to work in harmony with others, and to make judgements about people and relationships. This happened to coincide with the views of employers who claimed that school leavers and university graduates often lacked precisely those abilities that they needed. This presented another pressure on the over-crowded curriculum, but by now, psychologists such as Bruner had long been advocating less specification of detail to be memorised and encouraging teachers to concentrate on developing understanding of the processes involved.

More recently, some psychologists have preferred to explain human learning and intelligence by likening the working of the brain to a computer that processes information. Such psychologists give themselves the same kind of problem as the behaviourists: they have no means of explaining the most interesting features of human intelligence, what Gardner describes as 'the open-ended creativity that is crucial at the highest levels of human intellectual achievement'.[36] The computer is a very poor model for understanding the human mind, especially for teachers, but the metaphor will probably continue to be used in ways which will tend to mislead rather than help in the process of teaching and learning.

OTHER SOCIAL SCIENCES

It would be unwise to conclude this chapter by risking the assumption that only sociology and psychology have influenced education. Whilst those two subjects have exerted very strong influences, politics, economics and other social sciences have also been important. It would be possible to write a good deal about the economics of education and other ways in which the 'dismal science' has exerted pressures on schools and universities. 'Value for money' has changed education policies on many occasions in the later twentieth century, and some critics of the modern world complain that whereas non-economic values were once taken for granted in education, now the dominant force is clearly economic: education has to be justified in terms of commercial or industrial efficiency and competition rather than being concerned with 'a good life'. Similarly, politics has been so influential in education that we shall devote a whole chapter, Chapter 13, to this topic.

REFERENCES

1. H. Lamennais, 'L'Avenir', *Oeuvres Completes* (Brussels, 1839), vol.2, p. 440; quoted by R.A. Nisbet in *The Sociological Tradition* (Heinemann, 1966) p. 115.
2. A. Comte, *Cours de Philosophie Positive*, quoted by Nisbet, op. cit., p. 56.
3. F. Wheen, *Karl Marx* (Fourth Estate, 1999), p. 196.
4. K. Popper, *The Poverty of Historicism* (Routledge & Kegan Paul, 1961), *passim*.
5. P. Bourdieu and J.C. Passeron, *Reproduction* (Sage, 1990).
6. B. Bernstein, *Class, Codes and Control* (Routledge & Kegan Paul, 1975).
7. K. Marx and F. Engels, *The Communist Manifesto* in *Basic Writings in Politics and Philosophy* (Moscow, 1959, reprinted in *The Revolution of 1848*) (Penguin, 1973), p. 5.
8. R.A. Nisbet, op. cit., p. 221.

9. R. Peters, *Authority, Responsibility and Education* (Routledge & Kegan Paul, 1959), p. 5.
10. Nisbet, op. cit., p. 264.
11. Ibid., p. 300.
12. B.F. Skinner, *Science and Human Behaviour* (Macmillan, 1953).
13. This is not to be confused with the Skinner Box, an invention by which the behaviour of animals could be measured to calculate the effect of drugs on their behaviour.
14. B.F. Skinner, *Verbal Behaviour* (Methuen, New York, 1957).
15. N. Chomsky, 'Review of Verbal Behaviour by B.F. Skinner', *Language*, 35, 959, pp. 26–58.
16. L. Stenhouse, *An Introduction to Curriculum Research and Development* (Heinemann, 1975), pp. 81–3.
17. A.N. Whitehead, *The Aims of Education* (Williams and Norgate, 1929).
18. J. Piaget, *The Science of Education and the Psychology of the Child* (Longman, 1972).
19. L.S. Vygotsky, *Mind in Society* (MIT Press, MA, 1962).
20. J. Bruner, *Towards a Theory of Instruction* (Harvard, 1966).
21. Bruner, op. cit., p. 7.
22. N. Chomsky, *Syntactic Structures* (Mouton, The Hague and New York, 1957).
23. Kingman Report, *The Report of the Committee of Inquiry into the Teaching of the English Language* (Department of Education and Science, 1988).
24. Cox Report, *Report of the English Working Party 5–16 (National Curriculum)* (Department of Education and Science, 1989).
25. R. Carter (ed.), *Knowledge about Language and the Curriculum: the LINC Reader* (Hodder & Stoughton, 1990).
26. Department for Education and Employment, *Teaching: High Status, High Standards* (Circular 4/98) (Department for Education and Employment, 2000).
27. H.J. Eysenck, *The Structure of Human Personality* (Methuen, 1960).
28. B. Simon, 'Why No Pedagogy in England?' in B. Simon and W. Taylor, *Education in the Eighties* (Batsford, 1981), pp. 124–5.
29. M. Bloomer and P. Hodkinson, *Moving into Further Education: The Voice of the Learner* (Further Education Development Agency, 1997).
30. J.P. Guilford, 'The Structure of Intellect', *Psychology Bulletin*, 53, 1956, p. 267.
31. H.A. Witkin, *Psychological Differentiation* (Wiley, New York, 1962).
32. G. Pask, 'A Fresh Look at Cognition and the Individual', *International Journal of Man–Machine Studies* 4, 1972, pp. 211–16.
33. P. Vernon, *Secondary School Selection* (Methuen, 1957) .
34. H. Gardner, *Frames of Mind* (Fontana, 1993).
35. D. Golman, *Emotional Intelligence: Why it can matter more than IQ* (Bloomsbury, 1996).
36. Gardner, op. cit., p. 23.

Further Reading

Bottomore, T. and R. Nisbet (eds), *A History of Sociological Analysis* (Heinemann, 1979).
McCulloch, G., *Failing the Ordinary Child* (Open University Press, 1998).

13
The Influence of Politics and Political Ideologies on Educational Ideas

INTRODUCTION

It is sometimes suggested that education should be kept out of politics. This is an impossible demand because education necessarily involves making choices, such as who should be educated and what should be taught, and these choices are determined by values, including political values. Part of the purpose of this chapter will be to see how political ideas have influenced the history of educational ideas.

Perhaps the strongest political values influencing education throughout the world today are those connected with fairness, equality and democratic government. However, this age of democracy is a recent development which emerged gradually. Throughout the nineteenth century there was a steady growth in educational opportunity and in political enfranchisement in the West. In England during the eighteenth century, schools had been regarded as largely middle-class institutions, with some notable exceptions. In the first quarter of the nineteenth century, very few working-class children in England had access to schools of any kind. One of the reasons for increasing the number of elementary schools and later for the establishment of secondary schools was the idea that every man (and eventually every woman) had the right to vote and to participate in the government of the country; they should also have the right to education, not least so that the electorate should be educated and informed. Such democratic values did not go unchallenged, but they were accepted and developed by Robert Owen (1771–1858) for example, who not only preached the gospel of socialism but built schools for children of the workers in his factory in New Lanark. In his day Owen's ideas were seen as eccentric or even revolutionary – certainly a threat to established order. During the twentieth century in England, democracy has been accepted by all major political parties, although, as we shall see, they might define it differently. In the nineteenth century, classical liberal thought was *laissez faire* rather than democratic; conservatism only reluctantly accepted the extension of the franchise, still tending to look back nostalgically to a world which never really existed, where everyone knew their place in a feudal or semi-feudal society.

By the end of the First World War (1918) it seemed that democracy was the dominant political ideology in the West, if not in the whole world, but two points should be noted. First, democracy often failed to be practised in schools which retained many nineteenth-century features. Second, there were various anti-democratic movements in Europe that not only held back the development of democratic education but also presented ideological visions of education to be striven for. The first part of this chapter will be concerned with democracy and education; the second part will discuss the communist vision of education in the USSR, fascist policies on education in Italy and Nazi versions of totalitarian education in Hitler's Germany.

DEMOCRACY AND EDUCATION

In a series of books, Brian Simon[1] has shown the relationship between the development of education in England and the slow growth of democratic practices from the eighteenth to the twentieth centuries. Raymond Williams has theorised, especially in *The Long Revolution*,[2] about the development of democratic education and the various kinds of resistance to it. We will not attempt to summarise that narrative in this chapter, except to note once again the fact that education was lagging behind other democratic developments, and probably still is. We should not be surprised by this: education is to some extent necessarily backward-looking, being concerned partly with cultural heritage, and is also conservative in many of its practices.

T.H. Marshall[3] also discussed the development of democratic institutions in terms of three elements in his appropriately titled essay 'Citizenship and Social Class: civil, political and social'. Marshall put the elements in that order deliberately, giving an 'elastic'framework of civil in the eighteenth century, political in the nineteenth and social in the twentieth century. Civil rights, such as freedom of speech and thought, property rights and the right to justice came before the political right to vote and to participate in government. Finally, Marshall defined 'social' as rights to economic welfare and social heritage – 'to live the life of a civilised being'. The right to education was clearly included as a very important aspect of the final element. (It is interesting that the appropriateness of the three-element classification was good enough to withstand the test of time and appear as three headings for citizenship education in the English revised curriculum 1999–2000.) Marshall also made a far-sighted distinction between the right of a child to go to school

170

and the right of an adult citizen to have been educated:

> The duty to improve and civilise oneself is therefore a social duty, and not merely a personal one, because the social health of a society depends upon the civilisation of its members.[4]

Although democratic government in its present form is relatively new, it is now regarded almost everywhere as the norm, and at a late stage of the process of democratic development it has generated a number of educational ideas such as education for all, equality of opportunity in education, mixed ability teaching, and comprehensive schools (the avoidance of unfair selection and segregation). At an even later stage other concepts are incorporated: schools' councils, participation, student rights, contracts and the idea that every student is equally worthwhile – no child is ineducable. However, schools have found it difficult to become institutions which live up to the ideals of a democratic society. They often get stuck at the stage of nineteenth-century institutions.

We have seen that in England it was not useful to associate the development of education with any one individual. Education grew within a developing framework of democracy, but slowly and without an explicit philosophy or ideology. In the USA the situation was different because John Dewey (1859–1952) was not only a philosopher who wrote about democracy, education and the relation between them, he also put his ideas to the test in a model school. More importantly he brought together three kinds of theory: political theory about democracy, and philosophical ideas about both knowledge and education.

Dewey was writing at a time of contradictions. The USA claimed to be a society based on freedom and equal opportunities in education, but in reality society was deeply divided between the rich and the poor, and the education service was failing to provide satisfactory education for large numbers of young people, despite an ostensibly democratic educational structure stressing equality. It has often been pointed out that Dewey was born in the year that Darwin published *On the Origin of Species* and Marx produced *The Critique of Political Economy*. It would not be an exaggeration to suggest that in the more limited field of education Dewey was destined to become as influential as the other two. There was another connection between Marx and Dewey: both were influenced by Hegel and both eventually rejected his ideas, including the metaphysical notion of the State being superior to the individual.

Dewey considered education to be one of his highest priorities. When he was invited to the Chair of Philosophy in Chicago University in 1894, he accepted on condition that he could also lecture on education. By this time Dewey had progressed from Hegelian philosophy to some of the more practical ideas of anthropology, sociology and psychology as well as the pragmatism being expounded by C.S. Peirce (1839–1914). For this reason Dewey has been attacked by critics, especially in England, for relativism. This will be discussed in more detail below. Dewey began to see philosophy as 'the generalised theory of education' and by applying pragmatic criteria to what went on in schools, he came to the conclusion that education was not working and much of it was meaningless. Dewey's condemnation of the schools of his time was based on the fact that most schools were operating in very traditional ways, attempting to use formal instruction to teach academic 'subjects'. Dewey attacked this traditionalism on a number of fronts. First, he disagreed with the traditional notion of knowledge as a fixed body of information parcelled up into discrete subjects. Second, he did not accept the view of the mind as a blank slate or an empty vessel that needed to be filled. Dewey wanted to change the focus of education away from memorisation of 'subject-matter' to understanding the processes by which problems are solved. Finally, Dewey wanted to see a move away from the model of a passive student receiving information from the teacher to that of an active learner solving problems, as will be explained in Chapter 16.

It should be stressed that Dewey was not alone in criticising the accepted teaching methods of his time: there were plenty of 'reformers', but what Dewey did was to provide a theoretical, philosophical framework for the reforms. It is no accident that before Dewey became a professional philosopher, he had been a schoolteacher and had personal experience as well as theories to draw upon. He also saw the contradiction of the authoritarian nature of traditional schools and teachers in a society which claimed to be dedicated to democracy.

What was Dewey's alternative theoretical framework? Dewey saw education as an essentially practical question of helping the young to understand their environment, broadly defined, and to be able to function effectively within a world that was continuously evolving. A fundamental concept for Dewey was 'growth', but growth in an open-ended sense. The essence of education was learning to cope with change and uncertainty in creative ways. This did not mean that social heritage, including history, was unimportant, but Dewey wanted such knowledge to be acquired not as dead information to be memorised but as living problems to be experienced and solved. Student involvement and activity were essential and could be related to understanding and experiencing the continuity of past and present. The school should be a laboratory not a museum, and it should be democratic.

Dewey saw this view of education as scientific, and proposed a scientific method of approaching thinking and problem-solving. There were five stages: first, we begin to think when presented with a problem; second, we gather data; third, we think of steps to a solution and construct a hypothesis; fourth, we test the hypothesis; and finally, the problem is solved or we return to the data to create another hypothesis. Dewey also rejected some of the concepts of traditional educational theory such as mind, intelligence, interest, attention, motivation and, above all, discipline. These were distractions from the real task of involving young people in experiences that led to growth. Dewey assumed that if teachers used better methods and relied on scientific enquiry, then problems of order and coercion would disappear.

Among his enemies of education Dewey included two kinds of 'dualism': first, academic knowledge contrasted with vocational education; second, leisure and work. He also departed from the notion of 'liberal education'. Dewey also believed that morality should not be imposed from above but learned, experientially, in social contexts, including the context of the school. Schools, therefore, had to be moral institutions providing good models for practising moral behaviour. Children would learn to apply 'scientific' methods of problem-solving to social as well as technical issues.

Unfortunately, many of Dewey's ideas have been misunderstood and simplified. Later in life, Dewey found it necessary to dissociate himself from many 'progressive' practices and schools which simple allowed children to follow their own interests and learn whatever they wanted to by discovery. The debate continues: Sir Keith Joseph, as British education secretary (1981–86), criticised British educationists for even discussing Dewey's theories, and blamed him for preaching relativism; New Labour seems to have ignored the real theories of Dewey, preferring the traditional, back to basics approach which Dewey disapproved of. Dewey was, of course, well aware of the problems of trying to operate his methods, and discusses them in his books (for example, *Democracy and Education*⁵). However, he insists that many problems of schools were of their own making. Dewey may have underestimated the problems of modern education but his contribution to the discussion of education in a democracy was enormous.

We have already commented on the general tendency for schools and education to fall behind other aspects of social development. This 'cultural lag' was evident in the first half of twentieth century England, partly as a result of a reluctance to spend money on education, but partly also because educational ideas tended to remain nineteenth century or pre-democratic. One of the books which helped to change attitudes significantly was *Education: Its Data and First Principles* by Percy Nunn[6] (1870–1944), an outstanding British educationist. It was reprinted several times and translated into many languages, and also influenced some of the official reports such as Hadow.[7] Nunn was anxious to oppose what he regarded as the evil influence of German idealists, such as Hegel, whom he blamed for the growth of German nationalism and the idea of a superhuman State. Nunn's counter-attack took the form of praising the English version of moderate individualism. His book was regarded as progressive in the sense of being child-centred rather than dominated by State needs. In later editions of his book, he was conscious of the dangers of the Nazi State, but even in the first edition his individualism was clearly a response to what he saw as a dangerous continental trend:

> From the idealism of Hegel more than from any other source, the Prussian mind derived its fanatical belief in the absolute value of the State, its deadly doctrine that the State can admit no moral authority greater than its own, and the corollary that the educational system, from the primary schools to the university, should be used as an instrument to engrain these notions into the soul of the whole people.[8]

Nunn's views were complemented by those of R.H. Tawney (1880–1962) who wrote from the point of view of a committed democrat and member of the Labour Party. As professor of Economic History at the London School of Economics from 1931 to 1949, he wrote a good deal about the development of education and other democratic trends, and as president of the Workers' Education Association he became increasingly aware of inequalities of educational opportunity. His major contributions were two-fold. First, his book *Equality*[9] (1931) which argued convincingly against the class divisions that were impeding both educational and democratic developments. Second, his political activities within the Labour Party, in particular his draft of the Labour Party document *Secondary Education for All*[10] (1922). Before this document, official policy had been content with the 'ladder of opportunity' approach to secondary education which meant only a small minority of pupils leaving elementary schools at the age of 11 with a scholarship to a grammar school. Tawney's writings helped to change the metaphor from the minimalist ladder to the much more democratic 'broad highway' approach of free and compulsory secondary education for all. There was a clear connection between the 1922 Labour Party document and the Hadow Report *The Education of the Adolescent* (1926). The message was the same: genuine democracy needs an educated population and also offers equality of opportunity to all.

When the Second World War broke out in 1939, the government found itself in the position of having to take responsibility for a wide range of activities which included not only the education of children but the evacuation of large numbers of pupils and supervision of their welfare in the safer areas. This pattern of rationing and controls set a precedent for planning the Welfare State in England after the war. One writer on education who justified the continuation of planning after the war was Karl Mannheim (1893–1947) a refugee from the Nazis who had settled in London and for a short time was professor of Education at the Institute of Education. One of his books was *Diagnosis of Our Time*[11] which advocated planning for a free society. This was in direct conflict with the views of another refugee, Friedrich Hayek,[12] at the London School of Economics, who advocated traditional liberal economic values of *laissez faire*. Hayek inspired Sir Keith Joseph and others in Margaret Thatcher's governments (1979–92) to want to rely on the market as a policy for education rather than planning. A theoretical justification for privatising education had been provided, but it was never completely accepted by the majority within the Conservative Party.

In the immediate post-war period, however, planning had majority support, and William Beveridge's Report (1943) provided a basis for a 'cradle to the grave' welfare service, including education. The 1944 Education Act was regarded as a major reform, not least for 'secondary education for all' as envisaged by Tawney in 1922. Much of the work of sociologists from the 1950s onwards, however, was to show that the policy of free access to education was by no means a solution to problems of unequal life chances. The work of A.H. Halsey, David Glass, Jean Floud and others showed that social class was still a powerful factor. In Basil Bernstein's words 'education cannot compensate for society'.[13]

ANTI-DEMOCRATIC IDEOLOGIES AND EDUCATION

A.V. Kelly[14] has pointed out that political theory over the centuries has been fundamentally anti-democratic for at least two reasons. First, pessimistic views of human nature such as those of Hobbes have suggested that the majority of human beings need to be controlled by a strong state of some kind. Second, a metaphysical view that a superhuman entity, such as the Roman Catholic Church or the Prussian State has to take priority over the wishes of individual human beings. Operating with such views of human nature, educational theorists have often tended to stress obedience and subjection of individual liberty to the greater good.

Education in Communist Russia

Before 1917, education in Russia was backward compared with Western Europe and the USA. Education had been one of the reforms following the abortive revolution of 1905, but only limited progress had been made by the outbreak of the First World War in 1914. After 1917, Lenin's wife, Nadezhda Krupskaya (1869–1939), became a leading member of the Education Commission. She worked with Anatoly Lunacharsky (1875–1933), who was the first Commissar for Education. In 1917 they outlined a revolutionary programme which included free and compulsory education up to the age of 17; pre-school education for all children; universities and professional training to be open to all; and a form of adult education especially designed to promote communist thinking. It was difficult to give priority to all these 'reforms' but Lenin supported them because he wanted to improve literacy and saw better education as a prerequisite for a communist, industrial society.

For a while schools were left to their own devices, to experiment with curricula and pedagogy. Encouraged by Lunacharsky, some schools attempted experiments based on Dewey; others simply carried on with traditional curricula and formal methods of instruction. The elimination of illiteracy was an early priority, not only for schools but for the Young Communist League and for trade unions. The policy continued into the first Five Year Plan in 1929. Dewey had visited Russia in 1928 and his books remained popular for some years. S.T. Shatsky, a progressive educator, had translated passages from *Democracy and Education* and for a while the project method of teaching remained popular in some schools. The Five Year Plan, however, insisted on greater uniformity, and Dewey's influence declined.

Krupskaya continued to be an influential member of the Education Commission and many reforms were introduced as part of the Five Year Plan, including an 'integrated curriculum' for the first four years of the common or Labour School. By the end of the fourth year pupils were expected to be able to take part in meetings and play the role of chairman or secretary; they were also expected to be active in their own education and to organise various kinds of social activity; they also prepared articles for the 'Wall Newspaper'. All of this was different from the traditional passive role of pupils who had been simply expected to listen and obey.

Another important innovation was 'polytechnical education': part of the curriculum was devoted, not to preparation for work in the traditional sense, but to understanding mechanised agriculture and industry so that when they left school they would be ready for any role that was allocated to them. Krupskaya was a leading exponent of polytechnic theory and she was backed by Lenin until his death in 1924. However, in 1931 a significant change came when the Central Committee of the Communist Party declared that all experiments should cease. Polytechnic education continued but in a less flexible form. 'Progressive' forms of pedagogy (called pedology) were looked upon with suspicion and in 1936 pedology was abolished as a practice and a theory. Other theoretical work continued, however, including that of L.S. Vygotsky.[15] He died of tubercolosis at the early age of 38 but his work on language and thought was continued by A. R. Luria[16] and others.

In 1929 Lunacharsky had been dismissed as Education Commissar: it was thought that education was not improving quickly enough to provide the economy with the necessary manpower. He was replaced by A.S. Bubnov who remained in office until 1937. Bubnov had previously been Political Commissar for the Red Army and brought with him a concern for military efficiency: his task was to make education more useful for economic purposes; his method was to revert to tradition and discipline in schools. Krupskaya did not oppose these changes, but the Council for Education on which she had served since 1917 was abolished. Further centralisation and uniformity was introduced, and patriotism was stressed, especially in history books which were consequently rewritten. In some cases vocational education, which was particularly favoured by Stalin, replaced polytechnic education. Factory schools for young workers were developed. An even more important priority came with the drive for 'education for leadership': young people were selected for special training in Party Schools and youth organisations (the *Komsomol*). Although general education for all continued, there was a shift in priority towards leadership and training for leadership.

On the other hand, one of the heroes of communist education who was celebrated throughout his life was Anton Makarenko (1888–1939) who worked at the other end of the social scale. Makarenko developed a system for dealing humanely with the destitute orphans who existed in large numbers, organising collectives for these young people which were admired by many visitors from the West. As we have seen, until very recently, education theory was usually derived from other disciplines and then applied to educational issues. Makarenko was a theorist as well as a successful practitioner, and would have none of this. In one of his published lectures 'Methods of Upbringing' (1938, published 1965) he said:

I am convinced that educational methods cannot be evolved from what is suggested by adjacent sciences, no matter how far developed such sciences as psychology and biology...may be. I am convinced that deriving an educational means directly from these sciences' findings is something we have not the right to do.[17]

Only in recent writings in the West has this principle been accepted.

A second educational idea derived from Makarenko was the emphasis he placed on the social context of learning. In the West, the principle of individual liberty had sometimes led to methods which involved individual instruction and the search for individual learning styles. Makarenko's emphasis on the social is a healthy reminder of another point of view even if Makarenko took the principle of the superiority of the collective too far for many Western educationists.

After Stalin's death in 1953, attempts were made to apply the idea of polytechnic education to all schools as had originally been intended, but it was not seen as a success. With the collapse of communism in Russia any pretence of the continuation of a unique Russian system disappeared.

Education in Fascist Italy 1919–45

It would have been possible to have written about several variants of right-wing totalitarian systems in Europe such as Franco's Spain or Salazar's Portugal. We have limited ourselves to just two examples – Italy and Germany – but similar ideas (including education ideas) spread much further, for example, to South Africa, and to Argentina under Peron.

Fascist ideology in its Italian form is associated with Benito Mussolini (1883–1945) who first used the word 'fascist' in 1919 (derived from the Roman symbol of a bundle of rods plus an axe, *fasces*). In the social and economic chaos of Italy following the First World War, it was not surprising that many people were looking for an alternative form of government to that of democracy which appeared to be failing. The Enlightenment, liberalism and democracy emphasised the importance of individual freedom and equality. Fascism, by contrast, gave priority to the State and the need for individuals to subordinate their wishes to the corporate needs of the nation as a whole. In some ways, fascism represented an extreme twentieth-century version of the nationalism that had developed during the nineteenth century, but it was more than that. The Italian fascist slogan of 'believe, obey, fight' was an alternative to the 'liberty, equality, fraternity' of the French Revolution and its democratic aftermath, but it would be an exaggeration to talk of 'fascist philosophy', although one of Mussolini's followers, Giovanni Gentile (1875–1944), attempted to justify Mussolini's actions in philosophical terms.

At first, Mussolini was a socialist looking forward to a revolution of the kind that Marx had predicted. He eventually came to the conclusion that what was needed to change society was a great man: he wrote *La dottrina del facismo* (Doctrine of Fascism), which stated simply that he had wished to govern Italy and had taken power for the sake of a better nation. It was not until later that he found the more sophisticated philosophy of Gentile. The essential tenet of this ideology was by no means original: the State was the metaphysical source of all morality, guiding ideas and power. In this respect Gentile was following the ideas of Hegel and Fichte in Germany; he also for a while co-operated with Benedetto Croce (1866–1952) who later became a critic of Mussolini's fascism and Gentile's writing.

From 1922 to 1924, Gentile was minister of education and attempted a series of education reforms: the key factor here was to see education as an integral part of the corporate state. Gentile was also head of a Commission on Education (1926–28). Gentile's philosophy was a version of Idealism in which individual minds were – if they existed at all, subordinate to the collective, corporate state. This version of Idealism denied distinctions such as theory and practice, or past and present. Education was seen as the process of 'self-consciousness' or clarification of thought. His views on education were criticised by the Marxist writer Antonio Gramsci (1891–1937), who saw Gentile's reforms in practice as being extremely reactionary and denying opportunities to working-class children. Gramsci was imprisoned by the fascists for his views and died in captivity in 1937.

A more generous view of Gentile's philosophy might see his version of neo-Hegelian idealism as a reaction against Positivism, which in Italy had rejected anything spiritual or metaphysical, including the Church. In a strange way, Gentile's Idealism allowed for both, but it is difficult to reconcile Gentile's philosophy with Mussolini's ruthless totalitarian police state. Mussolini was never handicapped by any philosophy: he was the all-powerful leader, *il Duce*, embodying the state and it was the duty of all Italians to obey him; radio, press and education became instruments to ensure obedience. His concordat with the Roman Catholic Church (the Lateran Treaty of 1929) allowed some religious teaching in schools. His control over education was, however, never as total or as effective as Hitler's.

It is only possible to understand fascism in the light of the pessimism of post-war Europe where traditional values and modes of government seemed to have broken down. Education policy in Italy was subordinated to nationalistic and ultimately irrational ways of thinking. Perhaps the real

179

lesson for the history of educational ideas was that the anti-Enlightenment view of human beings was so readily accepted. The fact that Mussolini was, for a time, supported by many outside Italy ranging from the American poet Ezra Pound to politicians such as Winston Churchill, was not due to his education policy.

Education in Nazi Germany

Nazism should be seen not only as a reaction against German democracy but also in the context of other historical events. Noakes and Pridham,[18] two specialists in this period, have stated: 'Nazism was as a political movement essentially a product of the First World War, of defeat and of the revolutionary upheaval which followed. Its ideological roots, however, go back to pre-war Germany. They lay, first, in the new wave of anti-Semitism which began with the 'great depression' of 1873–96; and second, in the emergence of a new radical form of right-wing movement which began in the 1890s and found expression in the imperialist pressure groups and anti-democratic organisations such as the Pan-German League. Both of these developments were, in turn, responses to the social dislocation produced by the rapid and uneven industrialisation and urbanisation which followed national unification.'[19]

The story of Hitler's rise to power is well known and will not be summarised here. After many years operating as an extremist right-wing minority party, the Nazis were eventually reluctantly accepted by President Hindenburg, and Hitler became Chancellor. Through a mixture of terror and persuasion the Nazis were soon in control of the capitalist State, although sharing power with other right-wing parties. The Nazis were openly contemptuous of democracy and saw 'education' and propaganda as means of ensuring 'followership' as well as patriotism and anti-Semitism. Control of education involved close supervision of radio and other media. In March 1933 Joseph Goebbels, in overall charge of education and propaganda, spoke to the controllers of German radio stations in no uncertain terms:

> We make no bones about the fact that the radio belongs to us and to no-one else. And we will place the radio in the service of our ideology and no other ideology will find expression here … The radio must subordinate itself to the goals which the Government of the national revolution has set itself.[20]

Noakes and Pridham go on to describe how the Nazis ensured that they would have a sizeable audience: they arranged with industrialists to produce cheap radios. One-and-a-half million were produced in 1933 alone; by 1939, 70 per cent of German homes had a radio – the highest percentage in the world. The cheap radios could not receive foreign broadcasts.[21] Measures were also taken to control the press and the arts. In May 1933 the infamous 'burning of the books' ceremony took place, organised, perhaps significantly, by the students themselves, or at least by the official student body; the burning was immediately followed by the issuing of a list of forbidden books to public libraries. This kind of activity was justified in terms of protecting young Germans from 'a decadent culture'. The leader of the Nazi Teachers League, Hans Schemm, said: 'Those who have youth on their side control the future', a theme which Hitler took up in his own speeches in 1935 and 1938 in which he stressed the total claim of Nazism on young Germans.[22] Great pressure was accordingly put on young Germans to join the Hitler Youth which controlled access to work and sport.

The only alternative ideology that continued to exist openly was that of the Churches. Hitler did his best to silence any religious opposition and secured an agreement with the Roman Catholic Church. The opposition from the churches was – with some notable exceptions – feeble and ineffective. The Nazi equivalent of Mussolini's Gentile was Ernst Krieck (1882–1947), who was less of a philosopher than a Gentile – apologist for Hitler might be a better description. According to Krieck, the Nazi state was essentially total, and education was an inextricable part of the totality, not limited to schools and universities but permeating the whole of life. The Nazi philosophy saw 'educational' potential in all aspects of social life, hence the importance of symbols and rituals, such as the 'Heil Hitler' greeting and the rallies at Nuremberg. Education was part of the political framework designed to produce disciplined Germans who would, under the Führer, rule the world. Health education and sport were just as important as traditional academic subjects. Education was for all, but education for leadership was a priority. Krieck wrote approvingly about Schools for the Elite:

> The élite to be trained should be a carefully selected political–military group rigorously disciplined and bound together by a common national idea devoted to a life of honour, valour, loyalty, and preparedness for service and sacrifice … and committed to the values of national, military and political life.[23]

In 1933, a number of boarding schools for boys aged between 12 and 18 were established for future leaders who were carefully selected and tested from time to time to ensure that 'moral' and physical standards were maintained. Those failing the tests were excluded, but successful students proceeded to further leadership training in 'castles' within the Hitler Youth structure. Hitler described the programme in this way:

> Weakness has to be hammered out of them. In my castle of the Teutonic Order a youth will grow up before whom the world will crumble. I want a violent, domineering, undaunted, cruel youth. Youth must be all that. They must bear pain. There must be nothing weak and gentle about them ... I will have no intellectual training. Knowledge is ruin to my young men. I would have them learn only what takes their fancy. But one thing they must learn – self-command! They shall learn to overcome the fear of death under the severest tests. That is the intrepid and heroic stage of youth.[24]

In 1934 Bernhard Rust became the national minister of education, the semi-autonomous individual states having been abolished. He was a fanatical Nazi and took the opportunity to centralise and control the work of all schools. Teachers were required to read *Mein Kampf* and to study Nazi ideology. Surprisingly, a large number of teachers were already sympathetic to the Nazi cause: there was little resistance to the new education either in schools or in universities. Richard Evans, for example, said that most German historians 'collaborated willingly in the Nazi seizure of power and the Nazification of university education'.[25]

CONCLUSION: BACK TO DEMOCRACY?

By 1945 both Germany and Italy returned to democracy and democratic education. The communist regime continued in Russia but eventually collapsed, and although this might appear to be an account of the triumph of democracy and democratic forms of education, that would be misleading. Perhaps the real lesson to be learned from this chapter is the fact that modern societies can so easily turn into totalitarian states. It may be salutary to think about the warnings of the sociologists reviewed in Chapter 12, who emphasised the dangers facing modern societies.

One distinguished writer on this question, Erich Fromm[26] (1900–80), brought to bear psychology and sociology as well as politics and direct experience of Nazi Germany. The first chapter of his book, written during the Second World War, is devoted to 'Freedom – a Psychological Problem' in which he argued that it would be unwise to try to account for the Nazi regime using only economic and political explanations. Fromm put forward psychological reasons based on a neo-Freudian perspective for the failure of democracy in Germany, arguing that there were general lessons to be learned in all societies that had moved from medieval social solidarity via the Reformation to the modern urban industrial world of individual freedom. He quoted Dewey:

> The serious threat to our democracy is not the existence of foreign totalitarian states. It is the existence within our own personal attitudes and within our own institutions of conditions which have given a victory to external authority, discipline, uniformity and dependence upon The Leader in foreign countries. The battlefield is also accordingly here – within ourselves and our institutions.[27]

Fromm predicted difficulties later in the century for the USA and Western Europe, connected with the problem of individualism, which we have commented on from an educational point of view in earlier chapters. It is no coincidence, for example, that the Tawney we quoted on educational planning in this chapter is the same Tawney we referred to in our chapter on the Reformation: the contrast between traditional (medieval) society and the modern (urban–industrial) world has been a recurring theme in this book. In Chapter 12 we mentioned the fears of some sociologists; Fromm adds a psychological perspective to explain the emergence of authoritarianism in the 1920s and 1930s, and to warn of future dangers.

Much more recently concerns have been expressed about the future of democracy in England, for example, in the Demos publication *Freedom's Children*,[28] the title of which is significant. The Demos study (and several others) focused particularly upon the low voting rates among young citizens, but saw the problem much more widely as political apathy connected with a fragmenting value system. A number of suggestions were made in this book about repairing the social damage; in 1997 the Education Secretary, David Blunkett, lent his support to a programme of citizenship education which was accepted by government and will be implemented early in the twenty-first century.[29] It remains to be seen how successful this 'Aristotelian' addition to the curriculum will be. It soon became clear, however, that citizenship education would have to be placed in the much wider context of social and moral education.

REFERENCES

1. B. Simon, *History of Education 1780–1870* (Lawrence & Wishart, 1960); B. Simon, *Education and the Labour Movement 1870–1920* (Lawrence & Wishart, 1965); B. Simon, *The Politics of Educational Reform 1920–1940* (Lawrence & Wishart, 1974); B. Simon, *Education and the Social Order 1940–1990* (Lawrence & Wishart, 1991).
2. R. Williams, *The Long Revolution* (Penguin, 1961).
3. T.H. Marshall, *Citizenship and Social Class* (Cambridge University Press, Cambridge, 1950), p. 48.
4. Ibid., p. 85.
5. J. Dewey, *Democracy and Education* (Macmillan, New York, 1916).
6. P. Nunn, *Education: Its Data and First Principles* (Edward Arnold, 1920).
7. Hadow Report, *The Education of the Adolescent* (Board of Education, 1926).
8. P. Nunn, op. cit., p. 3.
9. R.H. Tawney, *Equality* (Allen & Unwin, 1931).
10. Labour Party, *Secondary Education for All* (Labour Party, 1922).
11. K. Mannheim, *Diagnosis of Our Time* (Routledge & Kegan Paul, 1943).
12. F. Hayek, *The Road to Serfdom* (Routledge & Kegan Paul, 1946).
13. B. Bernstein, 'Open School, Open Society', *New Society*, 14 September 1967.
14. A.V. Kelly, *Education and Democracy* (Paul Chapman, 1995), p. 17.
15. L.S. Vygotsky, *Thought and Language* (MIT Press, 1962).
16. A.R. Luria and I. Yudovich, *Speech and the Development of Mental Processes in the Child* (Staples Press, 1959).
17. Quoted by J. Bowen and P.R. Hobson, *Theories of Education* (Wiley, Brisbane, 1974), p. 230.
18. J. Noakes and G. Pridham, *Nazism 1919–45* (University of Exeter, Exeter, 1983–84), 2 vols.
19. Noakes, op. cit., vol. 1, p. 1.
20. Noakes, op. cit., vol. 2., p. 385.
21. Noakes, op. cit., vol. 2, p. 386.
22. Noakes, op. cit., vol. 2, p. 416.
23. Quoted by W.F. Connell, *A History of Education in the Twentieth Century World* (Curriculum Development Centre, Canberra, 1980), p. 257.
24. Quoted by Connell, op. cit., p. 258.
25. R.J. Evans, *In Defence of History* (Granta Books, 1997), p. 13.
26. E. Fromm, *Fear of Freedom* (Routledge & Kegan Paul, 1942).
27. J. Dewey, *Freedom and Culture* (Allen & Unwin, 1940).
28. H. Wilkinson and G. Mulgan, *Freedom's Children* (Demos, 1995).
29. Department for Education and Employment, *The Review of the National Curriculum in England: the Secretary of State's Proposals* (Qualifications and Curriculum Authority, 1999).

Further Reading

Carr, W. and Hartnett, A., *Education and the Struggle for Democracy* (Open University Press, 1996).
Lawton, D., Cairns, J. and Gardner, R., *Education for Citizenship* (Continuum, 2000).

14
The Second World War and After: Peace, Internationalism and Universal Literacy

INTRODUCTION

In Chapter 13, we discussed the growth of democracy and the influence of that political ideology on the history of educational ideas. The years of the Second World War represented a high point of that development. The result was a victory for the democratic powers and the general defeat of the anti-democratic forces followed by a programme of re-education in Germany, Italy and Japan.

Soon after the end of the war, other non-democratic countries such as Spain and Portugal adopted democratic constitutions with consciously democratic educational programmes involving free universal education including secondary education. Later still, in the 1980s and 1990s countries in the Eastern block including the USSR renounced communist or Marxist policies and their education systems. Apart from China and a few other Far Eastern nations, most of the world, including South Africa, were committed to democracy, and, officially, to democratic education systems. In addition to the initiatives of individual countries, a number of international agencies began to promulgate aspects of democratic education, especially the goal of universal literacy. UNESCO, OECD and the World Bank were particularly influential in the second half of the twentieth century.

At this stage it will be helpful to go back some years, before the end of the Second World War, to see the origins of some of these more recent but highly significant educational ideas and their application in the context of 'internationalism'.

International understanding

International co-operation in education can be traced back at least as far as the seventeenth century in post-reformation Europe when Comenius, who had experienced the horrors of the Thirty Years' War, planned a pansophic college to promote the idea of mutual understanding among all the varieties of Christianity and all the nations involved.[1] The college failed for a number of reasons, including financial problems, but the ideas of international co-operation in education and education as a means of encouraging peace lived on and were discussed again in the eighteenth century by Rousseau and, in different ways, by Kant and others. Comenius was also an early advocate of universal literacy.

In the nineteenth century, after the Napoleonic wars, the French educator Marc-Antoine Julien (1775–1848) recommended an international organisation to collect and analyse educational ideas and data. Influenced by both Rousseau and Pestalozzi, Julien was also international in his educational thinking and wanted to establish a science of education that included comparative education which he saw as a means of promoting trust and co-operation among politicians and educators.

In the twentieth century, Edward Peters established, in 1908, a publishing house in Ostend which was later connected with the start of the International Bureau of Education (IBE). The First World War interrupted the activities of that organisation, but they were revived after the war under the aegis of the League of Nations. Unfortunately, the early IBE organisation was soon reduced in scope and all but excluded education because at that time many countries were unwilling to submit their own systems to international scrutiny. In 1925 a compromise alternative was found: a privately funded IBE which produced much useful work not least in the field of comparative education, although it lacked the status of an official international organisation. After the Second World War, the IBE became part of the wider UNESCO group of organisations devoted to international education.

THE UNITED NATIONS EDUCATIONAL, SOCIAL AND CULTURAL ORGANISATION (UNESCO)

During the Second World War, the Allied Ministers of Education in Exile met in London and discussed education in the post-war world. In April 1944 the allies set up a United Nations Organisation for Educational and Cultural Reconstruction which was followed by the London meeting in 1945 which drafted the constitution of UNESCO. It was attended by such scholars as Julian Huxley (1887–1975) who became the first director-general. UNESCO was soon an organisation which was neither an aid organisation nor a funding agency, but an international organisation concerned with the development of human potential. The word often used in connection with UNESCO is 'facilitate'. Its role is to encourage and assist the transfer and sharing of knowledge on how to improve education systems; knowledge needed to protect the environment; and knowledge giving access to science and technology, as well as strengthening communication capacities, fostering mutual respect and tolerance, democratic participation and awareness of human rights. Another key word is co-operation: UNESCO co-operates with its institutional partners within the United Nations, with member states, as well as non-governmental organisations. Priority is given to education and the 'sharing and transfer of knowledge' in every one of UNESCO's fields of competence.

By November 1946, 20 states had accepted the UNESCO Constitution, but only one was in Africa and three in Asia. Gradually, especially following decolonisation, more and more African and Asian countries joined UNESCO which became a truly global organisation associated with many significant education reforms throughout the world. From 1947, following the independence of India and Pakistan, increasing numbers of colonial territories became independent nations in Africa and elsewhere. UNESCO provided assistance in many cases. They established experimental and training projects on various aspects of education considered to be particularly relevant to underdeveloped countries. An early example was an institute for training teachers in Mexico in 1951 which was particularly concerned with fundamental education in tropical areas. By the 1990s there was some pressure for UNESCO, and its Institutes, to be less dominated by Western European cultures and education models.

The aims of UNESCO: peace and universal literacy

The aims of UNESCO, as expressed in its Constitution in 1957, include as a major purpose 'to contribute to peace and security by promoting collaboration among the nations through education, science and culture to further universal respect for justice, for the rule of law and for the human rights and fundamental freedoms which are affirmed for the peoples of the world, without distinction of race, sex, language or religion'.

Literacy was an enormous problem for most underdeveloped countries. From the 1970s onwards efforts were made to overcome illiteracy by extending primary schooling, and, by experimenting with a new adult education structure or system – development education – building the four elements of agricultural improvement, health care, self-government and literacy education into a simple practical programme. As poorer countries developed they tended to try to copy the developed world by instituting secondary education for large proportions of the population, often without adequate financing to provide an efficient system, including teacher training. Such overambitious programmes frequently conflicted with more modest but realistic principles of development education, although both shared the aim of universal literacy.

UNESCO/International Institute for Education Planning (IIEP)

In 1963 an institute of educational planning had been set up in Paris to advise and train educational administrators, especially those from developing countries. This International Institute for Educational Planning arranged seminars and working parties on problems in developing countries, sent experts to advise and work in those countries and held large conferences to plan development for whole regions: for example, the conference in Karachi (1960) for South and East Asia and Addis Ababa (1961) for Africa. The essential feature was to assist nations in the preparation of their own plans, as well as experimenting with literacy projects and improving curricula. Technical education was a priority, but was often less successful than general education projects. Following the 1990 Jomtien Conference on Education for All, the IIEP took the lead in developing strategies for educational planning and management at times of crisis, with ideas on flexible planning and strategic choice being developed for member states. IIEP is funded by a UNESCO financial allocation, but also by voluntary contributions from individual member states, from other national entities, and by contracts for specific projects.

UNESCO/The International Bureau for Education (IBE)

As we observed above, an earlier form of the IBE pre-dated UNESCO. It was founded in 1925 in Geneva as a non-governmental institution, as part of the education reform movement of the 1920s and the beginning of intergovernmental co-operation within the League of Nations. In 1969, the IBE became an integral part of UNESCO, whilst retaining intellectual autonomy. The IBE is responsible for the International Conference on Education (ICE) which normally meets every two years in Geneva, convened by the Director-General of UNESCO. The IBE houses a documentation centre which includes a large collection of national reports of educational development. IBE also organises training activities and has published such reference works as the *International Yearbook of Education* as well as *Prospects* which is an international review of comparative education. Despite its illustrious history, including being headed for some years by Jean Piaget, the IBE has found it more difficult to develop a truly distinctive role within the UNESCO structure, and has become an international centre for information on educational content and methods (curriculum) and their renewal.

UNESCO/United Nations Institute of Education (UIE)

The UIE was established in Hamburg in 1951, when the Federal Republic of Germany joined UNESCO. It began as an international institute promoting dialogue between educators and researchers. It now specialises in adult and non-formal education within a framework for lifelong learning, and its work includes research, training and documentation dissemination. There is an extensive exchange network on Literacy and Adult Learning in Industrialised and Developing Countries. The Institute also has a documentation centre, and publishes the well-known *International Review of Education*. Currently the three priorities agreed by the governing board for UIE are: (1) following up the Fifth International Conference on Adult Education; (2) reinforcing national capacity for promoting the right for all to learn, and the provision of adult learning opportunities; (3) analysing the transitions of education systems towards lifelong learning.

All three institutes are established within the framework of UNESCO, have a governing body elected or appointed according to statutes approved by UNESCO, reporting to the General Conference of UNESCO, and receive funding from UNESCO. The Director of each institute is appointed by the Director-General of UNESCO.

UNESCO and Developing Countries

The United Nations also set up a special development fund which UNESCO helps to administer. UNESCO produces reports, statistical analyses, journals and books intended to guide educators in developing countries.

North African countries were among the first to achieve independence: Libya in 1951, Tunisia and Morocco in 1956 and Algeria in 1962. In sub-Saharan Africa, the Gold Coast became independent Ghana in 1959, soon followed by Nigeria in 1960, Sierra Leone in 1961 and Gambia in 1965. In many of these countries vast sums of money have been spent on education but not always with great success. This has sometimes been blamed on 'the colonial legacy' of over-formal teaching and academic curricula, but attempts to introduce practical work on non-Western models, as in Tanzania under Nyere, have not stood the test of time either.

There was an important UNESCO conference on Education and Scientific and Technical Training in relation to development in Africa in Nairobi in 1968. It would seem to be true that no complete solution has yet been found to education in developing countries either copying Western models or trying to develop a uniquely African or Asian alternative.

The work of UNESCO has sometimes been criticised on grounds of political bias. Certainly some programmes appeared to encourage anti-capitalist propaganda. In 1984 the USA, which contributed 25 per cent of the UNESCO budget withdrew its support having attacked its 'over-politicisation'. The United Kingdom followed the United States' example and withdrew in 1985. After a change of Director-General and the election of a Labour Government, the United Kingdom rejoined in 1997.

The Organisation for Economic Co-operation and Development (OECD)

The Organisation for Economic Co-operation and Development (OECD) was founded in 1961 to stimulate economic development and world trade, especially but not exclusively among its member states; it has sometimes been criticised for being a 'rich man's club' of affluent, developed countries. In some respects it was an extension internationally of the Organisation for European Economic Co-operation, which had been set up in 1948 to co-ordinate the application of post-war US aid to Europe under the Marshall Plan. A major purpose of the OECD is to achieve the highest sustainable economic growth and employment and a rising standard of living in member countries, whilst maintaining financial stability. This aim is achieved partly by liberalising international trade and the movement of capital. A second aim is the co-ordination of economic aid to underdeveloped countries. Much of the educational work of OECD is carried out by the Centre for Educational Research and Innovation (CERI) which is based in Paris. The OECD/CERI publish reviews of national policies for education of its member countries and in recent years has been concerned particularly with the question of quality in education, which is only partly a question of 'value for money'. The work of OECD/CERI also illustrates the close connection in the post-war world between education and economic efficiency.

The World Bank

The International Bank for Reconstruction and Development (the World Bank) is affiliated with the United Nations and is dedicated to the purpose of financing productive projects that further the economic development of member nations. Like OECD and UNESCO, the World Bank is a post-war development, initially set up in 1946 as a result of the United Nations Monetary and Financial Conference (1944) at Bretton Woods in the USA. At first, World Bank loans were directly concerned with post-war reconstruction projects, but by 1949 the focus moved towards loans for economic development outside Europe. By the end of the century the World Bank was by far the largest organisation concerned with development, and education was seen as an important prerequisite for many kinds of economic progress. In addition to negotiating loans for developing countries, the World Bank provides technical assistance, including educational advice. Its activities illustrate the close connection between economics and education; but the Bank has sometimes been criticised for having a narrowly economic view of the purpose of education.

Since 1945, education has ceased to be a purely local or national concern. It has become international in a number of ways and for a variety of reasons. Individual nations have realised that just as 'no man is an island' we are now, as independent nations, all part of a global community sharing such problems as peace, the environment, global warming and overpopulation. To some extent these are all educational issues of a political kind. International agencies have encouraged co-operation of various kinds and they have also promoted comparative studies, including the evaluation of standards achieved in different education systems. Co-operation can only be helpful in education as in many other spheres, but there are dangers. For example, comparative educationists have warned about 'naive cultural borrowing', and there may also be a danger of agencies like the World Bank wanting to promote one single model of educational development. There is a narrow path to be trodden between extreme cultural relativism and cultural imperialism.

UNIVERSAL LITERACY, MULTICULTURAL EDUCATION AND INTERCULTURALISM

Part of the ideal of universal literacy was a concern for equality of opportunity. Some educationists, for example, Paolo Freire,[2] always linked literacy to a teaching method, or pedagogy, which dealt with the real, everyday concerns of the under-privileged, or in his terms, 'The oppressed'. For Freire, literacy was part of a programme of civic liberation for those who had been denied access to formal education or who had been failed by it.

International comparisons of adult literacy have shown that even advanced industrial countries have high levels of functional illiteracy, that is, the inability to read and write to cope with everyday needs such as filling in job application forms or reading a bus timetable. The reasons for this kind of illiteracy are at least two-fold: the failure of conventional schooling systems to deal adequately with those who in the past were excluded from schooling systems, for example, peasants in Brazil or lower working-class children in England. The second reason for failure, in many European countries, is the presence of large numbers of children of immigrants who do not easily fit into the normal school system either for reasons of language or cultural differences or both. The response of some countries, including England, to the latter problem was 'multicultural education'. This was an attempt to promote respect for minority cultures by teachers, pupils and others, and to make special efforts to overcome linguistic difficulties. This approach has, in some places, evolved into more positive cultural programmes distinguished by the title 'inter-cultural'. One aspect of such programmes is to oppose the idea of cultural uniqueness (such as the supposed cultural purity of Aryan Germany) and to emphasise the interdependence of cultures and national traditions. At the Institute of Education, University of London, for example, the Centre for Multicultural Education has been renamed and redeveloped as the International Centre for Intercultural Studies (ICIS). In an article he has written Jagdish Gundara[3] reminds us that Ancient Greece, the cradle of European civilisation, owed much to Egypt and Phoenicia.

Applying these ideas to the educational scene, Gundara is fond of using the word 'entitlement' in the context of literacy and educational opportunity. This is not surprising since 'entitlement' is part of the discourse of 'rights' in the tradition of UNESCO programmes. He makes the valid point that to establish a national curriculum by legislation is by no means the same as making it accessible to all. In a separate article on citizenship education, Gundara relates citizenship to both entitlement and the need to look beyond schools for the education solution:

> It is not only what children are taught and what they learn but also their actual experiences at school which contribute to their understanding of their rights and their responsibilities as future citizens. So, a democractic school ethos is important and this needs to be experienced in the context of the wider community. The role of youth work, further and other formal and non-formal life-long learning are all-important. There is an African adage that 'It takes a whole village to educate a child.' There is obviously a lot to this

adage but nowadays it is possible that the village itself will need re-educating. This is especially true because both young people and adults are not sufficiently educated to understand the historical and contemporary underpinnings of society and issues of citizenship and belonging within it.[4]

Perhaps the key to entitlement in education is citizenship: all members of a community should feel they have a right or entitlement to literacy and other kinds of access to education; those responsible for education policies must make sure that not only is education available but is also genuinely accessible to all. Hence the term 'inclusive education' which is increasingly used in educational discourse about those sections of the community deprived of access to education – the excluded.

REFERENCES

1. D. Murphy, *Comenius* (Irish Academic Press, 1995), p. 25.
2. P. Freire, *Pedagogy of the Oppressed* (Penguin, 1971).
3. J. Gundara, 'Values, National Curriculum and Diversity in British Society', in P. O'Hear and J. White (eds), *Assessing the National Curriculum* (Paul Chapman, 1993), p. 72.
4. J. Gundara, 'Social Diversity, Inclusiveness and Citizenship Education', in D. Lawton, J. Cairns and R. Gardner (eds), *Education for Citizenship* (Continuum, 2000), pp. 14–26.

Further Reading

Coombs, P., *The World Crisis in Education* (Oxford University Press, Oxford and New York, 1968).
Mayor, F., *UNESCO – An Ideal in Action* (UNESCO, Paris, 1997).

15
Liberal Education

One of the ideas that emerged from the culture of fourth-century BC Greece was 'liberal education' which has been discussed, challenged and adapted in various ways ever since. The classical Greek economy was based largely on slavery. Slaves were trained to do manual work, while education for future citizens was concerned with freedom, leisure pursuits and ideas. This was the beginning of the education of the free man or 'liberal' education. We should beware of exaggerating the dichotomy between work and leisure, but it was deeply engrained in Greek culture.

Plato's ideas on education were very complex, but he did make a connection between 'freedom' and 'education for its own sake', untrammeled by any notions of useful knowledge, or training for a specific kind of work. Plato's outline of his ideal education system in the *Republic* would, in many respects, not meet the requirements of liberal education by some modern definitions: it was, for example, undemocratic, even anti-democratic, but it has survived as a powerful model. A more extreme version of the Greek idea was that 'practical' activities debased a free man's soul. According to this theory an essential feature of the human 'rational animal' was his ability to think theoretically. Most Greek men would have limited this capacity to the male gender, but Plato did at least speculate about the possibility of women being admitted to the highest form of education and becoming guardians. Aristotle continued to think within the Greek tradition when he made his well-known distinction within the Arts between pure forms of art and the more practical, and inferior, aspects of designing and making.

The idea of liberal education has survived but has over the years been adapted to serve different cultural priorities. For example, although Roman culture was essentially practical, involving engineering, military training and administration, the notion of a superior kind of education for the future leaders of society survived in the form of training for oratory or rhetoric which was expounded by both Cicero and Quintilian. In the Middle Ages, as has been mentioned, the liberal education of the élite took the form of the *trivium* and the *quadrivium* which lasted at least until the Renaissance.

During the Renaissance, as was explained in Chapter 6, the education of the courtier was another version of liberal education. Castiglione and others described the leisure pursuits which were the essential requirements for an aristocrat – a man of action, a courtier–soldier who needed to be well-versed in literature and languages as well as the clear logical thought associated with the study of rhetoric; but there was still an association between rank (the lower orders) and manual work. In the seventeenth and eighteenth centuries, there was a good deal of speculation about the nature of education, but despite Rousseau's attack on the inappropriateness of traditional education, the liberal model survived the Enlightenment and continued to be distinguished from the acquisition of useful knowledge and skills.

By the nineteenth century, in English public schools the liberal education curriculum was modified, and classics with some mathematics became the basis for educating sons of 'gentlemen' who would become leaders of society at home or administrators of the Empire. Matthew Arnold[1] was not, however, optimistic. He talked about inadequate education among both the Barbarians (the upper classes) and the Philistines (the middle classes). Arnold wanted to transform education by exposing as many as possible to the best examples of literature and art, but he did not think that such 'culture' could ever be made available to all. Thus, Raymond Williams[2] saw nineteenth- and early twentieth-century educators in three groups: those who wanted to preserve culture as a minority liberal education for the élite: the 'classical humanists'; the 'industrial trainers' who wanted more useful vocational preparation for the working classes; and, thirdly, the 'public educators' who would have liked to plan a common curriculum for all.

During the twentieth century, other subjects were gradually added but the traditional secondary school curriculum was essentially non-vocational in the sense that it specified academic rather than practical knowledge, although sometimes the academic knowledge, such as Roman history, was justified as good preparation for a parliamentary or imperial career – relevance was not ruled out as long as it was remote. By this time, the distinction between an academic, liberal education and the so-called vocational training available for lower ranks in society was essentially specified in terms of practical, useful knowledge and skills. The education of the gentleman was deliberately general, and anything resembling practical skill-training tended to be despised. By now, a defining feature of liberal education tended to be the contrast with vocational training.

In 1970, the philosopher of education, Richard Peters,[3] was concerned to clarify the meaning of liberal education. Peters identified three current interpretations of liberal education. Whilst all three put a high value on knowledge and understanding they differed in some other respects. His first version stressed knowledge for its own sake, not inhibited by vocational or utilitarian ends. Peters suggested that this was an essentially Greek notion which had been revived in the nineteenth century by Matthew Arnold and others. The second version stressed the idea that education should be broad and balanced, not confined to one discipline by being overspecialised. Cardinal Newman, in his book *The Idea of a University*[4] (1852), had also stressed all-round development of the individual. Peters' third version was more concerned with methods of teaching: liberal education should not be constrained by dogmatic methods of instruction, because authoritarianism restricted the reasoning capacity of the individual. Peters pointed out that his three versions did not necessarily coincide, the term 'liberal education' was at that time being used to include at least one of the three sets of values.

We will need to refer back to Peters' three-fold classification which attempted to explain some of the ambiguities attaching to liberal education. At this stage, we will simply note that it has become increasingly common in education circles to deplore the contrast and barrier between liberal and vocational, partly for democratic reasons and partly because the distinction is unhelpful in terms of manpower planning. Peters' Version 2 (a broad and balanced curriculum) is generally regarded as desirable, although there may not be agreement about the meaning of either broad or balanced, and the desirable end is frequently ignored; for example, in English sixth forms, where there is a tendency for students to specialise in arts or science at the early age of 16, if not earlier. Finally, Version 3 (liberal pedagogy) is generally accepted, at least for older students, but it should be noted that this kind of teaching style can be applied to most curricula, whether labelled academic or not, and it is certainly possible to teach a supposedly liberal curriculum in a way that is very non-liberal according to Version 3 criteria.

Many writers have attempted to preserve the best of liberal education values whilst casting doubt on the academic/vocational distinction. One of the earliest was John Dewey[5] who was concerned to provide a worthwhile education for a much larger number of young people: he accordingly concentrated on a variant of Peters' Version 3 by defining education in terms of problem-solving teaching methods; Dewey also strongly advocated the inclusion in the curriculum of a critical approach to the understanding of industry and commerce. Dewey's notion was far from work-training and socialisation for work: he wanted a positive but critical attitude to the workplace. For Dewey, the content of the curriculum mattered less than the mode of learning: a so-called 'vocational curriculum' could be taught in such a way as to make it worthy of being called liberal education.

More recently, in England, Richard Pring has entered the fray, advocating in his book *Closing the Gap*[6] and indicating with the sub-title of his book where the gap was – 'Liberal Education and Vocational Preparation'. He identified two enemies: those who, when faced with change, retreat to a 'narrow concept of liberal education which leaves so many dispossessed'; and those who 'in trying to make education more relevant, betray the best that is preserved within liberal education'. Pring criticised those, including John Stuart Mill, who assumed that a liberal university education should not include professional training of any kind. Pring challenges that assumption and advocates, in the long run, the abolition of the two-track system which qualitatively divides young people into academic and vocational categories. Instead he recommends , in Stenhouse's[7] phrase, 'the community of educated people'.

In Ireland, Anton Trant[8] set out on a mission similar to Pring's, but in the context of a European Union Project. In *Reconciling Liberal and Vocational Education*, Trant described two traditional approaches to education, different but equally worthy, which should now be brought together as a single educational concept. One of the advantages of his study was that it involved empirical evidence, examples of schools and colleges which illustrated the reconciliation of the two traditions. Trant also discussed the impact of the Christian tradition on the Romano-Greek education model, suggesting that liberal education was able to include many practical activities such as manuscript illustration and metalwork – for example, in the Irish monasteries – without any difficulty. Similarly, some medieval universities had specialised in vocational studies, for instance, in Italy, law at Bologna and medicine at Salerno, without compromising liberal education. Other universities such as Paris taught theology as a vocational subject, in the more accurate sense of the word. Trant allies himself with Dewey and a contemporary educationist, Malcolm Skilbeck, in advocating an end to the disdain with which vocational education has sometimes been treated. OECD and the European Union are firmly on his side. Trant also quotes A.N. Whitehead:

> A technical or technological education, which is to have any chance of satisfying the practical needs of the nation must be conceived in a liberal spirit as a real intellectual enlightenment in regard to

principles applied and services rendered. In such an education, geometry and poetry are as essential as turning lathes.[9]

Another writer recently expressing concern about liberal education is the philosopher, Alan Ryan. In *Liberal Anxieties and Liberal Education*[10] Ryan discussed his anxieties about education in the USA, the UK and elsewhere. After reading Dewey's writings and broadly, but not entirely, agreeing with his views on education, Ryan unfortunately completely ignored the other writers on education quoted earlier in this chapter. This is a pity because he struggled to cope with the ambiguity of the term 'liberal education' and he might have found R.S. Peters' three versions of liberal education helpful in his own analysis. Instead, he admits to the distinction between liberal education and vocational education being 'decidedly suspect' but does not elaborate on the problem. Ryan's main intention would appear to be to preserve liberal education in complex and rapidly changing societies.

With that aim in mind Ryan made his own attempt to sort out the meaning of liberal education which, he suggests, has two distinct meanings: 'liberal education' and 'liberal-education'. He associates the former with the kind of education that sustains a liberal society (not defined) and the latter with the education of a gentleman. Part of his diagnosis is that a widely disseminated liberal education in the gentlemanly sense is often perceived as an essential element of education in a liberal society.

Perhaps the key to the puzzle lies in the fact that Ryan is primarily a political philosopher: so what does he mean by liberal society? His answer is scattered throughout the rest of the book: 'an educating society'[11] which is not the same as the 'planned society' rejected by Dewey; 'a society that embodies liberal social and political values – that encourages economic ambition, emphasises individual choice and the meritocratic route to social mobility, and takes for granted the variability of our tastes and allegiances';[12] it is also an 'open' society in the sense of 'democratic, argumentative, changeable';[13] and it is 'concerned for truth and individual freedom'.[14]

Now that we have a much clearer view of Ryan's 'liberal society', it may be useful to examine his 'liberal anxieties'. There are three: first, the cultural estrangement, or brutalisation of the underclass; second, unease about Weber's concept 'disenchantment', the loss of religion and spiritual meaning of life; and finally, a political fear of revolution of the 'Terror' kind. It would seem to be a tall order to expect education to relieve all three of these anxieties.

Ryan proceeds to discuss liberal education and non-liberal education in an interesting way. He accepts the fact that education should be concerned with the problem of earning a living, but rightly says that it is not the main concern of education, especially liberal education. Similarly, education for citizenship is important but not the central concern of education. At this point Ryan agrees with Dewey: 'liberal education is defined less by content than by purpose: the provision of a general intellectual training'.

Like Dewey, Ryan wants to distance himself from the excesses of child-centred education but questions the adequacy of Dewey's concept of 'growth' as the mainspring of an educational philosophy. Ryan thinks, however, that Dewey went some way to providing an answer, not least in his concentration on the learning process itself rather than the content; but surely some content is essential? How can we specify a core curriculum which will not be so demanding that it is beyond many students and so prescriptive that it will alienate the teachers? Ryan suggests that in reaching this conclusion he has come to much the same conclusion about the liberal–vocational divide as Dewey. All that remains is to specify exactly how trainee plumbers and bricklayers are to be taught in a liberal way.

CONCLUSION

In summary, it is probably enough to say that the distinction between liberal and vocational preparation was essentially a pre-democratic social differentiation which becomes increasingly irrelevant and offensive in a truly democratic age. However, in our search for reconciliation between the two traditions there is no need to ignore or to abolish the useful distinction between education and training – both are essential but it is sometimes necessary to emphasise the differences. It would be a pity to lose such meaningful distinctions as teaching/instructing, for example. In the Army, you will find weapon-training instructors who train soldiers to strip and fire rifles in the approved manner. Instruction and training are the correct words because in that situation there is only one right way. Therefore no discussion or argument is appropriate – there is only room for obedience to the rules and 100 per cent competence. The context is training, not education. That does not mean, of course, that some things we now call training could not be seen as an opportunity for education. For example, business studies can be just as liberal as academic economics and geography, perhaps more so if the curriculum and pedagogy are carefully planned. The debate about liberal education is by no means over.

REFERENCES

1. M. Arnold, *Culture and Anarchy* (Cambridge University Press, Cambridge, 1869).
2. R. Williams, *The Long Revolution* (Penguin, 1961), pp. 143–76.
3. R. Peters, 'Ambiguities in Liberal Education', in *Education and the Education of Teachers* (Routledge & Kegan Paul, 1970), p. 35.
4. J.H. Newman, *The Idea of a University* (Yale University Press, 1899) (1996 edn).
5. J. Dewey, *Democracy and Education* (New York Free Press, 1916).
6. R. Pring, *Closing the Gap: Liberal Education and Vocational Preparation* (Hodder & Stoughton, 1995), p. 183.
7. L. Stenhouse, *Culture and Education* (Nelson, 1967).
8. A. Trant (ed.), *Reconciling Liberal and Vocational Education* (Curriculum Development Unit, Dublin, 1999).
9. A.N. Whitehead, *The Aims of Education* (Williams and Norgate, 1929), p. 7.
10. A. Ryan, *Liberal Anxieties and Liberal Education* (Profile Books, 1999).
11. Ibid., p. 34.
12. Ibid., p. 37
13. Ibid., p. 45.
14. Ibid., p. 47.

Further Reading

Spencer, H., 'What knowledge is of most worth?' in *Essays on Education* (Dent, 1861, 1911 edn).
Tawney, R.H., *Equality* (Allen & Unwin, 1931).

16
Pedagogy

Pedagogy, defined in the *Oxford Dictionary of Education* as 'the art or science of teaching', was, for most of the twentieth century, largely ignored by educationists. The term 'pedagogue' had come to be associated with pedantry and dogmatism, a teacher with a limited and narrow view. Nevertheless, pedagogy has a long and interesting history and its possible value is now becoming increasingly recognised.

Johann Amos Comenius

One of the earliest educators to become interested in a methodical study of pedagogy was Johann Amos Comenius (1592–1670) who was discussed in Chapter 7. Born in Moravia, where he later taught, his educational ideas were set out in his book *The Great Didactic* with the sub-title, 'the Whole Art of Teaching All things to all Men' (1657). Comenius wished to change the meaningless drill in grammar and rhetoric which characterised the schools of his day. He wrote:

> They are the terror of boys, and the slaughterhouses of minds –
> places where a hatred of literature and books is contracted, where
> ten or more years are spent in learning what might be acquired in
> one, where what ought to be poured in gently is violently forced in
> and beaten in, where what ought to be put clearly and perspicuously
> is presented in a confused and intricate way, as if it were a collection
> of puzzles – places where minds are fed on words.[1]

The Great Didactic set out 'to seek and to find a theory of instruction, to which teachers may teach less, but learners may learn more.' For this purpose, Comenius divided the period of a child's growth into four distinct phases – infancy, childhood, boyhood and youth – each with their own distinctive types of institutions: for infancy, the mother's knee, for childhood the vernacular school, for boyhood the Latin school or gymnasium and for youth, the university and travel.

Although Comenius did not specifically discuss psychology in his writings, nevertheless his method of instruction were based on a well-formed theory of the mental life and growth of children. Knowledge through the senses formed the basis of the principles of method which he applied in his schools of infancy and the vernacular school. The child's imagination was to be enlarged as his or her knowledge grew, and memory was to be developed and strengthened through practice, though not by mere cramming, but by exploring from the known to the unknown.[2]

One of Comenius's major contributions to the advancement of pedagogy was the fitting of instruction to the mental development stages of the child. He advocated firm discipline, but urged teachers to seek the motives which stimulated children to learn, and to relate schoolwork to life. Comenius provided instructional assistance by devising a series of attractive textbooks, often illustrated and graded in word difficulty, a practice subsequently adopted by generations of teachers. Thus, Comenius's programme contained a large pedagogical element, much of it addressed to the teacher. In many ways, he was ahead of his time, and for many decades his work was forgotten.

John Locke

Although no mention is made of Comenius in the educational writings of the English philosopher John Locke (1632–1704), nevertheless it is clear that he adopted many of his principles (see also Chapter 7). There were obviously differences in their philosophy: Locke saw the process of education as the hardening of the child's body and mind by restraining eating and drinking and by inculcating good habits. In his book *Some Thoughts Concerning Education* (1693), Locke saw the child as 'white paper on wax'; this contrasted with Comenius who wrote, 'Nature has implanted within us the seed of learning, of virtue, and of piety. The object of education is to bring these seeds to perfection.' On the other hand, Locke believed that unhappy experiences caused children to dislike those aspects of learning with which the experience was associated. Though the teacher's authority was to be firmly established, he urged that 'playing and childish actions are to be left perfectly free and unrestrained' and that parents should be aware of making rules which were beyond the capacities of children to keep.

Locke, like some of his contemporaries, was unhappy with the narrow and rigid methods of teaching practised in the seventeenth century grammar schools. In *Some Thoughts Concerning Education* he wrote:

Let the master's industry and skill be never so great, it is impossible he should have fifty or an hundred scholars under his eye, any longer that they are in the school together; nor can it be expected that he should instruct them successfully in anything but their books.[3]

Importantly, Locke recognises that because of differences in personalities and mental capacities, there is a need to treat each child as unique. 'Each man's mind has some peculiarity, as well as his face, that distinguishes him from all others; and there are possibly scarce two children who can be conducted by the same method'.[4] In relating his philosophy to the learning process, Locke initially dismisses 'excessive anxiety' by parents about their children's learning, since, to him, knowledge is secondary, with virtue the main object of education and culture. Nevertheless, he devotes a substantial section to the subjects which should form a curriculum and how they should be taught: Latin should be taught colloquially, learning by heart was 'useless', and arithmetic was to be encouraged, as 'the best sort of abstract reasoning'. Towards the end of this chapter, Locke states, 'This I am sure, nothing so much clears a learner's way, helps him so much on it, and makes him go so easy and so far in any inquiry, as a good method.'[5]

Locke's views can be criticised on a number of grounds, such as his assumption that the mind and the body were distinct entities which called for separate treatment; that the education of the senses should be of lesser importance (Locke believed, for instance, that the taste for poetry in children should be suppressed), and his assumption that the child could be credited with capacities like those of an adult. Nevertheless, he was one of the earliest educationists to make a link between pedagogy and theories of childhood.

DEVELOPMENTS IN GERMANY

Earlier Writers

During the eighteenth and nineteenth centuries particularly, Germany was the European country which paid most attention to pedagogy. Chairs at universities were established in the subject, often in harness with philosophy. One of the earliest writers was Johann Bernard Basedow (1723–90). He was inspired by Rousseau's *Emile,* though disagreeing with Rousseau on the extent to which morality could be left entirely to nature, and he also favoured direct instruction. Basedow's contribution to the advancement of the study of pedagogy was an encyclopaedic treatise entitled *Elementary Book* (1770–72), which set out methods of teaching curriculum content. His treatment of method was intended as much for parents as for teachers. The emphasis was on what was useful for everyday life, including physical education and vocational training, with a strong bias towards humanistic rather than the theological education then current. Languages and science were reduced to their purely practical aspects and art and drawing were encouraged.

The second part of Basedow's strategy was to open a school, called the 'Philanthropium', at Dessau, which would act as an experimental laboratory, where pupils could be taught on the lines set out in the *Elementary Book*, and also act as a training centre for future teachers. The school was based on the notion that education should be an enjoyable experience, and that children should be treated as children 'so that they might remain longer uncorrupted'. Like Comenius, Basedow emphasised the need to reduce memory work and instead, use children's senses to make acquaintance with the world. In many ways the activities of the Philanthropium was a forerunner of the modern activities curriculum. Goethe, who visited the school, praised Basedow's methods as did Kant in his treatise *On Pedagogy*, stating, 'It was the only school in which the teachers had liberty to work according to their own methods and schemes, and where they were in free communication with all learned men throughout Germany'.[6]

There were a number of other academics who took a close interest in the development of pedagogy. Friedrich Edward Beneke (1758–1854), a professor of philosophy at Göttingen University, applied his interest in psychology to education and the school room. His book *Doctrine of Education and Instruction* , which attempted to establish the phenomenon of mind on a scientific basis, was widely used in German normal schools. Another influential writer, Johann Charles Frederick Rosenkranz (1805–79), professor of Philosophy at Heidelberg University from 1831, published *Pedagogics as a System* in 1848. His system, designed to make pedagogics a science, consisted of an elaborate scheme which drew on examples from all parts of the world to demonstrate different aspects of the physical, intellectual, moral, national, theocratic and humanitarian modes.[7] Like many other overarching pedagogical schemes, its implementation would have been difficult, but it provided a useful framework for educationists to explore.

Friedrich Froebel

The work of Johann Heinrich Pestalozzi has already been discussed (see Chapter 8). Before taking up teaching, Friedrich Froebel (1782–1852), had spent two years at Yverdon, where Pestalozzi's school had been established. Although he admired Pestalozzi, Froebel was critical of the lack of system with which the institution was conducted, and believed he was too crudely empirical in his work. After undertaking subsequent further study, Froebel considered that 'The one thing needed for Man was unity of development, perfect evolution in accordance with the laws of his being, such evolution as science discovers in the other organisations of nature.' He argued that 'Education becomes a science when the educator himself practises the science of life.' Educational theory, he maintained, 'consists in the principles derived from such insights which ... enables intelligent beings to achieve the purpose for which they are created'. One writer has called this the first expression in the Western educational record that education is capable of becoming a science, and pedagogy a technology.[8]

Froebel drew his philosophy, which he set out in his book *The Education of Man* (1826), from four sources: (1) post-Kantian philosophy, especially pantheism, which states that everything is in God and is an expression of His creative will; (2) the development of scientific knowledge for the light it throws on the course of human development; (3) the writings of great educators, in order to create a teacher's own theories; and (4) the scientific observation of human development. The growth of the child, Froebel stated, was like the growth of a plant, to be cared for and tended. He also emphasised the importance of play which led to purposeful activity in the classroom.[9] Human growth took place in stages, and the nascent feature of each stage defines the educational aim of a particular stage

The kindergarten, a 'nursery school for little children', was opened in 1837 to put these theories into practice. Froebel developed a series of toys and apparatus called gifts and occupations, which, while providing for children's play, at the same time trained them in dexterity of movement and gave them insights into the laws of nature. Games and singing played an important part in the educational process. The Froebelian movement had become established within his own life time with about 20 kindergartens training mainly young girls in his method. The movement quickly spread to other countries and continents and was particularly well received in Great Britain.

Johann Friedrich Herbart

A more practical approach to pedagogy was formulated by Johann Friedrich Herbart (1776–1841). After attending university, Herbart studied the works of Pestalozzi and developed an interest in the philosophy and science of education. From 1809, he was professor of

Philosophy and Pedagogy at Königsberg University and from 1833, at Göttingen. As an early psychologist, Herbart visualised three levels in the development of the mind: first, sensations and perceptions; second, imagination and memory; and third, conceptual thinking and judgement. One special mental function, called by Herbart 'apperception', the linking of new knowledge with previous teaching and similar ideas already experienced by the student, is a notion which is now an accepted part of classroom teaching.

Unhappy with what was being taught in schools, Herbart believed that the acquisition of knowledge could be better assimilated if it were learned with genuine interest. Stored knowledge was useless and therefore Herbart formulated a pedagogy which accorded with the human mind. Education for Herbart meant instruction. There were five steps, each indispensable, in every process of instruction for knowledge to become an instrument of the mind. These were set out in his *Plan of Lectures on Pedagogy* (1835):

1. *Preparation*. Pupils' past ideas and memories relating to the topic being discussed in class are necessary for assimilation.
2. *Presentation*. The ordering of lesson material so that the pupil fully understands it.
3. *Association*. Comparison with ideas previously brought up in class to be thoroughly assimilated.
4. *Generalisation*. An essential step in the development of the mind involving the analysis of sensory experiences.
5. *Application*. The final stage in the acquisition of knowledge by using it in the interpretation of life.

Herbart's pedagogical and psychological theories are now out of date, formed as they were before the time of Darwin's work. Herbart's support of the doctrine of cultural stages in the development of the young and the somewhat mechanistic teaching approach which his system entailed are but two examples. On the positive side he demonstrated that faculty psychology was no longer valid, and his scientific and mathematical approach to education and his methodology in the training of teachers were of value for many decades. Herbart's practices were enthusiastically received in America and Britain and flourished in the last decade of the nineteenth century. Some of his basic principles have become educational commonplaces, such as using the child's interest, and the teacher's formulation of lesson plans.

Pedagogy

Maria Montessori

Another educationist who attempted a scientific approach to pedagogy was Maria Montessori (1870–1952). Like Froebel before her, she was concerned with the education of the younger age group, having worked with handicapped and poor children in Rome. Arising from this, Montessori evolved a pedagogy which she was able to put into practice. Based on the aim 'to aid the spontaneous development of the mental, spiritual and physical personality' the Montessori method has three main features:

1. *Treat children as individuals.* Pupils develop at different rates, so school work has to be adapted to the individuality of the child. The individual was important and he or she was encouraged to work at his or her own rate.
2. *Insistence upon freedom.* The child, through work, must be guided to arrive at independence. The teacher should not dominate as the pupil's self-control was the ultimate goal.
3. *Training of the senses.* Sensory education was the main distinguishing mark of the system. Montessori believed that there was a close relationship between the senses and the intellect. If sensory training was neglected the individual would be inadequate in later life.

It was the third aspect that gave rise to Montessori materials, specially designed didactic apparatus involving, for example, identification of materials by touch, apparatus with shapes and holes for matching, and frames for developing practical skills. The child proceeded at his or her own pace: this was made possible as the exercises are largely self-corrective.

The Montessorian system has been criticised as being too rigid, with an absence of social training or the development of aesthetic sensibilities, as well as little didactic instruction. One of the major objections to Montessori's pedagogical system was that it was based on a wrong notion of the mental characteristics of a young child.[10] Like Herbart's work, many of Montessori's ideas have been absorbed into educational practice, particularly the encouragement of independent learning on the part of the child.

Herbert Spencer

In England in the nineteenth century, Herbert Spencer (1820–1903), though not fully working out a theory of education, made a useful contribution towards formulating a rational pedagogy.[11] In his book *Education, Intellectual, Moral and Physical* (1861) Spencer included as a first chapter 'What knowledge is of most worth?' and in three following chapters on intellectual, moral and physical education, he examines the most appropriate methods for instruction for each of them, stemming from a scale of activities based on the evolution of man – from self-preservation to leisure and aesthetics.

It is in the second chapter, Intellectual Education, that Spencer draws up a list of necessary studies in a hierarchy, with science as the most important subject in the curriculum, which he saw as developing intellectual qualities, and with literary studies at the bottom. Spencer criticised the Pestalozzian system, believing it to be too sophisticated to operate. 'Knowing so little as we yet do of psychology, and ignorant as our teachers are of that little, what chance has a system which requires psychology for its basis?'.[12] Educational methods need to harmonise with mental faculties 'before we can be said to possess that *science* on which the *art* of education must be based'.[13]

In the meantime, Spencer put forward five maxims, in logical order, as a basis for method: (1) proceed from the simple to the complex; (2) proceed from the indefinite to the definite; (3) the education of the child ' must accord both in mode and arrangement, with the education of mankind, considered historically. In other words the genesis of knowledge in the individual must follow the same course as the genesis of knowledge in the race'; (4) proceed from the empirical to the rational; and (5) encouragement should be given to the process of self-development.

Criticisms of Spencer's principles are not too difficult to find. He can be accused of vagueness in not spelling out precise pedagogical procedures, for example, how to proceed from the simple to the complex without taking into account the age, abilities and outlook of the child. Again, the ordering in importance of subjects adopts a viewpoint of what may be valuable in later adult life rather than forming the basis of a school curriculum. However, his emphasis on the importance of science was welcomed at a time when such teaching was largely absent in schools. Perhaps the main value of Spencer's reflections on education was his advocacy a more scientific approach to it.

Alexander Bain

The call for a more scientific approach led in 1875 to one educationist, C.H. Lake, proposing a 'Society for the development of a knowledge of the Science of Education'. After its establishment it provided a useful forum for educationists interested in this topic.[14] One of the group,

Alexander Bain (1818–1903), professor of Logic at Aberdeen University, wrote a book entitled *Education as a Science* (1879) pointing out that previous writers had been overambitious in their search for a unitary theory of education. Bain wrote:

> I thus propose to remove from the Science of Education matters belonging to much wider departments of human conduct, and to concentrate the view upon what exclusively pertains to Education, the means of building up the acquired powers of human beings.[15]

The main value of Bain's work lay in the study of the relationship between psychology and physiology, and brain functioning and subjects, that is, how the child acquires capacities and functions. Bain's book became the leading manual used in teacher training colleges for students who were involved in studying theories of education and educational practice. In a series of lectures on the theory and practice of education, James Ward, professor of mental philosophy at Cambridge University, and an exact contemporary of Bain, noted that on the Continent, *Paedagogik* was usually one of the subjects pertaining to a philosophic chair, claiming that 'it is not hard to shew in a general way that a science of education is theoretically possible, and that such a science must be based on psychology and the cognate sciences'.[16]

LATER DEVELOPMENTS

Some interesting work was carried out in Britain in the later nineteenth century, especially in the area of science teaching. The prime mover in this field was H.E. Armstrong (1848–1937), professor of Chemistry at the London Institute. Armstrong was a firm believer in making scientific knowledge better known to the public. From the 1890s, he became involved in curriculum development in his subject, based on heurism. This led to the mounting of courses for elementary school teachers in his method.[17] Armstrong was also the author of an article in the Board of Education Special Report on Educational Subjects entitled 'The Heuristic Method of Teaching, or the Art of Making Children Discover Things for Themselves' (1898).

Unfortunately not all pedagogic advances were correctly interpreted. Herbartianism, which stressed the importance of the learner and the role of instruction in planning a curriculum, was popular in England in the last decade of the nineteenth century. This could lead to rigidity as in the following example from a text book of the time:

> *Aim.* How were the objects, which made Columbus decide there was land to the West, carried to the Eastern Atlantic?
> *Preparation.* Why did Columbus sail West? He hoped to find land. Why did he think there was land westward? Various objects had been found in the Eastern Atlantic which he thought had drifted from the West. Mention the objects. (a) Pieces of carved wood were found by a Portuguese pilot in the seas west of Portugal. (b) Reeds and trees were cast up on the western shores of the Azores. (c) The bodies of two men of an unknown race drifted on to the island of Flores.
> Require the pupils to quote from their literature Tennyson's *Columbus*, lines indicating the approach of land:
>
> > Still westward, and the weedy seas – at length
> > The landbird, and the branch with berries on it,
> > The carven staff.
>
> Had Columbus any other reason for thinking there was land westward?
> He had read accounts of it in old books.
> Recapitulation of Preparation.[18]

It has been suggested by Brian Simon that it was only at the end of the nineteenth century and the beginning of the twentieth that secondary education was involved in pedagogic approaches. Educational psychology associated with Cyril Burt and others looked to simple mental footrules and in the field of educational theory, mental testing, with its stress on individualism became dominant.[19] The advance towards a working pedagogy, it has been claimed, in primary schools, received a setback in 1967 with publication of the *Plowden Report on Children and their Primary Schools* which stressed the individual needs of children rather than identifying the needs and characteristics of children in general.[20]

John Dewey

In the United States of America, the psychologist and philosopher John Dewey (1859–1952), saw the need to attempt to match theory and practice in the quest for an efficient pedagogy. In 1896, like Basedow before him, he opened the School Laboratory at the University of Chicago, where 'theories and ideas might be demonstrated, tested, criticized, explored and the evolution of new truths discovered'. In his book *My Pedagogic Creed* (1897), Dewey wrote that education was not a preparation for future living but a 'continuing reconstruction of experience'. The School Laboratory was a community engaged in a social process of enriching the child's own activities: with well-disciplined thinking and co-operative behaviour, education was 'the fundamental method of social progress and reform'. The book opens with the words 'the only true education comes through the stimulation of a child's powers by the demands of the social situation in which he finds himself'. Dewey's ideas were more fully worked out in two further books *How We Think* and *Democracy and Education.* As he wrote in the latter, 'nothing has brought pedagogical theory into greater disrepute than the belief that it is identified with handing out to teachers recipes and models to be followed in teaching'.[21]

The teaching at the Laboratory School, a research centre where theories could be tried out, was a mixture of empiricism and inspiration. The emphasis was on co-operation, co-ordination, sharing and social responsibility. The other main characteristic of the school was its interest in activity: the child was placed in the centre of educational problems and situations were planned where children would have to deliberate in order to solve them. The pupils built up their own understanding through meaningful activities. The curriculum was based on social occupations, classified under four headings: the social, constructive, investigative and expressive impulses or interest. Studies were divided into three groups, science and mathematics, communication and expressive skills and social studies. Each activity involved three types of work, motor, intellectual and co-operative planning.[22]

The experiment which lasted for eight years was not independently evaluated and its success was not easy to judge. The work provided a vehicle for Dewey's theories to be put into action in an attempt to formulate a suitable pedagogy which would achieve satisfactory educational ends. Some of the more important gains were the confirmation of the importance of the doctrine of interest and socialisation, and the need for co-operative planning, all of which helped to bring about new thinking in the organisation of primary education in the twentieth century.

CONCLUSION

The *Cyclopaedia of Education* published in 1907 has an entry on pedagogy which mentions that 'the educational theorist has been too little in touch with the practical education. Without something like scientific discussion on educational subjects, without pedagogy, we shall never obtain a body of organised opinion on education'.[23] In the same year, a leading British teacher trainer commented on the current divorce of theory from practice:

> The reader is disappointed by the leanness of the land he has explored at considerable pains; and he passes with relief to the part labelled 'practice', which is often full of excellent empirical precepts which appear, however, to be strangely independent of the preceding 'theory'.[24]

In recent years there has been a world-wide revival of interest in pedagogy. For example, the advent of the national curriculum in Britain following the 1988 Education Reform Act attempted to define common objectives for all pupils in the main subjects, a first necessary condition for identifying effective pedagogical means.[25] Jerome Bruner has recently identified four dominant models of learners' minds: seeing children as imitative learners, as learning from didactic exposure, as thinkers, and as knowledgeable individuals, together with the implications of each of these models for pedagogy.[26]

There is an increasing research literature on pedagogy which focuses on different types of teachers, the context of teaching, and on teaching and learning, from which a suitable complex model of pedagogy is emerging.[27] Politicians and policy makers are also taking an increasing interest in pedagogy. It is salutary to conclude with a statement made by an educationist over a century ago:

> We may admit that a science of education can never do the half of what educational theorizers have supposed, can never be comparable for exactness and distinctiveness to , say, the theory of navigation or the theory of structures; and yet have reason to believe that such a science will be as valuable to the practical teacher as the theories just mentioned are to the navigator and the engineer.[28]

REFERENCES

1. L. Cole, *A History of Education. Socrates to Montessori* (Holt Reinhart & Winston, New York, 1964), p. 337.
2. F. Eby, *The Development of Modern Education* (Prentice Hall, New York, 1952), p. 199.
3. J. Locke, *Some Thoughts Concerning Education* (C. Daniel (ed.)) (National Society's Depository, 1693, 1880 edn), pp. 143–4.

4. Ibid., p. 363.
5. Ibid., p. 344.
6. R.H. Quick, *Essays on Educational Reformers* (Longmans, Green, 1895), p. 156.
7. K. von Raumer, *German Pedagogy. Education. The School and the Teacher* (Brown and Gross, Hartford, CN, 2nd edn. 1876), p. 26.
8. J. Bowen, *A History of Western Education, vol. 3. The Modern West:Europe and the New World* (Methuen, 1981), p. 339.
9. E. Laurence (ed.), *Freidrich Froebel and English Education* (Routledge & Kegan Paul, 1952, 1969 edn), p. 22.
10. W. Boyd, *From Locke to Montessori* (Harrop, 1914), p. 237.
11. G. Compayré, *The History of Pedagogy*, trans. W.H. Payne (Swann, Sonnenschein, 1905), p. 539.
12. H. Spencer, *Education. Intellectual, Moral and Physical* (Williams and Norgate, 1861, 1878 edn), p. 63.
13. Ibid., p. 64.
14. R.J.W. Selleck, *The New Education. The English Background, 1870–1914* (Pitman, 1968), p. 274.
15. A. Bain, *Education as a Science* (Kegan, Paul, Trench, Trübner, 1879, 1892 edn), p. 9.
16. J. Ward, *Psychology Applied to Education*, G. Davies Hicks (ed.) (Cambridge University Press, Cambridge, 1926), p. 1.
17. E.W. Jenkins and B.J. Swinnerton, *Junior School Science Education in England and Wales since 1900* (Woburn Press, 1998), p. 9.
18. C.I. Dodd, *Introduction to the Herbartian Principles of Teaching* (Swann, Sonnenschein, 1898), p. 160.
19. B. Simon, 'Why No Pedagogy in England?' in B. Simon and W. Taylor (eds), *Education in the Eighties* (Batsford, 1981), p. 133.
20. Ibid., p. 141.
21. J. Dewey, *Democracy and Education* (Collier Macmillan, 1916), p. 170.
22. W.F. Connell, *A History of Education in the Twentieth Century World* (Curriculum Development Centre, Canberra, 1980), pp. 74–80.
23. A.E. Fletcher (ed.), *Sonnenschein's Cyclopaedia of Education* (Allen and Unwin, 1907), p. 258.
24. T. Raymont, *The Principles of Education* (Longmans, Green, 1907), p. 23.
25. B. Simon, 'Some Problems of Pedagogy, Revisited', in *The State and Educational Change: Essays in the History of Education and Pedagogy* (Lawrence & Wishart, 1994), p. 153.
26. J. Bruner, 'Folk Pedagogies', in *The Culture of Education* (Harvard University Press, Cambridge, MA, 1996), pp. 53–61.
27. C. Watkins and P. Mortimore, 'Pedagogy: What Do We Know', in P. Mortimer (ed.), *Understanding Pedagogy and Its Impact on Learning* (Paul Chapman, 1999), pp. 3–8.
28. Ward, op. cit., pp. 2–3.

Further Reading

Adamson, J.W., *Pioneers of Modern Education 1600–1700* (Cambridge University Press, Cambridge, 1905).
Browning, O. (Butler, N.M.) (ed.) *Aspects of Education: A Study in the History of Pedagogy* (Industrial Education Society, New York, 1888).
Giroux, H.A., *Schooling for Democarcy: Critical Pedagogy in the Modern Age* (Routledge, 1988).
Millett, A., *Pedagogy – The Last Corner of the Secret Garden* (King's College School of Education, 1996).
Open University, *Schooling and Capitalism* E202, Block 1 (Open University Press, 1977).

17
Gender

One of the problems in discussing the topic of gender and education is the lack of any single feminist perspective on women's education, with reference to the past or the present. As Purvis[1] has pointed out, there are at least five different approaches which can be adopted – Marxist feminism, radical feminism, socialist feminism, liberal feminism and cultural feminism. Marxist feminism states that the oppression of women, through socialist inequalities and ownership of women by men, will end only when a communist society has been established; this will free women from the economic functions at present undertaken by families and will be taken over by the State. Radical feminism focuses on the power relationships between the sexes in a patriarchal society. Socialist feminism includes elements of the first two categories but argues that change can come about before a revolution in the ownership of the means of production. Liberal feminism posits a less radical approach, favouring gradual reform which would lead to the removal of legal, cultural and social constraints and equality with men. Cultural feminism favours the establishment of a separate women's culture which will endeavour to change the nature of society.

In what follows, it will become clear that educational thinkers have adopted some parts of these categories whilst ignoring others. Indeed, many leading writers on education have completely overlooked the needs of girls' and women's education. This may seem surprising in view of the fact that one of the earliest advocates of such education was as long ago as Plato in his books *Republic* and *Laws*.

GREECE

The *Republic*, written in 411 or 412 BC, consists of a dialogue between Socrates and a friend, Glaucon. The latter, in Book V, points out that, in the training for occupations, both men and women equally vary in their capacity for learning. He therefore concludes that 'none of the occupations which comprehend the ordering of a state belong to a woman as woman, nor yet to man as man; but natural gifts are to be found here and there, in both sexes alike; and, so far as her nature is concerned, the woman is admissible to all pursuits as well as the man'. One theme, however, that runs throughout the Book is that woman is weaker than the man. Nevertheless, women's love of knowledge might qualify her to be a guardian, and the two men discuss the practical arrangements which would be required for this to happen. They conclude that 'If the question is how to render a woman fit for the office of guardian, we shall not have one education for men, and another for women, especially as the nature to be wrought upon is the same in both cases.'

A much more detailed programme of women's education was outlined in Plato's later work, *Laws*. Universal, compulsory schooling for all free citizens was advocated for both boys and girls in order to produce good citizens. Play was an important part of early learning and both sexes should play together in a nursery day school until they were six years old. They would then be separated but would continue to receive similar instruction. 'In stating my doctrine,' Plato wrote, 'I intend no reservation on any point of horsemanship or physical training, as appropriate for men but not for women.' Science, mathematics and music also formed an important part of the curriculum.

However, Plato expressed reservations about women, that they had an 'inherent weakness of the soul' and were mischief makers. He assumed that boys would become soldiers and girls in due course were destined to become mothers and take up domestic duties. For that reason, girls should learn the arts and knowledge that would be useful in running a home.

EARLY CHRISTIAN

The Romans made little contribution to this topic and it was not until the early years of the fourth century AD, after Christianity had been accepted and established that theologians such as St Jerome (340–420) turned their attention to the analysis of girls' education. Jerome, who was renowned for his learning, propounded a philosophy which was to remain important in planning the curriculum of girls until as late as the eighteenth century. Jerome set out his beliefs in the form of letters. One important principle, in direct contradiction of Plato's, was that 'females should not know how to play with boys, nay, they should be afraid to do so. A girl should have no acquaintance with lewd talk, and if amid the noisy bustle of a household she hears an unclean word, she should not understand it.' The child should be taught to read and write, be adept at handicraft, especially needlework, and become immersed in the Holy Scriptures, both in Latin and Greek. No music was allowed – 'Paula must be deaf to all musical instruments, and never even know why the flute, the lyre, and the harp came into existence' – and dancing was also forbidden.[2] Modesty in dress, deportment and behaviour was essential and the virtues of virginity were emphasised. Those who longed for a continuity of a sheltered and secluded existence were encouraged to lead a holy life as nuns.

RENAISSANCE

The Renaissance, with its rediscovery of humanism and a revival of interest in Greek and Roman texts, was a stimulus for the founding of grammar schools offering a broad curriculum. Humanist scholars, such as Erasmus, More and Linacre, were advocates of girls' education, though it was a Spanish scholar, Joan Luis Vives (1492–1540) who was concerned with the theory as well as the practice of education for girls. He had been invited to England in 1523 by a fellow Spaniard, Catherine of Aragon, Henry VIII's wife, to suggest a plan for the studies of her seven-year-old daughter, Princess Mary, later Mary I.

Besides devising a course of studies which included attention to classical texts and poems, Plato's *Dialogues* and the New Testament, which was to be read every morning and night, Vives wrote two text books, *De Institutione Faeminae Christianae* (The Instruction of Christian Woman) and *De Ratione Studii* especially for the benefit of the young Mary. Vives advocated an education for women in order to make them suitable companions in marriage. Like St Jerome, he saw education as a protection against immorality and that 'nothing so completely preserves the modesty of young girls as learning'. One of the earliest writers to base education on psychology, he wrote, 'Observe the child and adapt your aims and methods to his needs.' He differed from other Renaissance tutors in recommending that mothers, rather than tutors, should instruct their offspring and guide them in infancy. Vives believed in life-long education for both sexes. He did not consider that too many concessions should be made to girls during their education. 'The daughter should be handled without any cherishing. For cherishing marreth sons, but it utterly destroys daughters.' Whilst Vives is often seen as taking an inferior view of women's intellect, nevertheless he adopted a pragmatic approach to their education. 'If any girl shows herself inclined for and capable of learning, she should be allowed to go further with it', a precept not acted upon in Britain until several centuries later.[3]

Within three years of Vives' arrival in England he fell into disfavour when Henry VIII began divorce proceedings against Catherine. However, Princess Mary's educational progress and accomplishments were a tribute to Vives' endeavours.

Another humanist writer, Richard Mulcaster (1530–1611), headmaster of Merchant Taylors' and St Paul's Schools, echoed sentiments similar to Vives. Whilst believing that girls a well as boys should be entitled to a sound education – 'Myself, I am for them tooth and nail.' – Mulcaster argued in his book *Positions, Wherein Those Primitive Circumstances be examined, which are necessie* [sic] *for the Training up of Children either for Skill in their Boke or Health in their Bodie* (1581) that there was a difference in the mental capacity of boys and girls:

> Though the girls seem commonly to have a quicker ripening in wit than boys have, for all that seeming yet it is not so. Their natural weakness, which cannot hold long, delivers very soon and yet there be as prating boy as there be prattling wenches. Besides, their brains be not so much charged, neither with weight nor with multitude of matters, as boys' heads be, and therefore like empty casks, they make the greater noise.

This supposed difference assumed great importance in the late nineteenth- and early twentieth-century debate on the provision of girls' education, as we shall see. Mulcaster, as a practical schoolmaster, though unlike other writers, drew attention to the need for appropriate training for girls who might not marry:

> If a young maiden is to be brought up with a view to marriage, obedience to authority and similar qualities must for the best kind of training, but if from necessity she has to learn how to earn her own living some technical training must prepare her for a definite calling.[4]

Unfortunately, both Vives' and Mulcaster's positive ideas on the nature of girls' education were not generally translated into action. Few schools or teachers were available, except for refugees from the Low Countries and France and then mainly for their own children. Educational practice, therefore, lagged behind theory during the Renaissance period.

ENLIGHTENMENT

Fashionable girls' boarding schools began to appear around London after the Restoration; we know for instance that Henry Purcell wrote his opera *Dido and Aeneas* for such a school at Chelsea in 1670. The movement received a stimulus with the writings in France of the cleric and teacher François de Solignac de la Mothe Fénelon (1651–1715). In his *Traité de l'Education des Filles* (1687) (Treatise on the Education of Girls). He emphasised the need for equal education. English women, such as Mary Astell (1668–1731) in her book *A Serious Proposal to the Ladies for the Advancement of True and Greatest Interest* (1694) showed that women were regarded as inferior not because of their nature but because of their lack of education. Mary Astell, who had studied both Locke and Descartes, also proposed that there should be established a college for the higher education of 'the most neglected part of the World as to all Real improvement, the Ladies'. In a publication three years later, *An Essay in Defence of the Female Sex*, she described the differences in education given to the two sexes, when at the age of six or seven, boys are sent to grammar school to learn Greek and Latin, while girls are sent to boarding schools to learn needlework, dancing and other accomplishments. She considered philosophy and a study of English important for women. 'The Men may have unrivalled the Glory of speaking as many Languages as Babel afforded; we only desire to express ourselves pertinently in One.'[5]

Even as progressive a writer as Jean Jacques Rousseau in his classic book *Émile* (1762), whilst drawing attention to the need to cultivate women's reasoning and understanding, also stated:

> The whole education of women should be related to that of men. To please them, to be useful to them, to become loved and honoured by them; to bring them up when young, to care for them when grown; to advise, to console them, to make life easy and pleasant for them – these are the duties of women at every age, and this is what they should be taught from childhood (Book 5).

Precisely the opposite argument was used by the radical feminist Mary Wollstonecroft (1759–97), who stated that such subordination limited women's physical, mental and moral powers. She believed in equal rights for women and in her book, *Vindication of the Rights of Women* (1792) condemned an education which was simply geared to marriage. Nor did Wollstonecroft approve of boarding schools for children; she favoured the establishment of co-educational day schools, organised by the State, in order to bring about better understanding between the sexes. 'Were boys and girls permitted to pursue the same studies together, those graceful decencies might early be inculcated which produce modesty without those sexual distinctions that taint the mind.'[6] Education should also prepare women for independence and to play a part in public affairs (she advocated the election of women to Parliament) and the curriculum was to be geared to women's future needs. Wollstonecroft's views were ahead of her time, but after her early death at the age of 38 they became very influential.

NINETEENTH CENTURY

The provision of education in England by the beginning of the nineteenth century was organised strictly on class lines. Elementary education, with its concentration on the 3Rs, and provided at minimum cost for the poor, was a purely instrumental one. A typical example was Samuel Wilderspin (1782–1866), the father of the infant school movement. In his book *On the Importance of Educating the Infant Children of the Poor*, he stated that these schools were

> for the acquisition of habits and cleanliness and decorum, of cheerful and ready subordination ... and of abstinence from everything impure and profane: a scene, in short, at once of activity and amusement, of intellectual improvement and moral discipline.

With the introduction of government financing of elementary education from 1833, there was increasing pressure for 'value for money'. One of Her Majesty's Inspectors of Schools, appointed to supervise the expenditure of such monies, wrote in his report for 1862:

> Girls have no knowledge of needlework, cannot cut out or mend, and darning stockings is an unknown science. But at an examination, a few will write lines upon a slate and cast up a sum, and the mistress will state that they are prepared to answer questions in history or geography, besides names of cities etc, etc. No needlework is ever displayed; no questions are asked on any subject which will be useful to them.

With the introduction of 'payment by results' in that same year, plain needlework became compulsory for girls. The effect of this was apparent some 26 years later when the Cross Commission on Elementary Education reported in 1888: 'As the time for the girls [in elementary schools] is largely taken up by needlework, the time they can give to arithmetic is less than that which can be given to boys.' The solution suggested was to modify the arithmetical requirements of the Code for girls, with exemptions from learning tables. Further differentiation of curriculum requirements followed in the next decade with the introduction into the Code of domestic economy for girls. Such differentiation represented the views of what seemed appropriate for the two sexes and continued into the twentieth century.

The question of co-education in elementary schools also indicates interesting attitudes towards girls and their education. A Committee of Council on Education pamphlet was issued to schools later in the century on the subject and was entitled *Mixed Schools and Good Manners*. HMI who reported on co-education argued that schools would be limited in their choice of masters 'for it is unavoidable that the master ought to be married. It is not right to place a young unmarried man in a position which undoubtedly may be one of temptation.' Furthermore, needlework was found to be inferior to those schools composed of girls only under the supervision of a mistress, and the teaching of girls by a master was not considered 'conducive to the early formation of habits and modesty'.

Middle-class education for girls followed a rather different pattern. Up to about 1850, many girls were educated at home under a governess. The main impetus to providing school education for girls came with the founding of the Governesses' Benevolent Institution which demonstrated the need for their suitable training starting at school level. Queen's College, Harley Street, opened in 1848, provided such courses. Two years later the North London Collegiate School for Ladies was established by Frances Buss, and Dorothea Beale became principal of the Cheltenham Ladies' College in 1857. Both Miss Buss and Miss Beale had been pupils at Queen's College. One interesting feature of girls' middle-class schooling at this time was that their theory of emancipation from boys' schools was based on one of imitation; for example, girls adopted boys' sports, such as cricket, stressed the importance of classics in the curriculum and competed with boys in the Cambridge Local Examinations which, after a struggle, girls were allowed to enter for from 1863.[7] Not all headmistresses agreed that the new examinations were appropriate for girls. One who refused to enter any candidates did so on the grounds 'that no girl ought to go through anything that was public'.

There were three aspects of girls' education which reformers in the nineteenth century considered important:

1. *Humanistic*. This was reflected in the evidence given to the School Inquiry Commission into endowed schools, 1864–68, which pointed

to the need for women's education to be liberal and humane. 'Women make up one half of society and we cannot afford to leave one half of its members imperfectly educated.'

2. *Vocational*. With the opening up of opportunities for women in the professions, such as teaching, medicine, the Civil Service and social work, the aim of education was to prepare them for their vocations in the world. Latin, German and mathematics, known to be less congenial subjects to girls, were advocated because they were considered to afford good mental discipline.

3. *Economic*. The increasing problem of surplus women of marriageable age, given the demographic predictions, made it essential that, with the need for many to earn a living, there had to be some identity of curriculum and examinations offered to both boys and girls if opportunities were to be secured.

Although girls were increasingly well provided for after the setting up of the Girls' Public Day Schools Company in 1872, there was much male opposition at all levels to the concept of the need for women's education. Anthropological and anatomical studies from the 1860s showed that it was impossible for women to compete successfully with men. One researcher, for instance, demonstrated that as the brains of men and women were different in size and structure, so women must be less intelligent than men:

> The difference between the sexes as regards the cranial cavity increases with the development of the race, so that the male European excels more the female than does the negro the negress; and hence, with the progress of civilization, the men are in advance of the women, so that the inequality of the sexes increases with civilization.[8]

The opening of higher education to women, following Emily Davies' founding of the College at Hitchin in 1869 and transferred to Newnham, Cambridge in 1873, raised even more opposition. Physiologically, it was argued, they were unable to bear the strain of the necessary concentration required for a course of study and, it was claimed, they might become sterile as result; morally it was also unwise. One bitter opponent of women's education at Oxford was the Reverend John William Burgon. When women were allowed to enter for honours degree examinations, he gave a sermon which was published in 1884 entitled *To Educate Young Women Like Men, and With Young Men – a Thing Inexpedient and Immodest*. Some writers regarded women as temptresses and sinful, and

221

stated that they would prove to be distracting to hard-working male students. The fear of Cambridge becoming a mixed university, with the prospect of women sharing the power to participate in decision-making led the professor of Philology, William Skeat, to write to a colleague, 'Even the BA degree would enable them to take five books at a time out of University Library on a ticket countersigned by "their tutor". I am entirely opposed to the admission of women to "privileges" of this character. And I honestly believe they are better off as they are.'[9] There was also the threat of competition for employment if women showed talent for a discipline. The long battle to exclude women from training to become doctors in England is a good example of this. Much of the opposition, though, stemmed from the traditional male view of the place of women in society.

The basic dilemma confronting proponents of women's education in the nineteenth century was whether to map out a justification based on theories of feminism or to emulate the education considered suitable for males. Emily Davies favoured a middle-ground approach. Giving evidence before the Schools Inquiry Commission, she was asked, ' In fact, you wish very much to assimilate the general mental training of boys and girls?' She replied, 'I think so. If we could find out what is the best mental training it would be best for both, but I suppose nobody has found that out yet.' This problem was to be widely addressed in the next century.

TWENTIETH CENTURY

Social and political changes in the first half of the twentieth century did much to improve the educational chances of women. The suffragette movement was responsible for women obtaining the vote, service and clerical opportunities expanded and the Sex Disqualification Removal Act of 1919 broke down the barriers for women wishing to enter the professions. There was little change, however, in the proportion of women employed in wage labour between 1881 and 1951, some 25 per cent.

These changes did not have a dramatic effect on attitudes towards girls' education. Official reports and administrative memoranda reflect well the continuation of a traditional philosophy. The 1902 Education Act continued to provide, through the new Local Education Authorities, elementary education for the working class, though the 1907 Free Place Regulations allowed a sizeable number of bright working-class boys and girls to obtain free education at the newly established municipal grammar schools.

Differentiation of the curriculum prevailed in both types of school. The Boer War, which ended the same year that the Education Bill became law, revealed the poor physical condition of British Army volunteers, up to a third of whom were rejected as being unfit to serve. The subsequent Report of the Interdepartmental Committee on Physical Deterioration (1904) recommended that boys should be given more physical exercises and drill in schools while girls should prepare for their role as homemakers by lessons in cookery and domestic science. A series of Special Reports was issued on *School Training for the Home Duties of Women*.[10] The Board of Education Elementary School Code of that year stated:

> The purpose of the Public Elementary School is to form and strengthen the character and to develop the intelligence of the children entrusted to it, and to make the best of the school years available, in assisting both boys and girls, according to their different needs, to fit themselves, practically as well as intellectually, for the work of life.

At secondary school level, matters were little different. The Board of Education Regulations for 1904–05 laid down a four-year course for all pupils, with housewifery provided for girls. In 1906, the Board claimed that as the demands made on girls' lives out of school 'are greater and more various than is the case with boys, the risk of overpressure is much greater'. As a result, more elastic arrangements for the time spent on subjects were encouraged. The following year, Secondary School Regulations allowed girls aged 15 to replace science with practical housewifery and by 1913, the Board was warning of the overpressure on girls, but not boys, caused by a shorter school day combined with too many subjects. Interestingly, the situation was more acute in mixed than in single sex schools. The Board recommended that girls might, with advantage, postpone the taking of public examinations 'to an age rather later than that which is usual for boys'. Such delay was not seen as of great importance. In the same year, an eminent medical man, Sir Almnroth Wright, explained in his book *The Unexpurgated Case Against Women Suffrage*:

> It must, as it will have come home to us, be clear to every thoughtful mind that woman's belief that she will, through education and the culmination of its effects upon her through generations, become a more glorious being, rests, not upon any rational basis, but only on the physiological fact that what is congenial to woman impresses

itself upon her as true. All that sober science in the form of history and physiology would seem to entitle us to hope for the future of woman is that she will develop *pari passu* with man; and that education will teach her not to retard him overmuch by her lagging in the rear.[11]

Exactly ten years later, an authoritative survey by the Consultative Committee of the Board of Education was undertaken on the differentiation of curriculum between the two sexes in secondary schools. The recommendations of the Committee were liberal-minded. It advised the elevation of music and art to equal standing with other subjects in the School Leaving Certificate Examinations, and that girls should be responsible for taking the initiative and developing their own interests in school. More importantly, the Committee advised that there should be a greater assimilation of teaching methods for boys and girls, as the former were receiving superior instruction. Girls showing an aptitude for manual subjects should be allowed to pursue such courses. This potential breaking down of the gender-specific curriculum was, however, never implemented. The Committee mentioned that as secondary education for girls was only about 60 years old, it was still regarded as experimental. 'It would therefore,' the Report concluded, 'be too easy make mistakes, if far-reaching changes were made.' The sciences for many decades afterwards continued to be regarded as masculine subjects. Qualities such as 'ladylike behaviour' was stressed for girls attending secondary schools, whilst the new central schools, with their vocational bias, prepared girls for occupations such as nursing, office and the department store.[12]

It could be argued that one solution would have been the provision of a complete co-educational system of secondary education, as was the case for primary schools. However, in 1926 the Hadow Report on *The Education of the Adolescent*, based on current psychological research, came out in favour of separate schools for boys and girls, noting that 'such arrangements are especially desirable for pupils who are passing through the early years of adolescence'. Even after the Second World War, when some change in attitude might have been expected, the Ministry of Education pamphlet *The Nation's Schools* (1945) pronounced that 'where numbers permit, the balance of advantage may be held to be on the side of single-sex schools'.[13] It was not until 1966, with the reorganisation of secondary schools into a comprehensive system, that the tempo of providing co-educational schools was hastened.

Two later reports adopted a more enlightened attitude. The Crowther Report *15–18* (1959) was one of the first official documents to recognise that girls would find themselves as adults playing a dual role of workers and wives and it also stressed the importance of girls continuing their education after leaving school. It noted that girls tended to specialise in arts subjects rather than the sciences. However, it was disappointing that only four years later the Newsom Report, which dealt with the education of average and below average ability students, recommended that, as girls were more interested in marriage, motherhood and personal relationships, their curriculum might differ in some respects from that of boys'. To give one example:

> A boy is usually excited by the prospect of a science course... He experiences a sense of wonder and a sense of power. The growth of wheat, the birth of a lamb, the movement of clouds put him in awe of nature; the locomotive he sees as man's response; the switch and the throttle are his magic wands... The girl may come to the science lesson with a less eager curiosity than the boy but she too will need to feel at home with machinery.[14]

As long ago as 1923, the Committee on the Differentiation of Curriculum between the Sexes pursued three questions: Should boys and girls study the same subjects in secondary schools? Should they study all subjects in the same way and up to the same standard? And if any different treatment is desirable, what should the difference be?

It has been widely recognised that the 'hidden curriculum' of a school can be an important factor in determining the answer to these questions. Studies had shown that teachers reinforce sex-role stereotypes in many ways, not necessarily consciously. These extend to encouraging girls to take some subjects rather than others at examination level. For example, physics tends to be regarded in mixed schools as largely the province of boys. There are undoubtedly sex differences in cognitive skills and in academic performance: girls develop stronger reading and formal language skills at an earlier age than boys; more boys than girls are referred for learning disabilities. Girls' ability to solve visual spatial problems is of a lower order than boys', though whether it is due to genetic or environmental factors is still a matter for dispute.[15] As late as 1975, the Department of Education and Science Survey *Curricular Differences for Boys and Girls* commented on the fact that 'there are significant differences in subjects studied by girls and boys and these differences are too striking to be accepted without question.'

During the last 30 or 40 years there have been a number of policy and social changes which have affected the gender issue. The growing feminine movement has turned its attention to examining deficiencies in education for women. Policy changes, such as the introduction of comprehensivisation and the raising of the school leaving age in 1971–72; the setting up of the Equal Opportunities Commission; the Sex Discrimination Act of 1975; and the increased access to higher education for women following the Robbins Report in 1963, have all had important implications for changing attitudes in society towards women's role in respect of education. More recently, the Education Reform Act of 1988, when schools could opt of local education control, and the growing diversity of types of secondary schools encouraged by successive governments of both major political parties, has implications for gender education as has the introduction of a National Curriculum into schools. Many of these areas, particularly the effect of changing policy since the 1944 Education Act on gender education, require further research.[16]

CONCLUSION

This chapter has dealt largely with the way in which, historically, girls and women have underachieved through a combination of structural, legislative and policy factors and some of the theories which have been propounded through the centuries which may have contributed to this situation. In fact, the word 'gender', of course, includes both sexes and attention is now being increasingly paid to studying why boys are underachieving in relation to girls. For example, at GCSE and A Level examinations in the 1990s, girls' results have improved faster than boys' and boys' problems with schooling, particularly their motivation to learn, is now a matter of major concern. A better understanding of how students, both boys and girls, make sense of learning situations would help towards more equitable teaching assessment practice for both sexes.[17]

REFERENCES

1. J. Purvis, 'A Feminist Perspective on the History of Women's Education,' in *The Education of Girls and Women* (History of Education Society, 1984), pp. 2–3.
2. S.N. Kersey, *Classics in the Education of Girls and Women* (Scarecrow Press Inc., Metuchen, NJ, 1981), p. 13.
3. M.C. Borer, *Willingly to School. A History of Women's Education* (Lutterworth Press, Guildford, 1976), pp. 52–4.
4. D. Gardiner, *English Girlhood At School* (Oxford University Press, Oxford, 1929), p. 192.
5. A. Wallas, *Before the Bluestockings* (Allen and Unwin, 1929), p. 135.
6. M. Wollstonecroft, *Vindication of the Rights of Women* (1792, Penguin English Library, Harmondsworth, Middlesex, 1982 edn), p. 283.
7. J. Kamm, *Hope Deferred. Girls' Education in English History* (Methuen, 1965), p. 230.

8. J. Burstyn, *Victorian Education and the Ideal of Womanhood* (Croom Helm, 1980), p. 78.
9. R.M. Tullberg, *Women at Cambridge* (Cambridge University Press, Cambridge, 1998 edn), p. 73.
10. C. Dyhouse, *Girls Growing Up in Late Edwardian and Victorian England* (Routledge & Kegan Paul, 1981), p. 93.
11. Sir A. Wright, *The Unexpurgated Case Against Woman Suffrage* (Constable, 1913), pp. 39–40.
12. P. Gordon. R. Aldrich and D. Dean, *Education and Policy in England in the Twentieth Century* (Woburn Press, 1991), p. 192.
13. D.W. Dean, 'Education for Moral Improvement: Domesticity and Social Cohesion. The Labour Government, 1945–1951', in L. Dawtrey, *et al.* (eds), *Equality and Inequality in Educational Policy* (Multilingual Matters, Clevedon, Avon, 1995), p. 25.
14. R. Deem, *Women and Schooling* (Routledge & Kegan Paul, 1978), pp. 60–1.
15. L.A. Serbin, 'The Hidden Curriculum: Academic Consequences of Teacher Expectations', in M. Marland (ed.), *Sex Differences and Schooling* (Heinemann, 1983), p. 224.
16. S. Delamont, 'Gender', in P. Gordon (ed.), *A Guide to Educational Research* (Woburn Press, 1996), p. 345.
17. P. Murphy. and J. Elwood, 'Gendered Learning Outside and Inside School: Influence on Achievement', in D. Epstein *et al.* (eds), *Failing Boys? Issues in Gender and Achievement* (Open University Press, Buckingham, 1998), p. 179.

Further Reading

Delamont, S., *A Woman's Place in Education: Historical and Sociological Perspectives on Gender and Education* (Aldershot, Brookfield, 1996).
Diller, A. (ed.), *The Gender Question in Education: Theory, Pedagogy and Politics* (Westview, BO, 1996).
Equal Opportunities Commission / Chief Inspector of Schools, *The Gender Divide: Performance Differences between Boys and Girls at School* (Equal Opportunities Commission, 1996).
Goodman, J. and Martin, J., 'Breaking Boundaries: Gender, Politics and the History of Education', *History of Education*, 29, 5, 2000.
Hunt, F., *Gender and Policy in English Education. Schooling for Girls, 1902–44* (Harvester Wheatsheaf, Hemel Hempstead, 1991).

18
Conclusion: The End of Education?

INTRODUCTION

Part of the purpose of this book was to discuss the continuous development of educational thought over about 3,000 years. We have tried to show that whilst some ideas have fallen into disuse or disrepute others have been modified and refined and have continued to exist. We have seen that education is essentially concerned with the transmission of values, knowledge and beliefs from one generation to the next. Some values, knowledge and beliefs may change over time but there has often been a sense of continuity, sometimes even progress. Many would see the twentieth century as the rise of democracy over competing belief systems, and with democracy, ideas of universal education and equality of opportunity have gradually been accepted, in principle if not in practice.

Yet many problems remain, and perhaps one of the most important, from an educational point of view, is a challenge to democratic optimism in the form of extreme cultural relativism or some versions of postmodernism. In earlier chapters we have seen that the eighteenth-century Enlightenment, despite temporary periods of chaos and reaction, led to the growth of the social sciences and to the spread of humanistic beliefs in the latter part of the nineteenth century and for most of the twentieth century. Towards the end of the twentieth century, however, social theorists have developed more complex interpretations, some of which question fundamental values and beliefs.

We have seen that sociology as a discipline emerged from the Enlightenment. The so-called Enlightenment project of the eighteenth century was concerned to provide rational explanations not only for the physical universe but also for humanity itself. Enlightenment thinkers were, generally, optimistic. Critics of the Enlightenment have even attributed blame for the excesses of the French Revolution to an exaggerated faith in human reason, and too little respect for traditions which they saw as the inherited wisdom or culture of their society. The rise of social science in the nineteenth century was essentially a product of both traditional values and scientific rationality, taking into account the limited rationality of human beings and their institutions. Many of these social science explanations, sometimes referred to as 'grand narratives', have been called into question by postmodernism, along with many historical explanations.

One important part of the sociological account of late nineteenth and the twentieth centuries was the period described as 'economic nationalism'[1] which dominated the years from the end of the Second World War to the mid-1970s. The features of economic nationalism included the fact that education assumed a key political role in modern societies, and that there was sustained economic growth. Progress was seen in terms of national economic growth; and three political priorities emerged for governments – prosperity, security and opportunity. All three were linked together by government policies, business organisations, families and education.

Economic nationalism was reinforced by the forging of common, national cultures. But there were several outstanding problems of modern capitalism, including how to maintain social solidarity and control in a society based on inequalities of reward and status. An additional problem was how to avoid alienation and loss of personal identity. Part of the answer was seen as 'meritocracy',[2] itself associated with bureaucracy, which relies on the myth of fairness of life-chances, whilst the reality is class and privilege. A further question concerns the role of education: is the task allotted to education too great? Schools are required to be responsible not only for social control but also for education for democracy, manpower training and individual development.

The breakdown of economic nationalism was said to occur after the oil crisis in the 1970s. In the 1980s the doctrines of the New Right presented another threat to social consensus. More recently, there has been much discussion of globalisation and the demise of economic nationalism. However, one of the advantages of economic nationalism was consensus which was partly based on education. There were at least three important elements in the educational consensus: universal primary and secondary education; very high participation rates in tertiary education; and the vocationalising of education.

Tensions and contradictions existed in what was referred to as economic nationalism. They were discussed critically by intellectuals, sociologists and others, some of whom referred to themselves as postmodernists. Postmodernism is a set of theories, not necessarily coherent or consistent, which postulate a complete transformation from modern society, emphasising: relativism (the view that no theory of society is better than any other); scientific objective truth is non-existent;

grand theories or 'narratives' such as those of the Enlightenment or Marxism are meaningless; knowledge is not about truth but about power and oppression; symbols, signs and other forms of communication, not just language, are important in the human condition. Postmodern thinking leaves a series of major problems for education. Not least is the difficulty of deciding what to teach when nothing is more important than anything else. We saw in Chapter 1 how some historians have counter-attacked the postmodernist challenge; some social scientists have also dealt with the problems of high modernism within different theoretical perspectives.

CRITICAL THEORY

These theories owe much to the so-called Frankfurt School which originated at the Institute of Social Research at Frankfurt University in 1923. In the 1930s the rise of the Nazi Party caused most of the members to migrate to the USA: first to Columbia University and later to California. The group included not only sociologists but some who would achieve fame as social psychologists, such as Erich Fromm, and social philosophers such as Herbert Marcuse (1898–1979). Part of the idea of the Institute of Social Research was to integrate social science disciplines and to see society in a more holistic way, a return to the aspiration of Comte but not to his positivism. It has sometimes been suggested that the basis of this integration was a combination of Marx and Freud, but this would be to underestimate the originality of the Frankfurt approach to critical theory.

After the Second World War, some of the group remained in the USA, others returned to Germany, and although the Institute was officially dissolved the work has continued, notably through the research of Jurgen Habermas (1929–) at the Max Planck Institute, Frankfurt. In some respects critical theory is a continuation of the eighteenth-century Enlightenment project, attempting to apply critical reasoning or rational thinking to aspects of society which are taken for granted or considered to be 'commonsense'.

Critical theory has cast doubt on much traditional sociology, especially functionalism and positivism, as well as postmodernism. Critical theorists also reject 'pluralism' because it represents an acceptance or accommodation of many of the unjust and irrational features of capitalist society. One important method of critical sociology is 'unmasking', that is, exposing the contradictions between the public goals, values and mission statements of institutions and what happens in reality. For example, it is claimed that markets are 'free' when they are really manipulated or rigged; or it is claimed that bureaucracies operate 'rationally' when their real practices are often lacking in reason and fairness, frequently disobeying their own rules. Above all, the method of critical theory is to continue to attack, or at least to question, traditional methods of social science and institutions on the assumption that change, but not revolution, will eventually take place.

Some features of the thinking behind critical theory include the following ideas: the assertion that critical theory is emancipatory, in the sense that one of its aims is freedom from 'technical' or instrumental rationality, that is, short-term means without examining the end or purpose of an activity. An important technique of critical theory is to ask 'Whose interest are served by...?' (for example, a belief, or tradition or behaviour). Critical theory also attacks the obsession of many social scientists with calculation and measurement; it is often alleged that clever statistics become an end in themselves. Culture is a central concept for critical theorists who attack many other sociologists for their lack of attention to this important idea derived from social anthropology. Critical theorists also give examples of the fact that instrumental rationality is used to control and dominate. Critical theorists want to return to 'the individual in society', not to individual psychology or individualism but to social psychology and personality (for example, the famous study by Theodore Adorno, *The Authoritarian Personality*[3] published in 1950). Another key concept is ideology which is defined broadly by critical theorists as sets of beliefs which influence behaviour. Critical theory uses some of the ideas of Freud and psychoanalysis to discuss differences between surface appearances and deep structures, which may be irrational. Finally, critical theory emphasises the centrality of language and communication to cultural studies.

Habermas in particular sees the problem of modern society in terms of *Legitimation Crisis*[4] in which he suggests that a key question for modern society is to ask 'Why accept this authority?' The fact that this question has now been asked so often goes some way to explaining the instability of many capitalist societies. Habermas also suggests that there is a related crisis, that is, a motivation crisis (many citizens now ask 'Why bother to participate?'). A third crisis, according to Habermas is 'identity crisis' (the individual constantly asks 'who am I, where do I belong?') To some extent this is a return to Durkheim's concept of *anomie* in the context of late capitalism.

Habermas has been criticised by both left and right. He was a revisionist who criticised some student movements for 'left fascism'. He was preoccupied with rational decision making; and specifying the conditions for consensus governed by the 'force of the better argument', that is, rationality; he was concerned with language and communication as part of rationality. According to Habermas, rationality has less to do with knowledge than with how knowledge is used. For example, when X speaks to Y, X implicitly claims intelligibility, truth, justification and sincerity, that is, the lack of any intention to deceive.[5]

All four claims are contingent and fallible. The ideal of communicative rationality is Habermas' basis for countering relativism. In this context he also discusses myths. Myths are seen as concretised modes of thought, integrating different aspects of life within a single domain. They express the organisation of societies which have not generated separate intellectual domains or arenas of discourse. Habermas has thus an evolutionary view of society – the expansion, over time, of rationality. He claims that the more we are able rationally to ground the conduct of our lives in the three main spheres of existence, that is, relations with the material world, with others and in the expressive realm of aesthetics, the more advanced our form of society can be said to be. Thus, Habermas implies that the modern world is more 'enlightened'. In traditional cultures man is more at the mercy of nature, the contingencies of which are 'explained' by myth: the life-world is the taken-for-granted universe, what some people would refer to as 'commonsense'. Tradition in such societies is all important.

Social evolution is connected with 'decentring' and separating the three main spheres of existence. Habermas considers Max Weber's ideas to be central to this kind of thinking, but considered Weber's view of modern society to be too pessimistic. Habermas said we need to inject communicative rationality back into the everyday social world.

Habermas rejects relativism: the rational is superior to the pre-rational or the irrational, but what are the universal criteria of rationality? He sometimes seems to rely on the idea of social evolution but without the historicist mistake of inevitability. In this respect, critical theory offers an optimistic alternative to postmodernist, nihilistic interpretations of reality. It is important for education because many of the ideas of critical theory can be seen to be completely compatible with some of the educational ideas discussed earlier in this book, such as the need for young people to learn to be critically reflective in the learning process rather than to memorise information or to be socialised into conformity and obedience.

Postmodernism logically leaves no room for education in the normal meaning of the word: education implies a planned, purposive rational process, but planning, purpose and rationality have no place in the vision of the more extreme postmodernists. Educationists are likely to be more attracted to other visions of the future such as those of Habermas or Giddens.[6] Even so, educationists have to plan for the future without knowing exactly what it will be. That is why certain principles of living in society and education are essential. Aristotle said that no human being could live without other human beings: only a god or a beast could live alone. We are thus driven back to considering education about society and for society as the first priority, more important than education for work, for example.

In our view, educational ideas cannot move far in the direction of postmodernism. The more extreme versions of postmodernism reject value preferences, but education is essentially concerned with value priorities, and also requires visions of a better society and a better way of life. Socrates was right: the Sophists were wrong. For that reason, we have concluded the book with this chapter which presents rational alternatives to postmodernism in the form of other late modernist philosophies such as critical theory and the sociological views of Habermas and Giddens. Whereas postmodernism rejects the values of the Enlightenment and post-Enlightenment developments, we believe that twenty-first-century education will be a fulfilment of some Enlightenment ideas about education, as refined by the nineteenth- and twentieth-century experiences discussed in earlier chapters, but without the naïve optimism of the Enlightenment. Pedagogy will be central to this development: it is remarkable that so far educational practice has had comparatively little concern for the pupils, despite Comenius and many of the reformers who followed.

REFERENCES

1. P. Brown *et al.*, 'The Transformation of Education and Society: An Introduction', in A.H. Halsey *et al.* (eds), *Education: Culture, Economy and Society*. (Oxford University Press, Oxford, 1997), pp. 1–7.
2. M. Young, *The Rise of the Meritocracy* (Penguin, 1958).
3. T. Adorno *et al.*, *The Authoritarian Personality* (Harper, New York, 1950).
4. J. Habermas, *Legitimation Crisis* (Heinemann Educational, 1976).
5. J. Habermas, *The Theory of Communicative Competence* (Heinemann Educational, 1984, 1988), 2 vols.
6. A. Giddens, *Modernity and Self-Identity* (Polity, Cambridge, 1991).

Further Reading

Habermas, J., *The Philosophical Discourse of Modernity: Twelve Lectures* (Cambridge Polity Press, 1987).
Kumar, K., *From Post-Industrial to Post-Modern Society* (Blackwell, Oxford, 1995).

Bibliography

Acland, A.H.D., *The Education of Citizens* (Central Co-operative Board, Manchester, 1883).

Adams, J., *The Evolution of Educational Theory* (Macmillan, 1928).

Adamson, J.W., *Pioneers of Modern Education 1600–1700* (Cambridge University Press, Cambridge, 1905).

Adorno, T. *et al.*, *The Authoritarian Personality* (Harper, New York, 1950).

Ankersmith, F.R., 'Historiography and postmodernism', *History and Theory*, 28, 1989.

Aristotle, *Ethics* (Introduction by J. Barnes) (Penguin Classics, 1976).

Armytage, W.H.G., *Four Hundred Years of English Education* (Cambridge University Press, Cambridge, 1964).

Armytage, W.H.G., 'Battles for the best: some educational aspects of the welfar–warfare state in England,' in P. Nash (ed.), *History and Education. The Educational Uses of the Past* (Random House, New York, 1970).

Arnold, M., *Culture and Anarchy* (Cambridge University Press, Cambridge, 1869).

Ashby, E. and Anderson, M., *Portrait of Haldane at Work on Education* (Macmillan, 1974).

Bain, A., *Education as A Science* (Kegan, Paul, Trench, Trübner, 1879, 1892 edn).

Bantock, G.H., *Culture, Industrialisation and Education* (Routledge & Kegan Paul, 1968).

Beiser, F., 'Johann Gottfried Herder', in *Concise Routledge Encyclopaedia of Philosophy* (Routledge, 2000).

Berlin, Isaiah, *The Roots of Romanticism* (H. Hardy (ed.)) (Chatto and Windus, 1999).

Bernstein, B., 'Open school, open society', *New Society*, 14 September 1967.

Bernstein, B., *Class, Codes and Control* (Routledge & Kegan Paul, 1975).

Bloomer, M. and Hodkinson, P., *Moving into Further Education: The Voice of the Learner* (Further Education Development Agency, 1997).

Boardman, J., Griffin, J. and Murray, O. (eds), *The Roman World* (Oxford University Press , Oxford, 1986).

Borer, M.C., *Willingly to School. A History of Women's Education* (Lutterworth Press, Guildford, 1976).

Bosanquet, B., *Edward Caird, 1835–1908* (Proceedings of the British Academy, 1908).

Bottomore, T. and Nisbet, R. (eds), *A History of Sociological Analysis* (Heinemann, 1979).

Bourdieu, P. and Passeron, J.C., *Reproduction* (Sage, 1990).

Bowen, J. and Hobson, P.R., *Theories of Education* (Wiley, Brisbane, 1974).

Bowen, J., *A History of Western Education. Vol. 3. The Modern West: Europe and the New World* (Methuen, 1981).

Boyd, W., *From Locke to Montessori* (Harrop, 1914).

Britain, I., 'Education', in I. McCalman (ed.), *An Oxford Companion to the Romantic Age. British Culture 1776–1832* (Oxford University Press, Oxford, 1999).

Bronowski, J. and Mazlish, B., *The Western Intellectual Tradition: From Leonardo to Hegel* (Harper & Row, 1960).

Brown, P. *et al.*, 'The transformation of education and society: an introduction', in A.H. Halsey *et al.* (eds), *Education: Culture, Economy and Society* (Oxford University Press, Oxford, 1997).

Browning, O. (N.M. Butler (ed.)), *Aspects of Education: A Study in the History of Pedagogy* (Industrial Education Society, New York, 1888).

Bruner, J., 'Folk pedagogies', in *The Culture of Education* (Harvard University Press, Cambridge, MA, 1996).

Bruner, J., *Towards a Theory of Instruction* (Harvard, 1966).

Burn, W.L., *The Age of Equipoise* (Unwin, 1964, 1968 edn).

Burstyn, J., *Victorian Education and the Ideal of Womanhood* (Croom Helm, 1980).

Butler, J.D., *Idealism in Education* (Harper, New York, 1966).

Cacoullos, A.R., *Thomas Hill Green: Philosopher of Rights* (Twayne, New York, 1974).

Carcopino, J., *Daily Life in Ancient Rome* (Penguin, 1962).

Carr, E.H., *What Is History?* (George Macaulay Trevelyan Lectures delivered in the University of Cambridge January–March, 1961).

Carr, W. and Hartnett, A., *Education and the Struggle for Democracy* (Open University Press, 1996).

Carter, R. (ed.) *Knowledge About Language and the Curriculum: The LINC Reader* (Hodder & Stoughton, 1990).

Castle, E.B., *Ancient Education and Today* (Penguin, 1961).

Chadwick, O., *The Reformation* (Pelican, 1964).

Chomsky, N., *Syntactic Structures* (Mouton, The Hague and New York, 1957).

Chomsky, N., 'Review of Verbal Behaviour by B.F. Skinner' *Language*, 5, 1959.

Cole, L., *A History of Education. Socrates to Montessori* (Holt Reinhart and Winston, New York, 1964).

Collingwood, R.G., *An Autobiography* (Oxford University Press, Oxford, 1944).

Compayré, G., *The History of Pedagogy* (trans. W.H. Payne) (Swann, Sonnenschein, 1905).

Connell, W.F., *A History of Education in the Twentieth Century World* (Curriculum Development Centre, Canberra, 1980).

Coombs, P., *The World Crisis in Education* (Oxford University Press, Oxford and New York, 1968).

Cox Report, *Report of the English Working Party 5–16 (National Curriculum)* (Department of Education and Science, 1989).

Curtis, S.J. and Boultwood, M.E.A., *A Short History of Educational Ideas* (University Tutorial Press, 1953, 4th edn, 1965).

Dean, D.W., 'Education for Moral Improvement: Domesticity and Social Cohesion. The Labour Government, 1945–1951', in L. Dawtrey *et al.* (eds), *Equality and Inequality in Educational Policy* (Multilingual Matters, Clevedon, Avon, 1995).

Deem, R., *Women and Schooling* (Routledge & Kegan Paul, 1978).

Delamont, S.A., *A Woman's Place in Education: Historical and Sociological Perspectives on Gender and Education* (Aldershot, Brookfield, 1996).

Delamont, S., 'Gender', in P. Gordon (ed.), *A Guide to Educational Research* (Woburn Press, 1996).

Department for Education and Employment, *The Review of the National Curriculum in England: The Secretary of State's Proposals* (Qualifications and Curriculum Authority, 1999)

Department for Education and Employment, *Teaching: High Status, High Standards* (Circular 4/98) (Department for Education and Employment, 2000).

Devonshire Commission on the Scientific Instruction and the Advancement of Science. Minutes of Evidence, PP 1872, xxv.

Dewey, J., *Democracy and Education* (Collier Macmillan, 1916).

Dewey, J. , *Freedom and Culture* (Allen & Unwin, 1940).

Diller, A. (ed.), *The Gender Question in Education: Theory, Pedagogy and Politics* (Westview, BO, 1996).

Dodd, C.I., *Introduction to the Herbartian Principles of Teaching* (Swann, Sonnenschein, 1898).

Dyhouse, C., *Girls Growing Up in Late Edwardian and Victorian England* (Routledge & Kegan Paul, 1981).

Eby, F., *The Development of Modern Education* (Prentice-Hall, New York, 1952).

Education Code, 1878, Viscount Sandon's Instructions to Her Majesty's Inspectorate, 16 January 1879, reprinted in PP 1881, lxxii.

Elton, G., *The Practice of History* (Sydney University Press, Sydney, 1967).

Equal Opportunities Commission/Chief Inspector of Schools, *The Gender Divide: Performance Differences Between Boys and Girls at School* (Equal Opportunities Commission, 1996).

Esher, Viscount (ed.), *The Girlhood of Queen Victoria, vol. 1* (Murray, 1912).

Evans, R.J., *In Defence of History* (Granta Books, 1997).

Eysenck, H.J., *The Structure of Human Personality* (Methuen, 1960).

Fletcher, A.E. (ed.), *Sonnenschein's Cyclopaedia of Education* (Allen and Unwin, 1907).

Foss, C. and Magdalino, P., *Rome and Byzantium* (Elsevier-Phaidon, Oxford, 1977).

Freire, P., *Pedagogy of the Oppressed* (Penguin, 1971).

Friedenthal, R., *Goethe: His Life and Times* (Weidenfeld, 1993).

Fromm, E., *Fear of Freedom* (Routledge & Kegan Paul, 1942).

Gardiner, D., *English Girlhood At School* (Oxford University Press, Oxford, 1929).

Gardner, H., *Frames of Mind* (Fontana, 1993).

Giddens, A., *Modernity and Self-Identity* (Polity, Cambridge, 1991).

Gilbert, E.W., 'Sir John Halford Mackinder', *Dictionary of National Biography* (Oxford University Press, Oxford, 1959).

Giroux, H.A., *Schooling for Democracy: Critical Pedagogy in the Modern Age* (Routledge, 1988).

Goldman, L., *Dons and Workers. Oxford and Adult Education since 1850* (Clarendon Press, Oxford, 1995).

Goldstrom, J.M., 'The Content of Education and the Socialization of the Working-class Child, 1830–1860', in P. McCann (ed.), *Popular Education and Socialization in the Nineteenth Century* (Methuen, 1970).

Golman, D., *Emotional Intelligence: Why It can Matter More Than IQ* (Bloomsbury, 1996).

Goodman, J. and Martin, J., 'Breaking Boundaries: Gender, Politics and the History of Education', *History of Education*, 29, 5 (Woburn Press, 2000).

Gordon, P. (ed.), *Politics and Society: The Journals of Lady Knightley of Fawsley, 1885 to 1913* (Northamptonshire Record Society, Northampton, 1999).

Gordon, P. and Lawton, D., *Lessons From the Past*, forthcoming.

Gordon, P. and White, J., *Philosophers as Educational Reformers. The Influence of Idealism on British Educational Thought and Practice* (Routledge & Kegan Paul, 1979).

Gordon. P., Aldrich, R. and Dean, D., *Education and Policy in England in the Twentieth Century* (Woburn Press, 1991).

Gosden, P.H.J.H., *How They Were Taught* (Blackwell, Oxford, 1969).

Guilford, J.P., 'The Structure of Intellect', *Psychology Bulletin*, 53, 1956.

Gundara, J., 'Values, National Curriculum and Diversity in British Society', in P. O'Hear and J. White, *Assessing the National Curriculum* (Paul Chapman, 1993).

Gundara, J., 'Social Diversity, Inclusiveness and Citizenship Education', in D. Lawton, J. Cairns and R. Gardner (eds), *Education for Citizenship* (Continuum, 2000).

Gutek, G.I., *A History of Western Educational Experience* (Waveland Press Inc., Prospect Heights, IL, 1972).

Habermas, J., *Legitimation Crisis* (Heinemann Educational, 1976).

Habermas, J., *The Theory of Communicative Competence* (Heinemann Educational, 1984, 1988), 2 vols.

Habermas, J., *The Philosophical Discourse of Modernity: Twelve Lectures* (Cambridge Polity Press, 1987).

Hadow Report, *The Education of the Adolescent* (Board of Education, 1926).

Haldane, R.B., *An Autobiography* (Hodder & Stoughton, 1929).

Hale, J.R., *Renaissance Europe* (Fontana, 1971).

Hamilton, D., *Towards a Theory of Schooling* (Falmer, 1989).

Hampson, N., *The Enlightenment* (Penguin, 1968).

Hans, N., *Comparative Education* (Routledge & Kegan Paul, 1967).

Hansard, 3, 182, 13 March 1866.

Hargreaves, A., *Changing Teachers, Changing Times: Teachers' Work and Culture in the Postmodern Age* (Cassell, 1994).

Harris, R.W., *Romanticism and the Social Order 1780–1830* (Blandford Press, 1969).

Hayek, F., *The Road to Serfdom* (Routledge & Kegan Paul, 1946).

Hewins, W.A.S., *The Apologia of an Imperialist*, (Constable, 1929) 2 vols.

Hill, J.C. (ed.), *The Romantic Imagination* (Macmillan, 1977).

Hunt, F., *Gender and Policy in English Education. Schooling for Girls, 1902–44* (Harvester Wheatsheaf, Hemel Hempstead, 1991).

Huyghe, R. (ed.) *Byzantine and Medieval Art* (Paul Hamlyn, 1958).

Im Hof, U., *The Enlightenment* (Blackwell, Oxford, 1994).

Jasper, D., 'Samuel Taylor Coleridge', in J. Raimond and J.R. Watson (eds.), *A Handbook of English Romanticism* (Macmillan, 1992).

Jenkins, E.W. and Swinnerton, B.J., *Junior School Science Education in England and Wales since 1900* (Woburn Press, 1998).

Joyce, E., 'The Imperial Aspect of Girls' Friendly Society Emigration', *Imperial Colonist*, August 1913.

Kamm, J., *Hope Deferred. Girls' Education in English History* (Methuen, 1965).

Keech, A.W., 'Romanticism and Language', in S. Curran (ed.), *The Cambridge Companion to British Romanticism* (Cambridge University Press, Cambridge, 1993).

Keen, M., *Medieval Europe* (Penguin, 1968).

Kelly, A.V. , *Education and Democracy* (Paul Chapman, 1995).

Kersey, S.N., *Classics in the Education of Girls and Women* (Scarecrow Press Inc., Metuchen, NJ, 1981).

Kingman Report, *The Report of the Committee of Inquiry into the Teaching of the English Language* (Department of Education and Science, 1988).

Kumar, K., *From Post-Industrial to Post-Modern Society* (Blackwell, Oxford, 1995).

Labour Party, *Secondary Education for All* (Labour Party, 1922).

Lamennais, H., 'L'Avenir', *Oeuvres Completes, vol. 2* (Brussels, 1839).

Laurence, E. (ed.), *Friedrich Froebel and English Education* (Routledge & Kegan Paul, 1952, 1969 edn).

Lawson, J., *Medieval Education and the Reformation* (Routledge & Kegan Paul, 1967).

Lawson, J. and Silver, H., *A Social History of Education in England* (Methuen, 1973).

Lawton, D., Cairns, J., and Gardner, R., *Education for Citizenship* (Continuum, 2000).

Leach, A.F., *English Schools at the Reformation 1546–8* (Russell, NY, 1968).

Legouis, E. (trans. Matthews, J.W.), *The Early Life of William Wordsworth, 1770–1795* (Dent, 1897).

Lindsay, A.D., 'T. H. Green, and the idealists', in F.J.C. Hearnshaw (ed.), *The Social and Political Ideas of some Representative Thinkers of the Victorian Age* (Harrap, 1933).

Locke, J., *Some Thoughts Concerning Education*, C. Daniel (ed.) (National Society's Depository, 1693) (1880 edn).

Lowe, R., *Primary and Classical Education* (Edmonston and Douglas, Edinburgh, 1867).

Luria, A.R., and Yudovich, I., *Speech and the Development of Mental Processes in the Child* (Staples Press, 1959).

McCulloch, G., *Failing the Ordinary Child* (Open University Press, 1998).

McFarland, T., *Coleridge and the Pantheistic Tradition* (Clarendon Press, Oxford, 1960)

Mackenzie, M., *Hegel's Educational Theory and Practice* (Swann Sonnenschein, 1909).

Mangan, J.A., *The Games Ethic and Imperialism* (Frank Cass, 1998).

Mannheim, K., *Diagnosis of Our Time* (Routledge & Kegan Paul, 1943).

Marrou, H.I., *A History of Education in Antiquity* (Mentor, 1964).

Marshall, T.H., *Citizenship and Social Class* (Cambridge University Press, Cambridge, 1950).

Marx, K. and Engels, F., *The Communist Manifesto* in *Basic Writings in Politics and Philosophy* (Moscow, 1959, repr. in *The Revolution of 1848*) (Penguin, 1973).

Matthew, H.C.G., *The Liberal Imperialists. The Ideas and Politics of a Post-Gladstonian Elite* (Oxford University Press, Oxford, 1973).

Mayor, F., *UNESCO – An Ideal in Action* (UNESCO, Paris, 1997).

Meath, Earl of, 'The Empire Day Movement', *Imperial Colonist*, May 1906.

Menhennet, A., *The Romantic Movement 1785–1830* (Croom Helm, 1981).

Miller, R.D., *Schiller and the Ideal of Freedom* (Clarendon Press, Oxford, 1970).

Millet, A., *Pedagogy – the Last Corner of the Secret Garden* (King's College School of Education, 1996).

Minutes of the Committee of Council on Education, PP 1844, xxxviii.

Morris, P., *Industrialisation and Education* (Industrial Welfare Society, 1954).

Murphy, D., *Comenius* (Irish Academic Press, 1995).

Murphy, P. and Elwood, J., 'Gendered Learning Outside and Inside School: Influence on Achievement', in D. Epstein *et al.* (eds), *Failing Boys? Issues in Gender and Achievement* (Open University Press, Buckingham, 1998).

Nettleship, R.L., *The Theory of Education in Plato's Republic* (Oxford University Press, Oxford, 1935).

Newcastle Commission on the State of Popular Education in England, PP 1861, xxi.

Newman, J.H., *The Idea of a University* (Yale University Press, 1899) (1996 edn).

Nisbet, R.A., *The Sociological Tradition* (Heinemann, 1966).

Noakes, J. and Pridham, G., *Nazism 1919–45*, (University of Exeter, Exeter, 1983–84) 2 vols.

Norwich, J.J., *Byzantium: The Apogee* (Penguin, 1991).

Nunn, P., *Education: Its Data and First Principles* (Edward Arnold, 1920).

Open University, *Education and Production* E353, Block 3 (Open University Press, 1972).

Open University, *Schooling and Capitalism* E202, Block 1 (Open University Press, 1977).

Pask, G., 'A Fresh Look at Cognition and the Individual', *International Journal of Man–Machine Studies*, 4, 1972.

Penn, A., *Targeting Schools. Drill, Militarism and Imperialism* (Woburn Press, 1999).

Peters, R., 'Ambiguities in Liberal Education', in *Education and the Education of Teachers* (Routledge & Kegan Paul, 1970).

Peters, R., *Authority, Responsibility and Education* (Routledge & Kegan Paul, 1959).

Piaget, J., *The Science of Education and the Psychology of the Child* Longman, 1972).

Pieper, J., *Scholasticism* (trans. R. and C. Winston) (Faber & Faber, 1961).

Plato, *Plato's Dialogues* (trans. by F.M. Cornford) (Routledge & Kegan Paul, 1935).

Plato, *Republic* (trans. D. Lee) (Penguin Classics, 1987).

Ploscataska, L.M., 'Geographical Education, Empire and Citizenship' (PhD thesis, University of London, 1996).

Plumb, J.H., *The Penguin Book of the Renaissance* (Penguin, 1964).

Popper, K., *The Poverty of Historicism* (Routledge & Kegan Paul, 1961).

Porter, R., *Enlightenment: Britain and the Creation of the Modern World* (Allen Lane, Penguin Press, 2000).

Pring, R., *Closing the Gap: Liberal Education and Vocational Preparation* (Hodder & Stoughton, 1995).

Prichett, S. (ed.), *The Romantics* (Methuen, 1981).

Procacci, G., *History of the Italian People* (Pelican, 1973).

Purvis, J., 'A Feminist Perspective on the History of Women's Education', in J. Purvis (ed.), *The Education of Girls and Women* (History of Education Society, 1984).

Quick, R.H., *Essays on Educational Reformers* (Longmans, Green, 1895).

Raumer, K. von., *German Pedagogy. Education. The School and the Teacher* (Brown and Gross, Hartford, CT, 2nd edn. 1876).

Raymont, T., *The Principles of Education* (Longmans, Green, 1907).

Reisner, E.H., *Nationalism and Education since 1870* (Macmillan, 1922).

Reiss, S., *Goethe's Novels* (Macmillan, 1969).

Riasanovsky, N.V., *The Emergence of Romanticism* (Oxford University Press, Oxford, 1992).

Rice, T.T., *Everyday Life in Byzantium* (Barnes and Noble Books, New York, 1967).

Richter, M., *The Politics of Conscience. T.H. Green and His Age* (Weidenfeld & Nicolson, 1964).

Rust, L.R., *The Contours of European Romanticism* (Macmillan, 1979).

Ryan, A., *Liberal Anxieties and Liberal Education* (Profile Books,1999).

Searle, G.R., *The Quest for National Efficiency. A Study in British Political Thought, 1899–1914* (Blackwell, Oxford, 1971).

Selleck, R.J.W., *The New Education. The English Background, 1870–1914* (Pitman, 1968).

Serbin, L.A., 'The Hidden Curriculum: Academic Consequences of Teacher Expectations', in M. Marland (ed.), *Sex Differences and Schooling* (Heinemann, 1983).

Simon, B., *History of Education 1780–1870* (Lawrence & Wishart, 1960).

Simon, B., *Education and the Labour Movement 1870–1920* (Lawrence & Wishart, 1965).

Simon, B., *The Politics of Educational Reform 1920–1940* (Lawrence & Wishart, 1974).

Simon, B., 'Why No Pedgaogy in England?' in B. Simon and W. Taylor (eds.), *Education in the Eighties* (Batsford, 1981).

Simon, B., *Education and the Social Order 1940–1990* (Lawrence & Wishart, 1991).

Simon, B., 'Some Problems of Pedagogy, Revisited', in *The State and Educational Change: Essays in the History of Education and Pedagogy* (Lawrence & Wishart, 1994).

Simon, J., *The Social Origins of English Education* (Routledge & Kegan Paul, 1970).

Simpson, L.M., 'Education, Imperialism and National Efficiency in England 1895–1905' (PhD thesis, Glasgow University, 1979).

Skinner, B.F., *Science and Human Behaviour* (Macmillan, 1953).

Skinner, B.F., *Verbal Behaviour* (Methuen, New York, 1957).

Smith, A., *An Inquiry into the Nature and Causes of the Wealth of Nations* (The World Library of Standard Books, London, 1776, 1875 edn).

Spencer, H., 'What Knowledge is of Most Worth?' in H. Spencer (ed.), *Essays on Education* (Dent, 1861, 1911 edn).

Spencer, H., *Education. Intellectual, Moral and Physical* (Williams and Norgate, 1861, 1878 edn).

Springhall, J., *Youth, Empire and Society. British Youth Movements, 1883-1940* (Croom Helm, 1977).

Stenhouse, L., *Culture and Education* (Nelson, 1967).

Stenhouse, L., *An Introduction to Curriculum Research and Development* (Heinemann, 1975).

Stewart, W.A.C. and McCann, W.P., *The Educational Innovators, 1750–1880, vol. 3* (Macmillan, 1967).

Stone, L., *The Past and the Present Revisited* (Routledge & Kegan Paul, 1987).

Sylvester, D.W., *Robert Lowe and Education* (Cambridge University Press, 1974).

Tarnas, R., *The Passion of the Western Mind: Understanding the Ideas That Have Shaped our World View* (Random House, 1991).

Tawney, R.H., *Religion and the Rise of Capitalism* (Pelican, 1926).

Tawney, R.H., *Equality* (Allen & Unwin, 1931).

Toynbee, A., *'Progress and Poverty': A Criticism of Mr Henry George. Being Two Lectures Delivered in St Andrew's Hall, Newman Street, London* (Kegan Paul, 1883).

Trant, A. (ed.), *Reconciling Liberal and Vocational Education* (Curriculum Development Unit, Dublin, 1999).

Tullberg, R.M., *Women at Cambridge* (Cambridge University Press, Cambridge, 1998 edn).

Turnbull, G.H., *The Educational Theory of J.G. Fichte: A Critical Account Together with Translations* (Liverpool University Press, Liverpool, 1926).

Vernon, P., *Secondary School Selection* (Methuen, 1957).

Vygotsky, L.S., *Mind in Society* (MIT Press, Massachusetts,1962).

Vygotsky, L. S., *Thought and Language* (MIT Press, MA, 1962).

Wallas, A., *Before the Bluestockings* (Allen & Unwin, 1929).

Walsh, W., *The Use of Imagination: Educational Thought and the Literary Mind* (Chatto & Windus, 1959).

Ward, J., *Psychology Applied to Education* (G. Davies Hicks (ed.)) (Cambridge University Press, Cambridge, 1926).

Watkins, C. and Mortimore, P., 'Pedagogy: what do we know', in P. Mortimer (ed.), *Understanding Pedagogy and Its Impact on Learning* (Paul Chapman, 1999).

Wheen, F., *Karl Marx* (Fourth Estate, 1999).

Whitehead, A.N., *The Aims of Education* (Williams and Norgate, 1929).

Wilkinson, H. and Mulgan, G., *Freedom's Children* (Demos, 1995).

Williams, J.R., *The Life of Goethe. A Critical Biography* (Blackwell, Oxford, 1998).

Williams, R., *The Long Revolution* (Penguin, 1961).

Wiltshire, D., *The Social and Political Thought of Herbert Spencer* (Oxford University Press, Oxford, 1978).

Witkin, H.A., *Psychological Differentiation* (Wiley, New York, 1962).

Wodehouse, H., *A Survey of the History of Education* (Edward Arnold, 1929).

Wollstonecroft, M., *Vindication of the Rights of Women* (1792, Penguin English Library, Harmondsworth, Middlesex, 1982 edn).

Wright, Sir A., *The Unexpurgated Case Against Woman Suffrage* (Constable, 1913).

Young, M., *The Rise of the Meritocracy* (Penguin, 1958).

Zagorin, P., 'Historiography and Postmodernism: Reconsiderations', *History and Theory*, 29, 1990.

Zimmern, A.E., 'The Evolution of the Citizen', in O. Stanley (ed.), *The Way Out: Essays on the Meaning and Purpose of Adult Education* (Oxford University Press, Oxford, 1923).

Index

Index